# LITERARY LIFE

OF

# JAMES K. PAULDING.

J K Paulding

# LITERARY LIFE

OF

# JAMES K. PAULDING.

COMPILED BY HIS SON,

WILLIAM I. PAULDING.

IN ONE VOLUME.

NEW YORK:
CHARLES SCRIBNER AND COMPANY.
1867.

# PREFACE.

---

PROMINENT among the pioneers of American letters, before Literature had become a profession in this country, was James K. Paulding. One of the most popular of our authors for awhile, towards the close of his extended life various circumstances kept him much in the background. This may prove, upon the whole, a fortunate accident for his prospect of a living remembrance. To be too heavily weighted is a disadvantage in the struggle for a name; and very much of what he wrote in his life, having been of a merely temporary or controversial character, has lost its significance to men, and need not be packed again upon his back. There remains what, in my opinion, deserves to be brought again to light.

In justice to the talents of the man, it should be observed that he was in no exact sense an author. Early involved in political disquisition, and in the discussion of principles which he considered as being the very foundation stones of our system, he devoted almost the whole of his mature life, that was not absorbed in official routine, to newspaper writing upon subjects of this nature. His adventures in literature proper were rather the episodes of his intellectual activity than the real labors of his mind.

Holding a prolific and facile pen, and working so much for immediate demand, he fell into a hasty and careless style, impatient of correction; and, accordingly, he never found or made time to do himself justice. Notwithstanding this, throughout all his various productions and in the midst of his most heedless composition, occur passages of description, or little sketches of real or fictitious character or incident, or quaint vistas into the idiosyncrasies of his own mind, which, though dashed off *currente calamo*, are marked by a felicity of diction or originality of view which casts a new light or a novel grace over the most hackneyed subject. Many of these are so full of the spirit of the author or of his time, so complete in themselves, so admirable in all respects, that I felt that they ought not to be lost, without an effort to preserve them. I have, therefore, in the following pages, assembled enough to illustrate at least his great versatility.

I have been furnished, through the courtesy of Mr. Pierre M. Irving, with letters of my father to Washington Irving; by Mr. J. Carson Brevoort, with letters to his father, Henry Brevoort Jr.; and by Mr. Gouverneur Kemble, General Thomas Cadwallader of Trenton, and Mr. J. S. Sims of Pacolet Mills South Carolina, with letters to themselves respectively — which I have to regret that the plan of this volume, and the bounds I had set up for myself, prevented me from using, except to a limited extent.

But the life of a writer is the succession of his works. And this is more particularly true of our author. Little gifted with the dramatic faculty, neither was his best talent that of narration. Rather he was by nature an essayist, and, of all men, wrote most directly out of his own experience, observation, or reflection. His writings were the immediate out-pourings of his thought; his expression of sentiment was genuine. What he gave to the public was the manifestation of himself.

Feeling sure that I could frame a species of running commentary of the little studies, or "bits", (or call them what one may), before alluded to, which would build up a better idea of the individual, and be more interesting to the public, than any dry details of uneventful biography; and considering that they form in fact the delineation of his character, the true story of his mind; — I have woven them into the chronology of his days, and styled the whole, being the present volume, the LITERARY LIFE OF JAMES K. PAULDING. I propose to stand apart, furnishing only what links may be necessary to the chain of events, or what observations may seem to me essential to the thorough understanding of the author and the man; and it is my aim, in this and the ensuing volumes of this re-publication, to preserve what was most national, and, what in his case is almost synonymous, the most characteristic, of my father's writings.

Any one who should collate the forthcoming with previous editions of Mr. Paulding's works would find sundry changes of expression, and corrections of various kinds. For some of these I am responsible, and it is proper for me to explain why I have taken such liberties. Some years before my father's death, I had a conversation with him about his published works. They were at the time mainly beyond his control, but I urged him to put them in what he would like to be their permanent shape. He replied, that he was too old to undergo the labor, and that he meant to bequeath to me the care of his reputation, if worth caring for — or in words to that effect. In accordance, as I understood it, with this arrangement, he left to me all his literary property, to the exclusion of his other children. I have felt therefore that I was entitled to more than the ordinary latitude of an editor, and have seized upon that privilege of revision which the pre-occupation, or the indifference, of the author, allowed to escape himself.

The changes are mostly in the shape of omissions of tautological matter, or corrections of inaccuracies of language due to carelessness. The free substitutions of words are, in a great measure, mere transfers of his own expressions; though I have occasionally ventured to introduce one of my own. But I am confident that I have not, in any way, or in the least, distorted or disturbed that more ethereal part of his work which is the measure and figure of his mind.

EDITOR.

# CONTENTS.

## CHAPTER VI.

1816–1817. [ÆT. 38–39.]



## CHAPTER VII.

1818. [ÆT. 40.]



## CHAPTER VIII.

1818–1819. [ÆT. 40–41.]



## CHAPTER IX.

1819–1820. [ÆT. 41–42.]



## CHAPTER X.

1821–1822. [ÆT. 43–44.]



## CHAPTER XI.

1823. [ÆT. 45.]

## CHAPTER XII.

1823–1825. [ÆT. 45–47.]



## CHAPTER XIII.

1826. [ÆT. 48.]



## CHAPTER XIV.

1828–1832. [ÆT. 50–54.]



## CHAPTER XV.

1832–1835. [ÆT. 54–57.]



## CHAPTER XVI.

1835–1836. [ÆT. 57–58.]

## CHAPTER XVII.

1836–1838. [ÆT. 58–60.]



## CHAPTER XVIII.

1838–1840. [ÆT. 60–62.]



## CHAPTER XIX.

1841–1843. [ÆT. 63–65.]



## CHAPTER XX.

1844–1848. [ÆT. 66–70.]



## CHAPTER XXI.

1849. [ÆT. 71.]

## CHAPTER XXII.

1849. [ÆT. 71.]



## CHAPTER XXIII.

1850–1852. [ÆT. 72–74.]



## CHAPTER XXIV.

1852–1855. [ÆT. 74–77.]



## CHAPTER XXV.

1856–1858. [ÆT. 78–80.]



## CHAPTER XXVI.

1859 - APRIL 6, 1860. [ÆT. 81–81 yr. 7 mo. 15 days.]

# LITERARY LIFE

OF

# JAMES K. PAULDING.

---

## I.

Aug. 22, 1778–1797. [Æt. 0–19.]

BIRTH — FAMILY — FATHER — MOTHER — EARLY DAYS.

William Paulding married Catharine Ogden, in the city of New York, on the 25th of July, 1762. Of the nine children whom in the course of time they had, the eighth, JAMES KIRKE PAULDING, was born at Great-Nine-Partners in the County of Dutchess and State of New York, on the 22d of August, 1778, in the midst of the Revolutionary war.

From documents and records yet extant, it appears probable that the first of the name on this continent came hither at, or very shortly after, the surrender of the city of Nieuw Amsterdam to the English, in 1664: also, that there were two brothers. One of these settled in Ulster County, to which his descendants have adhered, with an occasional divergence to Dutchess; the other branch has fluctuated between Westchester County and the City of New York.

The Ulster men were evidently notabilities in their time — judges, colonels, high-sheriffs, and what not; great speculators likewise in wild lands. I do not know, however, that, though useful in their day, they ever did any thing to commend themselves especially to the remembrance of posterity. The others appear to have been simply respectable folk, cutting no particular figure in the world. Joost or Joseph Pauldinck, however, as early as 1683, is set down as "freeman of the city of New York." From him the descending line is traceable with tolerable clearness to William, the father of James.

This Joseph, Joost, or Yoost Pauldinck is mentioned in the records of Rye, Westchester County, in 1667; Henry Pawling in those of Kingston, Ulster County, in 1666. At first sight there seems to be some discrepancy between the names. But their proprietors, and others that came after them, lived in the days of that noble superiority to the trammels of spelling which sometimes so bewilders the antiquary. Moreover, the Dutch and English languages were battling for supremacy in the country, and were strangely mingled. Accordingly, the name appears, often with no initial capital, indifferently sometimes in the same document, as Pawling, Paelden, Pauling, Palingh, Paulding, Paeldin, Pauldin, Pauwldin, Pauldinck, Palding. One ingenious scribe was so plethoric of letters as to write Pauwldingh.

I suppose the name to have been properly Pawling, and the family English. My father, however, in a memorandum in my possession, states that his grandfather and grandmother spoke Dutch, and attended the old church at the entrance of Sleepy Hollow, where the preaching was entirely in that language. But, escaping from these speculations, I pass at once to the Revolutionary period.

It seems that William Paulding, father of James, ran away from home, took to the sea, rose to the command of several ships in succession sailing out of the port of New York, probably traded a little on his own account, and, about the year 1767, moved to Tarrytown in Westchester County, where he built himself a house, and opened a store. In the prosecution of his business he became well acquainted with and respected by the farmers of the county, and, at the breaking-out of the War of Independence was in comfortable, if not opulent, circumstances, and a man of considerable weight and influence in the community.

Every schoolboy knows one Paulding, named "John," and how he earned his motto of "Fidelity." This other, uncle of that popular hero, worked in his way too for the common cause. Member of the first "Committee of Safety" in New York; acting as a State Commissary to the Revolutionary forces; inhabitant of "The Neutral Ground;" standing forth as a representative man against the powerful Tory influences of this district; obnoxious to all manner of lawless characters in his neighborhood; obliged, in consequence, to remove his family from the sphere of his duties; and expected, in behalf of a government with little credit and no cash, to procure supplies from an impoverished people — altogether, his was not a pleasant position, or course of life. But he did not shirk it, nor, when the time came, the last responsibility. Himself a man of considerable property for those days, at length the crisis arrived, when, on an urgent occasion, the promises he could make as a public agent absolutely failed. Nevertheless it was necessary that the troops should be fed. Whereupon he marched into the gulf, pledged his entire fortune, surmounted the emergency, and felt himself a ruined man.

So it proved. In 1784 — (Independence acknowledged) — he presented the following brief statement of his claims: —

" *To the Honb$^{le}$ the Legislature of the State of New York*

*The Petition of William Paulding humbly sheweth* —

That your Petitioner was appointed to supply the Militia under the Command of General Clinton as will appear by his Appointment dated August 1776, a true Copy of which is hereunto annexed — That your Petitioner took charge as directed and supply'd them with Rations, agreeable to the Continental establishment; after leaving the service, your Petitioner with considerable expence, got his accounts Liquidated by Jonathan Trumbull Esq$^{r}$ Commissioner for settling accounts for the Continent and as the Legislature having as yet made no provision for the payment of his Accounts leaves your Petitioner liable to Arrest for monies due in consequence of the said Appointment and for which he has given his private Obligations — therefore

Your Petitioner Humbly Prays that he may have permission granted to him of purchasing by Appraisement, of the Commissioners, as much forfeited Lands as amounts to the ball$^{a}$ of his Accounts or such other relief as you in your wisdom shall think best —

WILLIAM PAULDING.

NEW YORK 17$^{th}$ OCTOBER 1784."

This was no great matter to ask or to grant. But the day of need was passed, and the Honorable the Legislature turned a deaf ear to the disabled patriot. As anticipated, he was arrested for debt, and confined in a log prison at White Plains, about six miles from Tarrytown to which place the family had now returned. My father writes, late in life:—

"As my elder brothers were absent at school in Hackinsack, it fell to my lot every Saturday to carry him a supply of those little comforts which we could afford to send."

"An old borrowed horse" transported the boy, with his "supply of clean clothes and other little necessaries."

"It was a melancholy journey, and I cannot think on it, even at this distant period, without painful emotions. He had not been there many months before the jail took fire; my father was released by this accident, and, nobody opposing, walked home, where he remained ever afterward undisturbed by his creditors. He had given them all he had, and they left him to enjoy his poverty in quiet. He was a proud man, and the ingratitude of his country, joined to the disgrace of a prison, though they did not produce despair, so operated on his mind that he ever afterward neglected the means of retrieving his fortune."

Elsewhere my father declares: "He never made a second application for the settlement of his accounts," "which, so long as I can recollect, served as waste paper about the house."

In fact, yielding himself up to a disgust for the world, not to be commended, but perhaps excusable, he turned himself graveward, at which bourn in process of time he arrived — not however till February 20th, 1825 — in his ninetieth year. Doubtless stirring incidents occurred in his experience: but he was not a person to prate of his own deeds, and they have perished from human memory. My father testifies that, after his misfortunes, "he resorted to books for employment, perhaps consolation, and it is probably to his example I owe a habit of reading which has accompanied me through life." Again, he says: "He was a man of very extensive reading, as well as great experience of the world, having as a navigator visited various quarters, and in latter years of his life one of his favorite recreations was to gather around him his younger children and those of the neighbors, and tell them stories of his own adventures, or those of Sindbad the sailor, or some other hero of the Arabian Nights."

A granddaughter describes him as a small man, with blue eyes, light complexion, and fine white hair, always studying newspapers. Indeed, according to her account, if he found a piece anywhere, though but six inches square, he would pick it up, smooth it out, and come to anchor in the first convenient spot to decipher it. Reading matter was not so plentiful in those days as now, and he had probably exhausted his stock. My father says of himself: "We had a few books saved from the wreck; but still, at this moment, [1852], I am conscious that this very circumstance gave to my early reading a value far beyond that of my subsequent life. What I read I read thoroughly, and what I learned I learned well. A book was then a treasure, now it is a superfluity. They follow so closely at each others' heels, that the footsteps of one obliterate those of the preceding, like the waves of the ocean."

Leading this harmless and placid life his days rolled on unmarked; and so, of the later years of this long-lived man remains now but a single specific record. Out of the dim past looms a quaint picture from the hand of a grandson who saw him once, an old old man, sitting in the sunlight and poring over the pages of Hoole's Ariosto.

The mother was gifted with greater energy. After her husband succumbed to his cruel stroke, she became almost literally the life of the entire family. In a burst of gratitude, her son James wrote of "a series of kindness and benefits received from my dear mother, such as few children ever knew, and none can ever repay." And again, in a memorandum addressed to his children: —

"I will give you a sketch of her character and person, for well does she deserve to be remembered with gratitude and veneration by us all. She was small in stature, with dark complexion, sparkling black eyes, and raven hair. When the spirit of my father was broken by the ruin of his affairs and the imprisonment of his person, the whole weight of supporting the family, at least those who were too young to support themselves, fell on my mother. . . . To her conduct I can never do justice. By her thrift, her activity and industry, and by that almost magic with which some women seem to achieve impossibilities, she managed, with the aid of occasional acts of kindness from her married daughters and her sister in New York, not only to feed and clothe us, but to send us to school, not at the expense of the parish but her own. This she did by plying her needle, morning, noon, and night, with a cheerful alacrity that diffused itself over the whole house. . . . All that I have ever been I owe to her."

The granddaughter herein before mentioned recalls her in similar terms, as very small, but symmetrical; adding that she was light and active in her movements, and at seventy-eight used to trip up and down a steep flight of stairs in her house, like a girl.

At the period above referred to, as my father (in a communication addressed in 1852 to the Hon. Joseph S. Sims of South Carolina) strongly expresses it, the family "were not only poor, but steeped in poverty;" and in a letter to Gouverneur Kemble, in 1839, he observes: "In my early days I have all but known what it was to want bread." Nevertheless the mother lived to see all her children comfortable, and some wealthy and distinguished. At length she also died, November 25th, 1830, in her eighty-ninth year.

But I have been anticipating. To return to James K. Paulding — I have stated that he was born at Great-Nine-Partners. He supposes that his father owned property there. At one time the Ulster branch of the family certainly did. I imagine it was an additional inducement to sending his family there that the people of the neighborhood were sturdy opponents of the Crown — "a riotous people and Levellers by principle," as Captain Paul Ricaut of the British army reported in 1771.

In reference to his birthplace our author remarks: "The prominent part taken by my father in behalf of the liberties of his country had made him highly obnoxious to the British then in the possession of the city of New York, as well as the Tories who abounded in the lower parts of Westchester. It became unsafe to leave his family at Tarrytown, and he accordingly removed them to a place called The Nine Partners in the County of Dutchess. After their departure the marauding parties often threatened to set our house on fire, but were deterred by the fear of burning that of a staunch old Tory who lived directly opposite. The house therefore escaped with a few shot-holes from the firing of the British vessels passing up the river, the marks of which may still be seen.

"I was born during this exile from home, and my first recollections are connected with this spot. I visited it some years ago, and was pleased to find that though I left it a child of only three or four years"—[from what he subsequently says he must have been at least five]—"my memory had not altogether deceived me. The house was gone; but the little knoll on which it stood, the green meadow which spread out at its foot, and the fine clear brook that flowed through it in graceful windings, were still there just as I had pictured them in my mind. The country around was beautiful, and it was here in all probability I imbibed that taste, almost passion, for the charms of Nature, which to this day furnishes one of my most cherished enjoyments. I remember nothing but the scene; the incidents which occurred, if worth recollecting or recording, have passed away, and not a shadow remains.

"At the conclusion of the war, my father, who used to visit us when the army went into Winter quarters, came home, and took us shortly afterward to our old residence at Tarrytown. Here my recollections become more distinct. I remember coming down the hill, and most especially the fine spring which gushed from its foot directly opposite to our house. The house itself excited my admiration, for it was the largest I had ever seen. It looked to me like a church without a steeple, and I continued to view it in that light, until I first came home after residing in New York, when it seemed to have dwindled into a very insignificant building."

The influences upon the youthful mind of James K. Paulding were of a marked nature, and produced a corresponding effect. His very birth, (his mother a refugee from her home by reason of British hostility), was almost a pledge of inherited enmity. Again, he writes, "My father, William Paulding, married Catharine Ogden, of the family of that name in New Jersey. Her father's name was Nathaniel, and one of the earliest, as well as most painful recollections, of my childhood, is the figure of this aged man whose few remaining hairs were as white as snow. He had been brutally cut across the head by a party of British soldiers during the Revolutionary war, because he would not cry, 'God save the King.' A partial and permanent derangement of intellect was the consequence, and I remember him walking along the beach at Tarrytown, picking up sticks, and talking to himself about the reign of Queen Anne of which he had a history which he often read, and how the Tories were no better than highway robbers." When to all this is added the fact that he grew up in a district reeking with tales of British, Hessian, or Tory atrocities, none can wonder that he imbibed a lasting prejudice against England and every thing English.

His boyish days were but gloomy. "As to myself," he says, "there was little sunshine in my youth. . . . For some time after the conclusion of the war there were very few schools in our part of the country, and the nearest schoolhouse was upward of two miles from our residence. At this country school, which was a log hut, I received my education. It was — as intimated before — upward of two miles from home, and there I went, and thence returned every day, almost always without a companion. I never look back on that period of life which most people contemplate with so much regret as the season of blossoms, without a feeling of dreary sadness. From the experience of my early life I never wish to be young again."

He appears at this time to have been living with an uncle on Sawmill River, back of Tarrytown, for the convenience of attending this school; and, there being no young people in the house, his only companion was a dumb girl, daughter of an old soldier who was allowed free quarters on the farm. Leading this life he became dreamy and melancholy; fell sick; was exercised with the fear of death; and came near having his brain addled at a revival, which, he says, resulted in the suicide of a neighbor.

"As for myself, I know not what the result might have been, had not the squire" [his schoolmaster] "just about this time been appointed Surrogate of the county, whereupon he at once abandoned his divine vocation of teaching the young idea how to shoot, and devoted himself equally to the concerns of the living and the dead. On going to school next morning, a note was received from the shepherd dismissing his flock, which signalized its satisfaction by turning the tables and benches upside down, scattering the contents of the chimney over the floor, and themselves in all directions. I returned to the house of my mother, and thus ended my education, which first and last cost about fifteen dollars, certainly quite as much as it was worth.". . . "The only circumstance worthy of note which occurred during my stay at Sawmill River, and possibly gave a direction to my whole life, was my encountering among the few books of my uncle, Goldsmith's Citizen of the World. I read it, I believe twenty times at least, and if I have any taste or style, I owe them to that charming work of the most delightful of all English writers."

"At the time I returned home I was a good-sized boy, some twelve or thirteen years old. My disposition was proud and shy. . . . My life at Tarrytown after leaving school was weary and irksome. The present was a blank and the future almost a void. My mind was sufficiently active, but my body indolent. . . . There was never any employment for my idle hours. . . . I was always fond of reading, but we had few books, and there was no public library." He records himself as having become "the most conspicuous idler in the village;" and so reckless of public opinion, that when the old folk turned up the whites of their eyes and the palms of their hands at him and prophesied he would come to no good, it troubled him not.

About this time "my brother William had presented me with a gun, and I took to shooting, but in rambling about the woods and fields, instead of minding my business employed myself in building castles in the air, at which I was always very expert. One day, having cocked my gun on hearing a quail whistle, I neglected to uncock it after having frightened the bird away, and was leaning listlessly against a tree with the gun resting against my shoulder, when somehow or other my foot touched the trigger and it went off, carrying away a part of the brim of my hat, but doing no other harm. The conclusion I drew from this was that I was not cut out for a sportsman, and from that time I took to fishing which I found suited me exactly, as I could stick the end of my rod into a rock, and indulge myself in a brown study at pleasure. . . .

"The only time I ever distinguished myself in the piscatory line was in catching a bass twenty two inches long, the greatest feat I ever performed. In the winter I used to set traps and snares, and on one memorable occasion came down Tarrytown hill with five quails, a partridge, and a rabbit. Do you think any hero returning from the conquest of kingdoms ever felt half as proud as I did?"

I have dwelt upon these particulars of my father's childhood and boyish days, perhaps longer than necessary; but I have done so because they furnish a key to his character and conduct throughout life, and naturally lead on to nearly all the opinions and ideas he embodied in the writings of so many subsequent years.

"I lived," he says, "pretty much in a world of my own creating." He had grown up "to the age of eighteen or nineteen, without ever going five miles from home." Thus he went mooning about, and passed into the rhyming stage of existence, about as unfit for a struggle with the great world as any youth could well be.

# II.

1797–1807. [ÆT. 19–29.]

LAUNCH IN NEW YORK — BREAKING IN — FIRST POETIC EFFORT — LETTER TO WASHINGTON IRVING — A STUDY — THE SALMAGUNDI SET — SALMAGUNDI.

BUT the plunge was at hand. "At length the time came for emerging into that world I had hitherto only contemplated through the medium of fancy. My elder brother [William] had procured me a situation in a public office, and furnished me the means of making my debut respectably. I was forthwith launched from comparative solitude into the bustle of a great city, and I well remember the first shock given to my sensitiveness was being laughed at by the rabble about the wharf where I landed," [no doubt from the weekly market sloop], "for walking in the middle of the street. Previous to this, my first Avatär, one of my sisters had married Mr. William Irving, eldest brother to Washington Irving, who was afterwards a representative in Congress from New York, a man of great wit, genius, and originality. This had produced a boyish acquaintance between Washington and myself, which was renewed on my arrival in New York, and ripened into a solid friendship which has continued to this day.

"Thus I fell, as it were, among the Philistines; for the circle in which I moved — though I can scarcely say had a being — was composed of young men, many of whom have since made no inconsiderable figure in the world. I was excessively thin-skinned — I may say, perfectly raw — and nothing was so painful to me as ridicule. They broke me in by quizzing me most unmercifully; but, though the perspiration of almost agony sprung from the very hair of my head, I bore it like a martyr, for I was too proud to show how I suffered. By this course I was drilled into something like a citizen of the new world into which I had been thrown. It was a rough discipline to a lad of my temperament, but proved of great service in after-life; and, though I look back on it with something like horror, I have always considered the lessons worth the purchase. It was the best school in which I ever studied."

The name of James Paulding appears in the New-York City Directory for 1797, as resident at number 43 Vesey Street, being the same house in which lived his brother William Paulding, Jr. I think it probable that this was the year in which he went to town, and that the situation to which he refers was in the United-States Loan Office. At any rate it is certain that at one period he held a clerkship there. He was now nineteen, and, as I suppose, scribbled in Commonplace books, but made no confidants, undergoing as best he could the case-hardening process above alluded to. The first specific and complete effort I have encountered is dated 1799, although it was not published till more than half a century afterward, when he was contributing some articles to "The United-States Review," in which periodical it appeared, in September, 1853. As usual, the poetic faculty was the first developed; and the verses convey, as I imagine, the author's first impressions of the scenery whose title surmounts them:—

### DAWN IN THE HIGHLANDS OF THE HUDSON.

The opening eyelids of the waking morn
Now o'er the drowsy world begin to wink,
While the bright lustres that the skies adorn,
Before the coming glory, pale and shrink.

High in the East, yon shadowy fleece of clouds,
Edged with a rosy tint, begins to glow,
While darkling mist the humbler landscape shrouds,
Veiling the beauties of the world below;

Save where yon wood-crowned peak is seen to rise,
Like giant towering in majestic height,
Lifting its gilded head amid the skies,
Beyond the rolling scud's fantastic flight.

No songster carols from his lonely bower;
No insect chirps along the meadow green;
No sound of life disturbs the quiet hour,
And silence reigns o'er all the Sabbath scene;

Save, ever and anon, some wakeful bird
Twitters a welcome to the blue-eyed dawn;
Or some full-uddered cow afar is heard,
Calling the lagging milkmaid to the lawn.

But see! the sun through yon deep cleft appears,
Careering masterful into the sky!
His presence all the world of nature cheers,
And wakes the woodland's mingled melody.

At once the air is vocal with the strain
That quavers through the valleys far and wide,
Along the bubbling brooks, the jewelled plain,
Deep in the glen, and up the mountain side.

A swarm of bustling insects speed away
  On pleasant tour of merry morning flight,
And sport and glitter in the sunny ray,
  Or revel 'mid the flowers in full delight.

The ever-busy bee is on the wing,
  Eager to quaff his cup of honeyed dew
Where roses wild in red luxuriance spring,
  And oft his luscious morning draught renew.

The envious mists, whose unsubstantial veil
  Drooped o'er the face of nature, upward fly,
Athwart the mountain's brow like spectres quail,
  And give the laughing landscape to the eye.

Slowly its beauties open to my view;
  One at a time its blushing charms unfold;
And nature, to her sex's maxim true,
  With sweet delay permits me to behold.

Like some capricious beauty, she awhile
  Hides the full magic of her winning face,
The pouting ruby lip, the dimpled smile,
  And all her youthful, soft, bewitching, grace,

Till, as by chance, the veil is blown aside,
  And lo! the glowing cheek, the sparkling eye,
The snowy neck, by happy chance are spied,
  Blended in one delicious harmony.

Thus nature coquets with the lord of day;
  Now shrouds her face in mist, and now appears
Enwrapped in gloom, or pranked in colors gay;
  Now glowing joyously, and now all tears.

The goddess still her loveliness renews
  In twilight gravity or morning play,
Or, 'mid the silent stars and noiseless dews,
  When night's pale regent holds her lonely sway.

Whether in balmy Spring, bedecked with flowers,
  And bright with smiles, she shows her ruddy face,
Or panting in her sultry Summer bowers,
  Or clothed in Autumn's many-colored grace,

Or e'en when rigorous Winter rides the air,
  His snowy beard wild streaming to the wind,
Now wrapt in clouds, and now with angry glare
  Chiding the storm for lingering behind;

Still there is something in her glorious plan
  That wakes our noblest thoughts, and lifts the soul
To HIM who gave the wondrous work to man,
  And with it feeling to enjoy the whole.

Peter Irving, an elder brother of Washington, was editor of a newspaper, "The Morning Chronicle," in New York, from 1802 to 1805. To its columns it is well known that Washington contributed, and there also his friend first saw himself in print.

In May, 1804, Irving left the country for a tour in Europe on account of his health, and shortly after his departure began a correspondence between the two, which runs over more than fifty years. The opening letter, from Paulding, is a little curious, as indicating that they had already gathered a set of intimates and provided them with nicknames, for the bestowal of which Irving had throughout his life a special fancy and a happy knack. It is dated New York, 28th June, 1804. I introduce a couple of extracts.

TO W. IRVING.

Take notice my lad, you are to expect no news from me; all my letters shall be devoted to higher objects, sublime speculations, and other matters of moonshine. In return I expect from you a history, ancient and modern, of every place or object that strikes your senses — a narrative of your feelings on occasions when the scene of some heroic action bursts upon you, and recalls the idea of the chivalric virtue of departed chiefs. I wish to Heaven I was with you — Sblood! What battles we would fight o'er and o'er again! Battles that should make pale the blushing honours of the bridge of Bronx, and wither yellow with envy the laurels won on that memorable day. You cannot have forgotten how the Hessians were mauled on that occasion, and how "Victory like a towering eagle sat perched upon my beaver," on the Bridge, and how Majors Sturgeon and Molasses gained immortal honour.

. . . . . . . . . . .

You will hear by this same conveyance of the welfare of all your friends — of them I shall therefore say nothing. But for my "single self" I tender the best good wishes of my heart for your health and happiness. I have been called cold-hearted, and indifferent to the welfare of others, because my manners are perhaps so. But it was injustice, and among the many wishes you may receive be assured there will be none more sincere or more earnest than mine.

Yours affectionately, J. K. PAULDING.

I presume the embryo author employed himself about these years, in writing for the newspapers, and jotting down memoranda like the following: —

"It was not a light that dazzled, but a pure, distinguishing, and placid light which called forth every object to view in its most perfect form. The isle spread large before him like a sweet vision of imagination, where distance fades not on the sight, where nearness fatigues not the eye. It had its gently-swelling hills of tranquil green, nor was the sky unvaried by clouds. But the clouds were bright and gloriously transparent, involving each in its bosom the nourishment of some murmuring stream, whose wandering down the steep was like the faint echoes of the harp of the winds when swept by zephyrs of Spring. The valleys were open, and free to the ocean; trees, loaded with leaves which scarcely waved to the night breeze, were scattered on the green declivities and rising grounds. The rude winds walked not on the mountain; no storm took its course through the sky. All was calm, and serene, and bright; the pure sun of Autumn shone from his clear blue sky on the happy fields, not hastening to the West for repose, but for ever seated immovable on his throne of gold in the highest heaven."

In the Directory for the year 1806, James K. Paulding is set down as living at No. 287 Greenwich Street, the residence of his brother-in-law, William Irving, Jr. Washington Irving returned home with renovated health in the Spring of this year, and the two were naturally much thrown together. William Irving is described on all hands as a superior man. Gouverneur Kemble, the sole survivor of this circle, speaks of him as full of apt illustration, and humor, and conceives that both his brother Washington, and his brother-in-law James, owed no little of their literary success in after-life to his original impulse of sympathy and advice.

There was a special knot of good fellows that included Washington Irving and Paulding, to whom the latter alludes in letters of later years to Henry Brevoort, Jr., himself one of the set, as the "ancient and honorable order," and "the ancient club of New York." Pretty much all of them, and many other of their acquaintance, were furnished with aliases. Brevoort answered to "Nuncle"; Paulding was dubbed "Billy Taylor"; Kemble, "the Patroon"; William Irving "the membrane"; Ebenezer Irving took rank as "Captain Great-heart". Only Washington Irving has no secondary title; whence I conclude that he had labelled the rest.

Other nicknames occur in the subsequent correspondence of Paulding with Brevoort, such as "the old man", and "Sindbad"; the latter believed to be David Porter, of "Essex" renown. "The Supercargo" was Henry, or, as he generally figures, *Harry* Ogden, who was evidently a great favorite among them; apparently one of those cheerful and light-hearted men whose temperament seems to have been given them by Providence especially to enable them to bear (as we often see in the compensations of this life) the ill luck which for ever pursues them. Perhaps all the more for this he was in favor with "us jolly but poor rogues."

Nor did others, not of the clan, escape this process of transmutation. Thus Longworth, the publisher, became "the Dusky"; and Captain Philipse, a much older man than any of them, "the Chieftain", it is to be presumed in deference to his ownership of large tracts of land in the Highlands of the Hudson, the relics of a patent which once covered the entire County of Putnam.

Well, it was a gay company just fifty years ago; and the whole state of things is worth dwelling upon a little, as being so far removed in spirit from the present day and existing habits of thought. It would seem as if ages, and not a single life-time only, divided us from it. Here were a parcel of young men whom Uncle Mammon would undoubtedly now pronounce a pack of ne'er-do-weels, most of whom nevertheless turned out somewhat notable in life, and some loomed largely in the public view for many years.

Shreds of odd stories have floated down even to the present day — how Henry Brevoort's hat, taken by mistake after a dinner party, was recognized on the head of an individual found in the gutter in front of Trinity Church, whom the Dogberrys of the day, or rather night, bore carefully home to that gentleman's lodgings, and insisted upon the body's being his own; how Billy M. was once carried in procession by his still capable friends to his bed, and, with Mozart's requiem chanted over him, was buried under all the furniture of his room; how — but what skills it to repeat these things now? "Alack and alack!", of all those merry blades but one survives. That one is Gouverneur Kemble, "the patroon", probably so styled by way of joke in those days of great landed properties because he owned an old house and a few acres near Newark, New Jersey — the Cockloft Hall of Salmagundi.

There is another noticeable thing. Of this society, four in particular, namely Washington Irving, Henry Brevoort Jr., Gouverneur Kemble, and James K. Paulding, became more closely bound in an unusual friendship. The relations which united this little group were of the most intimate. A confidence even beyond that of brothers existed among them; a confidence which, it is believed, was never violated under any circumstances, on any hand. And there is no trace of any quarrel to the end of their days.

We have now arrived at a period important in the history of the two literary members of this fraternity. Both had before this dabbled in newspaper work; but the publication of the first number of SALMAGUNDI, January 24, 1807, (Mr. Paulding being then in his twenty-ninth year and his associate about five years younger), may be considered as the starting point in the literary career of both; for, though the former can scarcely be said to have pursued literature as the ambition of his life, the success of this venture, doubtless, fixed him in the natural turn he had for pursuits of that nature.

Salmagundi arose, no one knows exactly how, between the two. It was more probably an inspiration than a plan, and was worked out in a hap-hazard way consonant with its original conception. Mr. Paulding says: —

"It was when fairly initiated into the mysteries of the town that Washington Irving and myself commenced the publication of Salmagundi, an irregular issue, the object of which was to ridicule the follies and foibles of the fashionable world. Though we had not anticipated any thing beyond a local circulation, the work soon took a wider sphere; gradually extended throughout the United States; and acquired great popularity. It was, I believe, the first of its kind in this country; produced numerous similar publications, none of which, however, extended beyond a few numbers, and formed somewhat of an era in our Literature. It reached two volumes, and we could easily have continued it indefinitely. But the publisher, with that liberality so characteristic of these modern Mæcenases, declined to concede to us a share of the profits which had become very considerable, and the work was abruptly discontinued. It was one of those productions of youth that wise men — or those who think themselves wise — are very apt to be ashamed of when they grow old."

It appears that the authors received one hundred dollars a-piece from Longworth, as their share of the proceeds. This joint work has been republished at sundry times, in connexion with Mr. Irving's works or those of Mr. Paulding; and, since the death of both parties, as a pendant to the "National Edition" of the former's writings.

The allies never chose to separate their interest in the articles. Their judgment as to the merits of the production varied somewhat. In 1820 Mr. Irving was much out of conceit with it. In February, 1822, the original copyright having expired, Mr. Paulding proposed to his friend (through his brother Ebenezer), that they should revise the work and republish it for their joint benefit; observing that it still had a good sale, and adducing as an additional reason for the course suggested, that the publisher had "taken the liberty to add some of his own nonsense occasionally"; and that "it would therefore be desirable even on that account to get the work out of his diabolical clutches if possible." He adds that he "was debauching it with blunders, and vile pictures, &c., that were a disgrace to any decent publication." I find no answer to this proposition at that time; but two years later, as I gather from a letter of Paulding to his coadjutor, the latter had brought up the subject. Mr. Paulding writes, under date of March 20, 1824: "I approve your plan of a new edition of Salmagundi, and will set about my part as soon as the spirit moves me. I anticipate much barrenness in my attempts, having almost exhausted myself in this line. I don't hold this early bantling of ours in such utter contempt as you do, and can't help viewing it in the light of a careless popular thing that will always be read in spite of its faults, perhaps in consequence of these very faults."

This project also fell through, for some reason unknown. In 1834, when Mr. Paulding had made an arrangement with Harper & Brothers for the publication of a uniform edition of his works, he applied to Mr. Irving who was then a near neighbor, (one living in Whitehall St. and the other just round the corner in Bridge St.), in the following language: "I know you consider Old Sal as a sort of saucy flippant trollope, belonging to nobody, and not worth fathering, and therefore venture to ask if you have any objection to have her again presented to the public in connexion with the continuation, and for our joint benefit. It can be reprinted from the Paris edition which I have, and without any further sanction of the authors than that indicates." He adds, at the close of the letter: "I preferred writing to talking to you, because I am much more accustomed to one than the other, and can explain myself better."

This letter was dated Feb. 28th. Mr. Irving rejoins the next day, according permission, but remarking that he never allowed Murray to republish it; that Galignani had done so without his authority; and, on the whole, depreciating the work somewhat in the spirit of a respectable elderly gentleman when called upon to harvest the wild oats of his youth. I do not find any hint to this effect in Mr. Paulding's letter, but Mr. Irving seems to have taken up the impression that additions or alterations were proposed; and, after speaking of its demerits, continues: "These, however, are excusable in a juvenile production: as such, therefore, I wish it to be considered, and for that reason am disinclined to any additions or modifications that may appear to give it the sanction of our present taste, judgment, and opinions."

So ends that story.

## III.

1808–1813. [ÆT. 30–35.]

HABITS OF AUTHORSHIP — THE SUMMER MORN — THE DIVERTING HISTORY OF JOHN BULL AND BROTHER JONATHAN — THE LAY OF THE SCOTTISH FIDDLE — REVIEW BY WASHINGTON IRVING — SKETCH OF, AND EXTRACTS FROM, THE LAY.

OUR author now went "plodding on," as he expresses it, for some years, probably contributing to the newspapers, but not coming self-assertively before the public. Indeed it was a peculiarity of his that he never seemed to care much whether his work produced him reputation or emolument. He writes, late in life: — "I never put my name to any production, except it was made a condition by the publisher;" and the late George P. Morris told me, that when conducting the New-York Mirror, some twenty years after the period we are now considering, my father would continually come into his office, produce a paper from his pocket, poke it at him, and march out without a single word. He sums up his ambitions for himself in one of the papers in the Second Series of Salmagundi. "For my part, I solemnly assure my readers, that I would willingly forego all the praises I expect to receive, (from posterity at least), if I could only enjoy the delights of living among the present generation, and laughing a little at their foibles, without being known by a single soul."

He wrote, apparently, because he must needs get rid of what he had in his head, or because he found the use of his pen the readiest way of killing time. In this anonymous way some of his most delicious little bits were published. I find in an early Commonplace book a printed fragment cut out of a newspaper of about the year 1810, (as I suppose), which, I have no doubt, is of his composition.

THE SUMMER MORN.

Twilight lingers dim and deep,
Hushing earth in dewy sleep;
Till along the amber sky
Morning's fiery arrows fly,
And in a slow-surging fold
From the land the mist is rolled,
Nature's gorgeous theatre;
Showing splendors far and near,
Solemn wood, and sheltered bay,
Where some weary bark, that lay
All night neighbored by the bank,
Through the willows clustering dank
Shines along with hollow sail,
Shifting to the morning gale.
Village sounds are waking now:
Birds are singing on the bough;
Through the hoary umbraged oak
Slowly curls the cottage smoke;
To the forest far and gray
Chants the woodman on his way.
Now the fisher through the pool
Woodbine-shaded, clear and cool,
Where, by moss and tufted weed
Loves the speckled trout to feed,
Wades with cautious step and eye,
Flinging oft the gilded fly;
Yet, with deep-delighted ear,
Pausing in his sport, to hear

Where the milkmaid's merry song
Rings the primrose path along,
Some sweet measure of the time
When the heart was in the rhyme;
Or, along the distant hill,
Softened comes the whistle shrill,
Telling where, beside his team,
(That, ascending in the beam,
Like a fiery troop appear),
Toils the early wagoner!
Sights like these let sluggards scorn —
Joy is in the Summer Morn.

This recalls some of the eldest English poets. Indeed, it is remarkable how often this early laborer in the field of American, suggests the corresponding phase of English, literature. The introduction of singing milkmaids and woodmen is not so conventional as might seem at first. My father alludes in various places to this matter, specifying the songs sung. An example comes to hand in the same book from which this little poem is taken, and is in the shape of a memorandum; thus:—

"Highlands.

Rustic procession to the hay-field — Jacobs, Connor, Eben, Cyrus, &c., marching in a row, with forks rakes, &c., on their shoulders, singing the Quaker Lady."

At other times on the contrary he notices and regrets the decay, or the lack, of the singing impulse among our people. For the primrose path and the fly-fisher I cannot so well account. All his sport in angling heretofore must, I think, have been in rough mountain streams, unless mayhap the Sawmill River had furnished him game in his boyhood; and at that time he was not so sophisticated as to know anything about such delicate appliances. Probably Izaak Walton is responsible for this, as for many another fancy allusion to the piscatorial art.

About this period, or perhaps a year or two earlier, the set began to frequent "the Grange," a residence just built by Captain Philipse, "the chieftain," on his estate in Putnam County. This house was opposite West Point, at the turn of the river, commanding from its two fronts the whole extent of the Highlands from Anthony's Nose to Pollepells Island. It was burnt in 1860.

In this pleasant retreat Mr. Paulding's next letter to Irving found him, a few months after the opening of the war of 1812. The former had just published THE DIVERTING HISTORY OF JOHN BULL AND BROTHER JONATHAN, a political satire, which will form a portion of one volume of the re-publication to which this Life is intended to serve as a species of herald. All later critics have acknowledged the homely force of the style of this work, and the pertinent vigor of its plan and execution; but it must have hung fire at first. Mr. Paulding writes:

NEW YORK. 5th Sept. 1812.

DEAR WASHINGTON, I send you a copy of John Bull, who has made some talk here, but I believe don't sell very well; for what reason I leave you to judge — it being such an excellent work.

It has been several times reprinted.

In 1813 our author published a little squib, styled "THE LAY OF THE SCOTTISH FIDDLE: a Tale of Havre de Grace. Supposed to be written by Walter Scott, Esq. First American, from the fourth Edinburgh edition." The volume was diminutive; the publishers were Inskeep and Bradford, New York, and Bradford and Inskeep, Philadelphia.

A brief review in the Analectic Magazine of September, 1813, by Washington Irving, then editor, sufficiently expresses the scope of the book. " A little work, 'supposed to be written by Walter Scott, Esq.' with the above title, has just issued from the press, under the fashionable modern form of a poem *with notes:* the late period at which it was put into our hands prevents us from entering into a particular account of it. The writer appears to have more than one object in view. At first, his intention seems to be merely to satirize and parody the writings of Walter Scott, which have lately had such an all-pervading circulation in the fashionable world; but in the course of his work, he seems disposed to extend his lash to the follies and errors of his countrymen; to advocate the present war; and to retaliate in a good-humoured way on the British invaders in the Chesapeake, for their excesses at Havre de Grace. But though ridicule and merriment appear to be the leading features, the work is occasionally diversified by little passages of pathos and feeling; the descriptions of American scenery, and American manners, are touched off with much truth of pencil and felicity of manner, and there are several veins of thought that would do credit to a work of a more elevated and sober character.

" There are, however, some traces of political satire discernible in this volume, which, though managed with great good nature, we regret that the revising hand of the author had not expunged; as they are calculated to awaken angry feelings in some bosoms, and to injure the interests of a work, which would otherwise be read with pleasure and approbation throughout the Union."

The volume consists of a Preface, an "Introduction" and five Cantos, and Notes, in which last there is a good deal of pleasantry. This system of padding out a book appears to have especially aroused our author's caustic humor. In a review by him of "The Emerald Isle, a poem by Charles Phillips, Esq.," to be found in The Analectic Magazine for July, 1813, he thus writes:—"Indeed there is at least four times the solid quantity of notes that there is of poetry; and the complexion of this mighty mass resembles not a little that multifarious variety of broken chairs, ancient bureaus, worn-out tables, and other precious remains of antiquity, which every good housewife thinks it necessary to scour up, and carry along with her in her periodical migrations."

Returning to "The Lay", I should observe that the copy in my possession is much interlined with the author's corrections, and in some parts entirely re-written. The course of the story is this. A blind fiddler led by his dog, finds his way from New York to Princeton, where he brings up at "Lord" Joline's tavern. Here he is induced to sing his lay, and—(with the episode of a grand row of students from Nassau Hall, and others)—works through it, and is dismissed in a condition which seems to assure a comfortable close to his days. From the INTRODUCTION I extract a delicate bit of burlesque:—

Now crossed they noble Hudson's tide,
In steamboat, young Columbia's pride,
And meet it is the poet say
They paid no ferriage by the way.

Through Jersey city straight they wend
And Bergen hill-tops slow ascend,
Whence he who is possessed of eyes
A gallant prospect often spies.
Far off the noiseless ocean rolled,
A pure expanse of burnished gold,
And nearer spread a various view
Of objects beautiful and new;
Fair Hackinsack, Passaic smooth,
Whose gentle murmurs sweetly soothe;
And Newark bay, and Arthur's sound;
And many an island spread around,
Like fat green turtles fast asleep
On the still surface of the deep.
And Gotham might you see, whose spires
Shone in the sun, like meteor fires.
The vessels lay all side by side,
And spread a leafless forest wide;
And now and then the Yo heave O
Borne on the breeze, all sad and slow,
Seemed like the requiem of trade,
Low in its grave for ever laid.

CANTO I. introduces THE THREE KNIGHTS, Sir Bolus—(Admiral Sir John Borlase Warren)—Sir Beresford—(Sir John Beresford)—and Childe Cockburn—(Rear-admiral Cockburn)—pondering their mission of waste and plunder. The bulk of the expedition is thus made fun of:—

Bold sailors, bottle-loving race,
Stretched half-asleep at random lay,
Or urged in dreams the gallant chase
Of oyster boats far up the bay.
Full seven hundred of these tars
Would doff their hats when Sir Knight came by,
All famed afar in naval wars
And feats of Border Chivalry.
Six lieutenants stout and bold,
Twelve midshipmen, as I am told,

Jolly lads of metal true,
Officered this stalwart crew.
All of these were clad in blue,
And to their broad-swords stuck like glue;
They quitted not their steel so bright,
Neither by day, nor yet by night:
    They lay down to rest
    With doublet all braced,
Pillowed on plank so rough and hard;
    They carved at the meal
    With sword of true steel,
And they drank their small beer out of buckets all tarred.

CANTO II. describes THE COUNCIL. Near the opening of this occurred eight lines, for which the following were substituted in manuscript:—

Opens the morn her dewy eyes
To see if it is time to rise;
Slow o'er the surface of the deep
The lazy fog begins to sweep;
Part of the distant shore, deep green,
Shows here and there, a lovely scene,
And part is hid in mystic cloud
Enwrapping it like ghostly shroud.
Anon, along the mountain side,
Like spectres pale, great masses glide,
Coasting the steep and wood-crowned height,
And hiding all from human sight,
Save one bare peak, aspiring bold,
Like giant capped with helm of gold.
  As the light vapor upward flies
To seek its kindred of the skies,
New objects greet the wondering view,
Of various form and varied hue.
A jutting point, a circling cove,
Whose sandy beach the fishers love;
A glen retreating from the shore,
Down which the rushing waters pour;

A whitewashed cottage, bowered in trees
Scarce moving in the morning breeze;
Each in its turn, a fair array,
Stand cheerful in the eye of day,
Till, at the last, a beauteous whole
Combines to win the ravished soul.
So, on the morning of her birth,
From Chaos rose the smiling earth,
And, from the gloom of vapory night,
Rushed into order, beauty, light.

However delicious this, I fancy it rather a study from the Hudson than from Chesapeake Bay. But this by the way. The accident through which the contemplated foray takes the specific direction of Havre de Grace is amusingly told: —

He ceased, then cast his hopeless eye
On a huge map just lying by,
And straight that eye, with living fire
Was lighted up, in bitter ire;
In tones that quelled the ocean wave
Thus our good knight began to rave:
"The recreant wight, who dares to say,
In the bright face of this good day,
French influence stains not this fair land,
Lies in his teeth, by this right hand.
A living proof behold we here
In black and white distinct appear;
Behold, Sir Knights, a vile French place
Called Havre — with a d——d de Grace!

Canto III. is entitled The Progress. The following description and reflections, quoted in the review previously alluded to, are very much altered and improved in my father's copy of the book. I give the later version. —

And now they caught the brightening gleam
Of Susquehanna's noble stream,
As rolling down it came to pay
Its tribute to the lordly bay,
And on its beauteous margin spied
The little town in rural pride
Wrapt round in safety's folding arms,
Nor dreaming of those tristful harms
Which fortune in her fitful spite
Decreed should come, that fatal night.
The sun low in the West did wane;
Athwart the level of the plain
The shadow of each tree the while
Seemed lengthened into many a mile;
The purple hue of evening fell
Upon the deep, sequestered, dell;
And scarce a lingering sunbeam played
Around the distant mountain's head.
When, lo! what growing, grand, surprise,
Rich in the ruddy Western skies!
What splendid tints of red and gold
At that calm hour the clouds unfold!
Some in the pure translucent breast
Of the whole sea of heavens rest,
Like fairy islets scattered wide
Afar and near in fabled tide
Where as wild Eastern fancy feigns
Some potent Genius ever reigns;
Others, like vessels gilded fair,
Drift slowly in the upper air,
Bedecked with flaunting streamers gay,
While powers unseen direct their way.
In more than royal pomp and pride
With gorgeous sail they graceful glide,
Gay as the barque whose glittering sheen
Sparkled around the Egyptian queen,
On whom as gazed the Roman fool
The subject world slipped from his rule.
Anon the golden lustre fades;
A graver hue the sky invades;

The veil of twilight nature shrouds,
And dark and darker grow the clouds:
E'en as the deep and healthful flush
That gives the youthful cheek its blush,
In manhood fades, grows gray with age,
And dies long ere we quit this stage.
Then sunk the breeze into a calm;
Gathered refreshing dews, like balm;
The night-hawk, screaming through the sky,
Told that the evening shades were nigh;
The bat began his dusky flight;
The whip-poor-will, *our* bird of night,
Ever unseen however near,
Quavered his quaint note in the ear;
The blundering beetle forth did hie,
With drowsy drone and heedless eye;
The little watchman of the night,
The firefly, trimmed his lantern bright,
And took his merry, airy, round,
Along the meadow's fragrant bound,
Where blossomed clover, bathed in dew,
In sweet luxuriance blushing grew.
O nature! goddess ever dear,
What a fair scene of peace was here!
What pleasant sports, what calm delights,
What happy days, what blameless nights,
Might in such tranquil haunts be spent,
Lulled in the lap of bland content!
But vain it is that gracious Heaven
To wilful man this earth has given;
Vain, that its witching face displays
Such beauties to his reckless gaze,
While this same rash unreasoning worm
Raises the whirlwind and the storm,
Pollutes her bosom with hot blood,
Turns to rank poison all her good,
And plays before his Maker's eyes
The serpent of this paradise.
Who that had gazed on scene so fair
Had deemed this world a world of care,

Where evil thoughts for ever seek
To lure to ill our nature weak;
Where all around temptation lies,
And good beyond us, in the skies?
No man with angel wrestles here,
Like him whom Israel's tribes revere;
But trains of imps in angel guise
For aye assault the wariest wise;
One foiled, another still succeeds;
Triumph to harder trial leads;
Till, tired at last, we quit the field,
Or to the weakest tempter yield
The trophies of a life-long war,
Rather than fight one battle more.

I presume that when these alterations were made Mr. Paulding had in view another edition of the book, but as that, so far as I know, was never called for, he inserted the most of the preceding lines in "The Backwoodsman." It is curious to note how they have become weakened in the expansion of the eight-syllabled into the ten-syllabled line; offering a valuable illustration of the feebleness of mere "words, words, words."

Burlesque now reigns again: —

The fiddle stopped; and sudden rose
The music of the minstrel's nose.
Though hushed the song, the sonorous sound
Amazed the audience nodding round:
Now it seems far, and now a-near,
Now meets, and now eludes, the ear;
Now seems like conch-shell echoing wide
Along some misty mountain side;
Now like the low and solemn knell
Of village church, in distant dell;
Now the sad requiem loads the gale,
And seems like tithe-pig's smothered wail,
As pent in bag, to pay the tolls
Of parish priest — for saving souls.

I am tempted to introduce here, from another of our author's works, a companion snore,—perhaps the greatest on record. I am confident it was born in a North River steamboat.

"Sometimes it rolled up in a lofty diapason, and then suddenly sunk into thorough bass; sometimes it seemed whistling through a quill, and anon it burst forth with such stupendous and transcendent exuberance, as to threaten the total disruption of the instrument itself. Its variety was inexhaustible; its transitions, sometimes gentle and insinuating, at others abrupt and ferocious; and occasionally it sent forth a long, lingering, Alexandrine note, that gradually dwindled away like a distant expiring echo."

Just at the close of the minstrel's nap the students enter the tavern, and, being joined by a party of country folk, a dance is gotten up. This brings us to—

CANTO IV., or THE DIGRESSION. A portion of this the reviewer before mentioned quotes, with the remark: "The following picture is admirably descriptive of a country bumpkin in love; the scenery is delightfully managed." This episode is in fact the most compact portion of the poem, and the merit of it less unequal than the rest; but as I have not space for the whole, and am loth to break it, I content myself with a specimen of the notes.

NOTE X.

*Soothed her pleased ear with Rhino Die.*

It has been hitherto supposed that the people of America, like the birds of that country, are not naturally musical, because travellers have, I am told, drawn their conclusions, from what they observed in cities or along the public roads, without penetrating beyond the mere outside shell of the country. The genuine indigenous habits of any country are not to be gathered in the streets or by the roadside; but in lonely and remote situations where the traveller never comes, and where, with the exception of a wandering peddler, a stranger is seldom seen. It is at the fireside of the farmer that the ancient manners and customs, the natural tastes of a people, take their stand; and it is there and in his fields, that I am assured, morning, noon, and evening, you may hear old ballads often sung by the workmen and maids, with whom it is altogether common and customary. With regard to the ballad of Rhino Die, I have been able to procure but two lines of it, which are the concluding ones of every verse, occupying the place of a sort of chorus. There is a simplicity in them which seems to indicate considerable antiquity.

"My name is Rhino Die,
All on the mountains high."

This ballad is probably of American origin, as neither Mr. Ritson, Mr. Ellis, nor my friend Jacobus Porcus, has given any account of it. All I can gather from my correspondent, who, like most other Americans, is barbarously indifferent to genuine minstrelsy, is, that it is twelve cows in length. That is, according to the ancient system of measuring ballads; which was by the number of cows milked by the maid, while she was singing them. Formerly the Hollanders measured time by the pipe, as the learned Diedrich Knickerbocker affirms in his history; and at present the natives of the East, have a custom, somewhat analogous, of measuring distances by time.

CANTO V., styled THE BURNING, contains a sketch of the destruction of Havre de Grace by the enemy, and sundry thrusts at domestic faction; gives the later fortunes of "the minstrel;" and ends with a farewell to the fiddle.

# IV.

1813–1814. [Æt. 35–36.]

THE ANALECTIC MAGAZINE — THE IDEA OF A TRUE PATRIOT.

I HAVE alluded to a review by Mr. Paulding in The Analectic Magazine. To this periodical, early in 1813, he became a contributor, in connexion with Washington Irving, editor, and Gulian C. Verplanck; and was more or less interested in its fortunes for some years thereafter. I reproduce here an article from his pen, to be found in the number for February, 1814, which is a good specimen of a sort of subdued irony in which he delighted.

THE IDEA OF A TRUE PATRIOT.

Grave observers, who, by looking steadily at the troubled ocean of life, sometimes see a little beyond the surface, will be often struck with surprise at beholding the influence which mere names exercise over the opinions of the majority of the human race. They will indeed almost be inclined to believe that the generality of men have no other criterion to distinguish virtue from vice, and that Brutus was in the right when, in the bitterness of disappointment at the failure of his attempt to free his country, he exclaimed, " O virtue! thou art but a *name*."

Observing this propensity in mankind to be governed by names, wise men, I mean those enlightened persons who had cunning enough to perceive the foibles of their fellow creatures and knavery enough to take advantage of them, did, at a very early period, invent a nomenclature most admirably calculated to break down the barrier between virtue and vice, and to confound them in the minds of unenlightened men. It was thus that persecution became piety; ill nature, candour; avarice, prudence; cunning, wisdom; and self-interest, patriotism — till at last divers philosophers, observing the singular operation of these disguised vices, began to doubt the very existence of virtue.

When, for instance, they saw a man who chose to call himself a patriot, abandoning himself to dishonourable intrigues, inventing and giving currency to falsehood, and outraging all those duties which compose the ligaments of society, — losing sight of those honourable principles and feelings which constitute the true dignity of man, and debasing himself to the level of pitiful hypocrisy — when they saw all this, they came to the preposterous conclusion that there was no such thing as true patriotism. But the more enlarged and enlightened philosophy of the present day has furnished a remedy for these seeming incongruities, and, by a most happy distinction, reconciled private with public virtue, by demonstrating that they are entirely distinct, nay, often diametrically opposite to each other.

In no age or country, perhaps, has patriotism been so plenty as in this. In the most virtuous periods of Greece and Rome it is melancholy to observe the dearth of patriots, lawgivers, and wise men. Seven wise men living at one time in Greece, gave immortality to the age; Solon and Lycurgus, by making laws for a couple of insignificant cities, were held up as objects of infinite admiration; and such was the scarcity of patriots that they were obliged to enlist Timoleon, who killed his brother, and the elder Brutus, who killed his son, in order to eke out the number. These instances clearly indicate the great superiority of the moderns over those ancients who are so insolently held up by most writers as objects of imitation; for there is hardly a village of this country that does not contain a man at least as wise in his neighbour's opinion as Thales; and one single city, as we read, called Gotham, actually produced at one time three wise men equally renowned with those of ancient Greece. As for legislators and patriots every board of aldermen can turn out half a dozen of the one, and the others are as plenty and as cheap as mackerel.

In proportion, however, as the sect of patriots grew more numerous, it branched out into a variety of schisms, insomuch that the purity of its original source became polluted, and it is now extremely difficult to distinguish the genuine from the adulterated patriotism. I will therefore lay down some rules by which the true patriot may be recognised at first sight by persons of ordinary sagacity. There are certain characteristic and peculiar marks which enable an accurate observer at all times to discern which is the perfect, and which is the mixed or degenerate breed of animals. As I profess to have this power in a high degree, having handled many patriots in my time, the following marks may be relied on by those who may be inclined to the purchase of this species of live stock.

The true patriot is one who uniformly prefers his own interest to that of his country, and who has enlarged his mind to a perception of this great moral truth, that public is almost always incompatible with private virtue. These opinions are the foundation of the quality I am about analyzing, and without it no patriotism can be genuine, any more than Dr. Solomon's Balm of Gilead can be relied on without the doctor's own signature. Let us now inquire how the combination of these two great qualities operates to produce infinite benefit to the community at large.

This attachment of the true patriot to his own individual interest is founded on a most subtle construction, which is doubtless the true one, of the celebrated political axiom, that "the good of the whole is the same as the good of all its parts." This, rightly understood, inculcates the doctrine, that every man ought exclusively to take care of himself, which is in fact the great law of nature. Assuredly, if the good of society consists in the prosperity of all its parts, the true way to attain that good is for each individual to cultivate his own interest at the expense of that of everybody else. The greatest possible number of people will then become prosperous, and thus the good of the whole will be achieved in the easiest and most effectual manner.

Nothing in fact so forcibly exemplifies the presumptuous folly of mankind as their making a sacrifice of individual interest to the general benefit; or the arrogance of that patriotism which has for its object the good of a whole community. Attempts like these bespeak an utter ignorance of the limited powers of man, who, so far from being able to make others happy, can scarcely, with all his exertions, attain to a moderate degree of comfort himself. From this salutary conviction of the circumscribed sphere of mortal action, has doubtless arisen that indifference to the prosperity of others manifested by many good men and true patriots, who, wisely perceiving it was as much as they could do to make themselves tolerably easy in this world, very properly abandoned all solicitude for the welfare of others.

But, however this opinion may be reconcilable to the feelings of the wise, it would be manifest folly in the true patriot to admit for a moment in public that it influences his conduct. That kind of honour which is proverbial among thieves, and which I suppose consists in throwing off all disguise among themselves, may possibly prompt him to unfold to his fraternity the noble principle by which he is actuated, but it will by no means suit his exalted purposes to make it public. There exists among unenlightened men a singular prejudice in favor of disinterestedness, even when it approaches to prodigality, and the thoughtless spendthrift, who in their apologetic language is nobody's enemy but his own, is always preferred to the thrifty citizen who is nobody's friend.

It is therefore necessary that the true patriot should cautiously veil from the piercing eyes of the world this exclusive feeling of self-interest, and advance some ostensible motive more congenial to the feelings of those whom he intends to make the instruments of his prosperity. Now, I believe it will be found that mankind, when they adopt a disguise, generally choose one as different as possible from their ordinary habit; or, when they assume a character for the purpose of practising on the credulity of mankind, take that which is most opposite to their natures. Thus, the drunkard will endeavour to put on an air of demure sobriety; the glutton will affect temperance, and complain of his want of appetite; the hypocrite lament his incapacity to disguise any thing from the world; the mountebank, being generally a very silly fellow, attempt to pass for a conjurer; and the true patriot, being governed by the great motive of individual interest, affect the exclusive pursuit of the interests of others.

Distinguished philosophers have surmised that a great portion of the knowledge of mankind was derived from a profound observation of the habits and instincts of brutes. If this opinion, so complimentary to my fellow-men, should be just, we may suppose that the practice was suggested by the example of the bird, which cunningly allures the attention of the unpractised urchin from its nest, by seeming to direct her anxiety toward the opposite quarter. Thus we find the true patriot disavowing, with obtrusive clamour, his real intent, and decoying the suspicion of unwary observers from that point where all his hopes are centred.

Perhaps to those whose minds are stinted to the mere comprehension of plain, every-day, homespun virtue, this species of disguise may appear like hypocrisy. But as there are pious frauds, so there is, in the eye of sound patriotism, a pious hypocrisy. It is when a man condescends to deceive others, for the purpose of advancing the public good, or his own, which has been proved the same. And here I must beg leave to observe, that there is a most unreasonable and vulgar prejudice against the hypocrite, who in fact produces great benefit to society, and, though good for nothing himself, is the cause of much good in others. The mere appearance of virtue, say the casuists, is salutary, because it often leads others to be really good; as the impostor Mahomet drew after him thousands of sincere votaries.

I now come to the second grand principle of the true patriot, to wit, that the public welfare almost always demands the sacrifice of private virtue, or, in other words, that one cannot be a good man and a great patriot at the same time, according to the usual acceptation.

In the pursuit of great objects, such as promoting or destroying the happiness of a nation, the most profound reasoners have held it allowable, nay praiseworthy, to dispense, if necessary, with those ordinary rules of action which govern men in common circumstances. Thus a man may lawfully do that in the attainment of a kingdom, with great glory to himself, which, if done to gain a farm, would utterly demolish his reputation, and forthwith bring him to the gallows. In the usual routine of private life, it is held a crime against the society of which we are members, to utter or to publish wilful falsehoods; to blacken the good name of our neighbour; to vilify a large portion of our countrymen; or to make it our daily labour to foment divisions, sharpen animosities, and nourish the most unkind antipathies among the different classes of our fellow-citizens. Nothing indeed but the purest patriotism can justify these breaches of common-law virtue, and none but a true patriot possesses the chemical power of changing, by an analysis that would confound the experimental science of Sir Humphrey Davy himself, these breaches of private duties into public benefits.

But the solution of this difficulty is easy enough; this seeming inconsistency arising altogether out of that opposition which exists between private and public virtue, which are, by ignorant people, so preposterously confounded together. The true patriot is, however, aware of this distinction; accordingly, despising the little every-day duties that are eternally in a man's way, he frames a more enlarged and liberal code of morality, admirably adapted to a lofty genius elevated above the petty prejudices that circumscribe the actions of little men. The noble maxim that "The end justifies the means," forms the guide of his conduct, and he does not scruple to become a bad citizen, and a bad neighbour — a false friend, or an unprincipled betrayer, for the good of his country, or, what is the same thing, the good of himself. But it is only the true patriot, and one, too, of the first order, who can rise to that degree of sublime public virtue, which consists in the sacrifice of those heart-subduing ties that take such fast hold of weaker men, and restrain them from effectually contributing to the individual-general prosperity.

Indeed, it requires not only great strength of mind in the true patriot to enable him to practise this ardent species of virtue, but also great depth of reasoning to discover that it is really virtue, and that of the rarest kind, because its difficulties are increased by the opposition of early-imbibed modes of thinking, as well as natural feelings. It was this sublime patriotism which enabled the elder Brutus to condemn his offspring to death, and inspired the younger one to stab his benefactor. These exploits have accordingly been made the theme of historic eulogy; and nothing furnishes a stronger proof of the injustice of fame, than that nobody has thought proper to celebrate the singular virtue of Peter the Great of Russia, who condemned his only son to death; or of Francis Ravaillac, the assassin of Henry the Fourth of France. To be sure, the purity of the great Peter's act is sullied by the fact that the son deserved his fate; and Ravaillac is deprived of half the splendour of his achievement on account of his having had no tie of gratitude to restrain him. And besides, the one was a Muscovite, the other a Frenchman, while Brutus had the fortune of being a Roman, a name which, through the caprice of history, has become inseparably connected with virtue.

But ignorant people, who only comprehend that simple virtue which depends on no refinement of reasoning, and requires no metaphysical logic to define, nor any careful chemical analysis to ascertain its quality, are altogether incapable of conceiving this exalted species of patriotism, which consists in the sacrifice of our noblest feelings. The only instance I remember of the kind in this country, is that of the famous Indian chief, Colonel Brandt, who put his son to death with as little compunction as either Brutus or Peter the Great. But the detractors from his merit say he was intoxicated at the time; if so, the palm must still rest with the Roman, who performed his sacrifice in cold blood.

With regard, however, to what may be considered the relative duties of man in his social and political capacity, and how, as the member of a community, his duty as a citizen is at war with his feelings as a mere individual, the question is one of extreme nicety. People who suppose that it is as easy to find out what is really virtue, as it is to practise it, argue with an utter ignorance of the subject. All the subtlety of the most acute genius is necessary to ascertain the almost imperceptible line of distinction between moral turpitude and true patriotism; or how far it is the duty of a man to violate, in the character of a patriot, those principles which constitute his rule of action as a mere moralist. That such a difficulty does really exist is demonstrated by the vast number of great books which have been written for the purpose of defining virtue, in which she appears in as many forms as Proteus, and is sometimes treated as a goddess, at others like an impostor. In these books, dreadful are the conflicts between private and public duties, which seem, like the ancient English and Scottish borderers, to have been always at war and committing depredations on each others' territories.

The true patriot, having learned to distinguish between these conflicting duties, proceeds upon the only true principle, that of sacrificing the lesser virtues to the greater. Thus it is the duty of a man to speak the truth; to be faithful to his friend; and to deal justly with all mankind in common cases. But if the true patriot finds out, which in fact he can always do by the aid of his superior sagacity, that the government of his country is in the hands of the worst men in it, who will if let alone inevitably bring it to ruin; or, on the other hand, if he discovers that the party opposed to the administration only want to get the power into their hands to ruin the country themselves — in either of these cases it certainly becomes his duty to save it from destruction by every means in his power.

If, then, in the pursuit of this noble object, he descends to the most ignoble actions, and scruples not to violate the truth — to betray private confidence — to blast the good name of his neighbour — to resort to habitual calumnies, and, in short, descend to the level of unprincipled vice — still this dereliction of those principles which usually govern common minds, is precisely what constitutes the superiority of patriotism over every other virtue. It is no very extraordinary exertion to practise virtue, when it is attended with no violation of those feelings and attachments which are so closely connected with the human heart. But to enter into fellowship with fraud and hypocrisy; to break the early ties of youthful intimacy; to combat in the lowest arena of life, and to make a noble sacrifice of the respect of all men of honour, for the good of our country; — is a species of virtue incontestably allied to excellence, inasmuch as it possesses the unalienable attribute of all perfection, that of most nearly approaching its opposite extreme.

It has long been held a great stretch of virtue, to consent even for a little while to shroud the character —to become the voluntary martyr of infamy, and to *appear* vicious, for the sake of some eventual good. What, then, is due to that exemplary patriot who condescends to *be* so, in the pure hope that public happiness, and the individual-general good, will at last spring from this disinterested sacrifice, even as the safety of Rome was achieved by devoting to destruction whatever was most precious among its citizens.

Men of the ordinary level of virtue are apt to be governed by the old maxim, that evil must never be done that good may come of it — a maxim which if strictly adhered to, would demolish all true patriots under the sun. Their very vocation consists in doing evil that good may come of it, and in nobly sacrificing private feelings, that is, the private feelings of others, to their conception of the public advantage. For instance, now, some men of pure intentions but narrow views, would suppose they were acting the part of true patriots, by maintaining the truth; by inculcating a union of sentiment in points of importance among members of the same community; by doing every thing in their power to preserve their domestic peace; and by infusing into the minds of all within the sphere of their influence that national regard for our countrymen which forms the best cement of civil society. The genuine patriot, on the contrary, forthwith divests himself of these meaner principles that circumscribe the actions of little men, and, scorning that paltry fairness which deals justice even to an enemy — that narrow-minded bigotry which adheres to the truth even when falsehood might subserve its interests — that treasonable friendship which clings even to the remains of expiring confidence, and hovers over the dying embers of affection — and that chicken-hearted candour which impels us to acknowledge that men who differ in opinion may be equally honest — spurs on triumphantly to the attainment of that individual wealth, which has been demonstrated to be the only legitimate foundation of national prosperity.

# V.

## 1815–1816. [ÆT. 37–38.]

THE UNITED STATES AND ENGLAND — SECRETARY OF THE BOARD OF NAVY COMMISSIONERS — RUINS OF THE CAPITOL — MISSES HIS OLD FRIENDS — IMPRESSIONS OF WASHINGTON CITY — JAMES MADISON — SUNDRY CELEBRITIES.

EARLY in 1815 Mr. Paulding published "THE UNITED STATES AND ENGLAND: being a reply to the criticism on Inchiquin's Letters contained in the Quarterly Review for January, 1814." This was a pamphlet of 115 pages, published by Bradford and Inskeep, Philadelphia, and A. H. Inskeep, New York. It was wholly a controversial work, in which he hauled the presumed author of the objectionable article rather roughly over the coals. He had fixed upon Southey, the laureate, as the offender, but it appears by a letter of his to Washington Irving at the close of this year that he had been mistaken.

TO W. IRVING.

WASHINGTON, 15th Dec. 1815.

Southey's denial, which you mention, has been published in our newspapers, and, had it not been coupled with some observations which deprived him of all claim to an apology, I would have addressed a letter to him making such atonement as I hope would have been perfectly satisfactory. As it is, I shall content myself with silence, for I believe there is no prospect of a new edition ever being called for.

Of John Bull and Brother Jonathan, The Lay, and this last book, Mr. Paulding writes, many years later: "These were all political, and attracted the attention of Mr. Madison, who has since informed me that he gave directions to the different heads of Departments to apprise him when any office worthy of my acceptance became vacant. Before such an event occurred peace was concluded, and a Board of Navy Commissioners being initiated, I was appointed its Secretary." The appointment bears date April 28, 1815.

I presume he went at once to reside at Washington, and that the following lines, dreary and mournful as their subject, and which carry something impressive in the very indistinctness of the images, give his first impressions of the ruins of the Capitol burnt by the British in the summer of the previous year.

As through yon noble pile, at evening's fall,
  When the pale moonbeams mingled with the stain
Of black'ning fires upon the mouldering wall,
  I pensive strayed, and mourned the ruined fane;

A figure stalked athwart my wayward path,
  And stopped my musing, meditative way!
Stern was its look, as if in secret wrath
  It sought revenge, and shunned the tell-tale day.

And, as I gazed with wonder at the shade,
  A gleam of moonlight flickered on its head,
Whose whitened honors hoary age betrayed,
  And visage pale seemed borrowed from the dead.

I saw an hour-glass tremble in its hand,
  And on a scythe reclined its aged form;
Majestic though in ruin, sadly grand,
  It seemed t' have weathered many a pelting storm.

'Twas Time! — and indignation checked my fear: —
"Insatiate fiend," I cried, in angry voice,
"Hast come to view thy ruthless triumph here,
And o'er thy work of ravage to rejoice?"

Slowly he answered, with a bitter smile,
And voice that seemed to come from some old grave: —
"It was not I that blasted this fair pile;
I came to mourn the wreck I could not save.

"Thou know'st, as I know, how a splendid band
From far-famed Albion's gentle bosom came;
Thou know'st that *they* applied the reckless brand:
*I* but behold — *I* shall *record* — the shame."

He said — and vanished like a thing of dream!
I heard his wings slide through the silent air;
I saw his scythe emit a parting gleam,
And, like a meteor, stream his snowy hair.

Mr. Paulding found his position a pleasant one. In the letter to Irving last quoted, he writes: —

It gives me leisure, respect, and independence, which last is peculiarly gratifying from its novelty. All my life I have been fettered by poverty, and my vivacity checked by the hopelessness of the future. Now my spirits are good, my prospects fair, and the treatment I receive from all around is marked with respectful consideration. I tell you these things because I know they will give you pleasure. Though not of a talkative *gossiping* character, our friendship I trust is of a nature far more respectable and solid. Did I want assistance, advice, or consolation, I would ask it of you, and I would give it as freely. In every thing that would give you happiness or honour I would rejoice; and so feeling, I disclose to you circumstances that give me happiness and honour, that you may also rejoice on my account. The President is very friendly to me in deportment and little attentions, and so are the rest of the magnificos, particularly the Secretary of the Navy, who smokes my segars in the politest manner imaginable.

Toward the conclusion of this letter he alludes to an early associate of his correspondent and himself, and now a brother-in-law of the former: —

Mr. Clay speaks of spending some time at *Brummy*, [Birmingham], with Harry Van Wart, who, he says, is charmingly situated, and a fine fellow. I was feelingly pleased with this, for I remembered when Hal and I were vagabonds together, and never dreamed that he would entertain a noble ambassador at his house, or I sit at the table of a President of the United States. Ask him if he remembers what a couple of likely fellows we were, and assure him of my affectionate recollection. Remember me also to Sally, [Mrs. V. W.], and tell her to bring up her boys like true Americans.

Notwithstanding his agreeable situation, he missed his old New York friends. This is notably evinced in several letters of this period to Henry Brevoort, Jr. For example, it appears that Mr. Brevoort's life had been despaired of, in consequence of a relapse of the Influenza, and Paulding writes to him when on the mend, December 1st, 1815.

William Kemble wrote me an account of your late danger, and I pictured to myself the anxious solicitude of your good parents, and Margaret, who owes you so much, until I could hardly see. He also told me, that in your extreme illness, you remembered and spoke of me, and never believe that I shall forget this proof of your regard. Alone as I am here, my heart is wide open to impressions of past times, and to know that I am remembered, and cherished by my old associates, is one of the chief pleasures I now enjoy. Believe me

I most affectionately rejoice in your recovery being now certain, and say to your worthy father, your kind affectionate mother, and your good little sister, that I wish them joy a hundred times, and wish too that I could come and eat a roasted goose with them next Sunday, as I sometimes used to do in days of yore.

And again, February 14th, 1816.

Though I am in pretty good spirits here, yet I often feel homesick and lonely for want of old friends that I shall never replace. Trees that are transplanted after a certain age never take root again.

To the same correspondent he gives his first impressions of the seat of Government.

*Sept.* 25, 1815. You cannot conceive of what consequence a bachelor like myself is in this odd city, where there are at least one thousand women, who being too lazy to work and too stupid to read, "have no delight to pass away their hours" but by attending to the affairs of other people. The consequence of all this is that it is the most paltry tattling place in the whole world. A man can't put on a clean shirt, or turn round, or pay a visit, or speak to a lady, without a Tea-party being called to discuss the matter. I have occasionally fallen in with the tavern-keeping belle, and at the President's 4th July levee talked a good deal to a married lady from Ohio, one of the most beautiful creatures I ever saw. Two very substantial tea-party stories were got up on these foundations, and, as there is no end to the limits of gossiping, I should not be surprised if they travelled to New York. You will laugh at my commencing the hero of such gallant tales.

*December 1st,* 1815. This is an odd place, and everybody and every thing seems to hang upon the Government. There is a regular gradation from the President downward, and I believe I am the only independent man in Washington. Did you ever see a basket of crabs, lifted up body and soul, by taking hold of the top one? Just so it is here — take hold of the President, and you raise the whole city, one hanging at the tail of the other in a regular gradation of dependence.

*February 28th*, 1816. The society of this place principally consists of birds of passage. Of these by far the greater part are such as one wishes never to have seen — and a few such as having seen, one would wish never to part with.

Elsewhere, in print, he describes the condition of the city itself about this period. "Washington, though beautifully situated, is rather a dull place at this time of year, [Autumn], except to sportsmen, who find excellent shooting about the centre of the city. I have seen great numbers of quail, plover, and snipe, within a couple or three hundred yards of the President's mansion, and they *do* say that deer abound in the 'slashes' as they are called, about half a mile North of that building. I can't answer to that fact, but I have seen plenty of rabbits there."

In the queer capital thus outlined our author resided about eight years, during which he became acquainted with most of the distinguished public men of the day, with many of whom he maintained friendly relations as long as they lived. He would occasionally sketch one very happily. Mr. Madison, among others, remained a life-long friend. Of him he writes to Brevoort in February, 1816: —

The great men here seem disposed to treat me with considerable respect, and I have several times made the President laugh in a manner altogether unbecoming a great man; so that I think my fortune is made, snug enough. This same Chief Magistrate is a confounded sensible fellow, and talks about every thing like a professor. He is generally grave, but of an evening when the business of the day is done, he loves to talk about this that and the other thing, and enjoys a joke hugely — as a great man should do. I begin to have a great liking to him, which, considering he is a greater man than myself, I think discovers no small degree of magnanimity. The other day I dined there. The old squire was in a good humour, and gave us some famous Claret and Champagne; whereupon Speaker Clay, the little plump Vice-President Gaillard, and General Mason, and I, did get as it were a little beyond the line of gravity becoming great statesmen.

Though partly written many years after this, I give here some further observations on Mr. Madison.

"At the close of his Presidency, I accompanied him in the steamboat down the Potomac to Acquia creek, where his carriage waited for him, and if ever man rejoiced on being freed from the cares of public life, it was he. During the voyage he was as playful as a child; talked and jested with everybody on board; and reminded me of a schoolboy on a long vacation.

"The next summer I visited him, according to previous arrangement, and spent some weeks at Montpelier. Our daily routine, with little variation, except Sunday, was as follows. After breakfast, between seven and eight, I took my segar, and seated myself on the Western portico of the house, looking toward the Blue Ridge, while Mr. Madison would commence a conversation; sometimes on public affairs in connexion with his own life, in which he spoke without reserve, and from which I gathered many lessons of experience; sometimes on literary and philosophical subjects; while, not unfrequently, for he was a capital story-teller, he would relate anecdotes, highly amusing as well as interesting. He was a man of wit, relished wit in others, and his small bright blue eyes would twinkle most wickedly when lighted up by some whimsical conception or association.

"By and by the horses were brought, and we set out on a tour to visit the different parts of the estate where farming operations were going on. As he never encumbered himself with a servant on these occasions, it fell to his lot to open the gates, which he did with a crooked stick, without dismounting, a feat which required no little skill. He undertook to teach me, and in time I acquired something of the art, but never could arrive at his dexterity.

"In the course of these daily rides Mr. Madison gave me the private history of sundry important transactions, from which I gathered that many great events arise from little causes, and that, as relates to the real moving impulses of public measures, History knows about as much of the Past as she does of the Future. My own subsequent experience as a member of Mr. Van Buren's cabinet, has fully satisfied me that our statesmen themselves would often be puzzled to account for their own actions, or to select from the multiplicity of motives that which above all others was most influential in directing them.

"Mr. Madison had, in great perfection, the power of condensing in his speeches and writings, though he did not always exercise it, for such is the appetite of the people of this country for long orations and discussions, that they do not like to swallow the truth in an incontrovertible axiom, but prefer it strongly diluted with verbiage.

"Mr. Madison had not, perhaps, so much genius as Mr. Jefferson, but, in my opinion, his mind was more consummate, and his faculties more nicely balanced than those of his predecessor, who, though justly called the great apostle of Democracy, I think sometimes carried his doctrines to the verge of political fanaticism.

"In brief, I have always considered Mr. Madison as emphatically THE SAGE of his time."

With John Randolph, also, he struck up a species of intimacy. From certain early memoranda, it would seem that he had at first adopted the current prejudices against that extraordinary man. But the strange character grew upon him, and I find allusions to this personage at intervals of years; and, finally, an elaborated study, which I shall give in its proper place.

In May, 1816, he went to Annapolis on public business, and jots down for Brevoort memoranda of sundry celebrities he met:

I dined with old Carroll of Carrollton, who is a little old fellow almost eighty, but active sprightly and intelligent in a most extraordinary degree, and almost as good a laugher as Adam Drummond. I never saw a finer old fellow, and we took to each other hugely.

Here is a touch which brings back the awkward uniform of that day:—

Among the great men down at Annapolis was Genl. Scott, who, bating his length, looks like a yellow-jacket hornet, being covered with gold lace.

His excellency, Mr. Pinkney, was also there:—

He is a man of great powers of mind; but exceedingly vain

of his talents and *person*, and as punctilious as a Spanish don of the true Castilian blood. There is something splendid about him however.

Mr. Pinkney had at this time just been appointed ambassador to the Court of Naples. Mr. Paulding writes of him, many years later.

"I never expect any thing from a man who thinks of his clothes. And yet the late William Pinkney of Maryland, was, at fifty, more careful in his toilet than a dandy with nothing to recommend him but his dress. But he was an exception to a rule. He was by far the most finished speaker I ever heard at the bar, and his reasoning powers were equal to his eloquence. His application was commensurate with both; and his death was caused by sitting up two nights in succession, preparing himself to argue a great cause before the Supreme Court. He was the only really great man I ever knew who was afraid of soiling his boots."

# VI.

1816–1817. [ÆT. 38–39.]

LETTERS FROM THE SOUTH — LETTER TO IRVING — A RUSTIC FUNERAL — THE SHINPLASTER DYNASTY — CHARACTER OF BROTHER JONATHAN — THE CAPHON ROCK.

MR. PAULDING left Annapolis with the Navy Commissioners, on a survey of Chesapeake Bay, and about the middle of July, 1816, brought up at Norfolk. He started thence, in consequence of ill health, on a tour through Virginia, not reaching Washington again till late in the fall.

The first fruits of this journey were LETTERS FROM THE SOUTH, published in 1817, by "James Eastburn & Co., at the Literary Rooms, Broadway corner of Pine street, New York." These form two rambling volumes, in which the author digresses continually into matters which have no connexion whatever with his excursion. He entered the State by the way of York and Williamsburg, following up the Pamunkey river; thence across the Blue Ridge to the upper waters of the Shenandoah; thence across the mountains again, taking the Warm the White and the Sweet Sulphur Springs in his way; thence to the Natural Bridge, and so down the valley to Berkeley Springs; coming out finally at Harper's Ferry.

In a letter to Irving, April 5, 1818, our author thus alludes to himself and to this publication:—

For myself — who perhaps you will wish to hear something about — I am in possession of a situation just such as I like, affording me a little more than I spend although I restrict myself in none of my wishes, and ample time to devote to my favourite pursuits. I have taken up my abode at Commodore Porter's, who has built a stately castle on the hill immediately opposite, and about a mile distant from, the house of the President. Here, occupying the Western turret, which looks far down the Potomac and commands a noble prospect, I enjoy an agreeable home, and indulge my scribbling propensities, to which I have now taken a decided vocation, I believe for the remainder of my life. The state of my health for more than a year past has interfered with this pursuit, but in the midst of lassitude, bile, and headaches, I last summer produced a little work, partly consisting of some recollections of a tour made the summer before in Virginia, and partly fictitious, which I believe is popular enough, notwithstanding the unhappy auspices under which it was written.

This work is full of characteristic matter; disquisitions about any thing that chanced to come into his head, dainty little pictures of nature, anecdotes or short stories touched off with a careless but striking grace, together with some details of manners and customs which will one day be invaluable to the antiquary and the historian. I make a few quotations by way of sample. He chances upon a burial-scene amid the mountains, which is described in a vein of fine simplicity. It will be seen that he has ingrafted some recollections of his early days.

### A RUSTIC FUNERAL.

Having two or three hours to spare till dinner, we rambled about the churchyard, reading the records of mortality, which, though everywhere confined to a few simple items, concerning a few insignificant people, are always interesting. They are the history of high and low; and none can read them without being impressed with a conviction that all are his brothers at last—for all die. He who moulders below was born,—and died; and whether rich, or a beggar, his chronicle is that of kings. The struggles of restless ambition,—the reverses of the great,—and the story of the wreck of lofty pride, we read as an interesting romance, addressing itself solely to the imagination: but when a monarch or a hero dies, he becomes our equal; his death is an example equally with that of the meanest mortal; and we here realize our common nature, and common end.

While poring over these tomb-stones, our attention was attracted by a long procession, on foot, on horseback, and in carriages of various kinds, winding slowly over one of the hills at a distance. It came toward the churchyard, entered it, and stopped at a large oak, under which was a newly-dug grave we had not noticed before. The people of the village were attracted by it, and came up, one after another, until there were, I suppose, two hundred, men, women, and children, gathered together. Without a whisper, except that of the oaks around, the coffin was taken from the wagon, lowered into the grave, and covered with earth. I never witnessed a scene more solemn and affecting; and beautiful as is our church funeral service, I will venture to say it never raised a feeling of more deep and awful devotion, than that which impressed the dead silence around. There was no need of saying "dust to dust;" every clod of earth, as it fell hollowly on the coffin, proclaimed it; neither was any proof wanting that "man that is born of a woman," must die, for a thousand little hillocks around gave silent testimony to the fact. When the mound over the grave was smoothed with pious care, a little buzzing ran through the crowd — and as it slowly separated, some ventured to talk about the deceased person, who was, I found, a Quaker woman, who died — as others die, of some common malady or other. She was neither a belle, nor a beauty; — no crowd ever followed her at a ball, nor could I learn that she had ever received a single offer of marriage, except from the person we had left still standing by her grave. Yet there was something in the story I learned of her, that affected me, I can hardly tell why, for it was not the least romantic.

It seems that her husband, in consequence of imprudence or misfortune, had several years before been confined in a prison for debt, leaving a family of eight children destitute. By the rare magic of industry and economy united, this woman, by her own labours, kept the little ones together, — fed, clothed, and sent them to school, until the gaol accidentally took fire, and the prisoner walked home. Here he afterwards remained unmolested, for the virtues of his wife had sanctified his person. There is a species of calm, persevering, courageous, and unconquerable industry, that gets the better even of fate. Such, it seems, was the industry of this valuable woman, and it was rewarded even in this world. She lived — God bless her — to see her husband independent, and to share many years of independence with him. She reared all her children, saw them honourably settled, and heard the old people say, that, whatever had been her sacrifices for them, they had repaid her, by their dutiful affection and exemplary conduct. Then, when she at last died, neither poet made her an angel nor newspaper eulogy a saint; but the neighbours, — the *neighbours*, followed her to the grave without uttering a word, — and the husband and children stood round it with their faces covered.

Mr. Paulding was all his life an opponent of what is styled "the credit system", and of paper money. According to his own account he imbibed this prejudice when a mere child. Writing in 1852, he says, speaking of his first schooling: —

"It was impossible to send me to a distance, for the only remnant of my father's property was a great pocket-book filled with Continental bills, the frequent contemplation of which gave me such a distaste to paper money that I have ever since despised it, and to this day have no confidence in Bank notes or Bank solvency."

In a letter of Dec. 14, 1837, to Gouverneur Kemble, at that time a member of Congress, he thus expresses himself: —

> Your assurance that the old Deposit System will not be revived gives me great satisfaction. I was under some apprehension that nothing would be done until the Banks thought proper to resume specie payments, when the public money would as a matter of course be again confided to them, again to constitute a National gambling fund. In that case I had some thought of joining my old friend Commodore Porter [then U. S. minister to the Sublime Porte] at Constantinople, for I prefer the despotism of the scimitar to that of Shinplasters, and a bashaw of three tails to a bank director.

On this trip, away up in the solitudes of the Blue Ridge, he was taken with an access of this fury, and discharged himself in a fulmination to which I have ventured to give the title of

### THE SHIN-PLASTER DYNASTY.

THE "Old Ancients," as our friend W——, the bank director, used to call them, pictured the god of riches as lolling in the lap of peace, and glittering in ornaments of gold. The modern Plutus is quite a different sort of personage, who, if he had his dues, and came forth in his appropriate livery, would look very much like a scarecrow in a cornfield, which is generally a man of straw, clothed in rags. This beggarly Plutus, instead of being nursed by peace like his ancient namesake, is the offspring of war. By the exercise of a rare kind of magic, he converts the debts of an institution into a source of wealth, and is, consequently, rich in proportion to the number of his creditors, rather than of his debtors. This new system of enriching one's self under the patronage of the paper Plutus is a great improvement on the ancient one, since it is much easier for a man to get in debt to others than to get others in debt to him.

To illustrate this, I will simply give you the prominent features of the present fashionable banking process, which has set so many splendid paupers on horseback, and caused all those, with few exceptions, who are not connected with the system, to go on foot. A modern bank spins itself out of its own bowels, as a spider does the web with which he catches the silly flies that buzz about. I will give you the history of one of these, which is nearly the history of all, and which I learned from an ex-director.

In a certain city, over which there did *not* reign a

mighty monarch, but which was governed by an illustrious mayor and twenty-four fat aldermen, which is a great city on paper, and, like the famous *Terra Incognita*, makes a terrible figure on the map, but is just as difficult to be found elsewhere as the said unknown land — in this great city, certain tavern-keepers, stage-owners, and drivers of hackney-coaches, being in want of money, did incontinently gather themselves together, and make a bank. They first elected themselves directors, and after advertising that the capital stock of the bank, to wit, the paper not yet made, was all that they meant to appropriate to the payment of their debts, fell to work and printed as many bank-notes as the president could possibly sign. With these notes they paid up their instalments, by borrowing of the bank to pay the bank. The plan succeeded so famously, that Messrs. Tom, Dick, Harry, tag, rag, bobtail, and the rest of them, got up banks in the same way, until at last money became so plenty, that it was actually the cheapest thing at market — which was a great blessing. Thus it continued, until this great city contained more than a dozen banks, which, in a little time, issued more paper than all the property in the place above and under ground could redeem. Everybody could get as much money as he wanted; consequently everybody ran in debt, and nobody would work, because he could live without so degrading himself. The whole community became independent, except that everybody was dependent on banks, and no man could call his house his own. People talk of the golden age — but it was nothing to the age of paper. Houses grew up like mushrooms, and tumbled down as soon.

Property attained to such a high price that nobody could afford to buy it but those who had no money; and every man, disdaining the pursuits of regular industry, became a dashing speculator, and went neck or nothing — which was another very fine thing. The staple commodities of this town attained to such an enormous and extravagant value, owing to the great plenty of paper money, that they cost more at home than they would sell for abroad; and thus that pernicious race of men, the merchants, was ruined — which was another exceeding fine thing. But the beauty of the whole system was, that it enabled a man to live in splendor all his life, leaving it to his children to pay his debts, instead of ruining their morals by bequeathing them a great fortune, as had hitherto been fashionable. Having produced this consummation so devoutly to be wished, nothing was wanting but to render it as permanent as the nature of things would permit. So they petitioned the legislature, which presided over the destinies of this great city, stating that they had established these banks in the teeth of the laws, to the which they had been induced by their great respect for the legislature which enacted the laws, and that therefore justice demanded that this violation of the law, and this respect for the lawgivers, should be duly acknowledged, by legalizing these banks as a reward for their breach of the laws. This reasoning was irresistible, and charters were given them in a lump, as an inducement to others to break the laws and respect the legislature.

The example of this great paper city has been followed in the neighborhood, in all directions, so that there is scarcely a town, that is to say, a cluster of a dozen houses, in this part of the world, that has not one or more banks. Some are smitten with the prospect of sharing in the spoils of simple industry, which pays all the tax of the depreciation of money; and honest men are frequently forced to become accomplices rather than victims. The country is puffed into an appearance of bloated prosperity which deceives the unwary, but is in reality weakened most essentially by this precarious expansion, and impoverished, in fact, by the loss of a portion of its export trade, owing to the unnaturally high price of every staple article at home, as well as by the comparative decrease of the value of incomes arising from the solid source of real capital. Men of the largest landed estates cannot cope with the expenses of a dependent on a bank, and must either shrink from a comparison with these upstart, unreal pageants, who have bank directors for their friends, or join the current, mortgage their estates, live splendidly, die insolvent, and leave their children beggars.

To show the effect of country banks, I will relate a little example which came under my own observation a day or two ago, and perhaps gave rise to these speculations. We stopped in the evening to sleep at the house of a Dutchman, who kept a sort of travellers' rest, rather, I believe, lest he should be obliged to entertain wayfarers for nothing, than from any great desire to add to the profits of his farm. It was a scene, and an evening, that made me melancholy with the fear of some day dying, and leaving a world so lovely. The house was on a rising ground, behind which, and close at hand, rose a majestic mountain, not savage with rocks and rugged precipices, but exhibiting a green foliage unbroken to the very top, whose graceful, waving outline, brought to the mind images of peace. In front was spread the richest little vale I ever saw; where meadows, and cornfields, the latter rising half a dozen feet above the fences, and the former speckled with sheep and cattle, succeeded each other in rich luxuriance. At one extremity ran a branch of the river Shenandoah, half hid among the high elms and sycamores; and a little further on rose a peaked hill, behind which the sun was setting. Every thing seen was peace itself; and every thing heard akin to silence, and only serving to render it more striking in the intervals. Sometimes the cow-bell's far-off tinkle came fluctuating on a transient breeze — sometimes the negro's sonorous and resounding laugh waked the mountain echo — sometimes his inimitable whistle, emulating the fife; and occasionally his song, which, mellowed by the distance, was singularly melodious. As long as I live I shall never forget that scene.

It was, in truth, a place for a man to make his home; and the honest Dutchman, for such he approved himself, not only by his dialect, but by his invincible predilection for rich bottoms, seemed to think as much; for he appeared to be actually contented — a rare thing in this world. In the calm leisure of the dusk of evening, he and his dame — and a jolly dame was she — good-humored as a lark, and round as a dumpling — came and sat with us in the porch; he, with his pipe; she, with her snuff-box, bearing on its lid the likeness of Commodore Porter. This custom is highly eschewed by all orthodox English travellers; but for my part, if a man is not wilfully obtrusive, and transgresses no law of etiquette that he knows of, I like his company, and can generally get something amusing or instructive from him.

Mine host seemed such a rare comfortable dog, that I determined to know, if possible, how he became so; and in order to entitle myself to his history, told him mine beforehand, for country people are always a little curious. The story of the burgomaster, or justice, (for so he announced himself), in substance, was as follows: —

"I married," said he, "at the age of twenty-six, and my wife — though perhaps you won't believe it — was reckoned a beauty in her day. My fortune was three hundred and twenty-eight pounds, and a negro man; and my wife brought me a great chest filled with, I dare say, six hundred petticoats and short gowns, which have lasted till this day; so her clothing cost me nothing. This was what we had to begin the world with. After looking about a little, I bought this farm, which, being much worn and out of order, I got cheap. What I had was enough for the first payment, and the rest of the purchase was to be in three equal annual instalments.

"The farm, as I said, was then in poor order, the fields a good deal worn out, the fences bad, and the house very old. But there was no time to groan; for the year was coming about, and the money must be paid. So Tom and I, and often my wife, turned out early and late, and worked like horses; and after selling my harvest, I carried my first payment home in hard dollars.

"Well," continued the Dutchman, "the next year I went on still better, paid the money still easier, and at the end of the third year, my farm was my own. We now thought to make ourselves comfortable by building a better home, for we had but a poor one before; so in the spring I set to work as soon as the frost was out of the ground. I burnt my own bricks and lime, from my own limestone and clay, and furnished timber and boards from my own farm. In the meantime, the war came on; and, as it is an ill wind that blows nobody good, the number of wagons passing this way increased every day, because the produce could not go round by sea. I sold the entire yield of my land at my door, except the wheat. If that was high, I could afford to send the flour to market; and if not, I cut it into *shorts* to feed the wagoners' horses. By the time my house was finished, it was paid for; and now I don't know what I shall build next, for my part. I am forty-three years old. I have twelve hundred acres of as fine bottom as any in Virginia — a good grist and saw mill, a tolerably good wife, if I could only make a fine lady of her — but she sticks to the old chest of clothes like a moth — a decent house over my head; and I owe no man a shilling, except Tom, who, by now and then raising a little grain, shooting a deer, and waiting on travellers, has, in my hands, enough to buy his freedom. But he is free already, for that matter, and knows he can go where he pleases."

"Pray," said I, "did you ever get a discount?"

"A discount! — what's that?" said the Dutchman.

"Did you ever borrow money of a bank, and mortgage your land for it?"

"No, no," said he, "I wasn't such a fool as that. My poor neighbor, whose house you see over the river yonder, with the windows broken and no smoke to the chimney, played a trick of that kind; but his farm is soon to be sold at vendue, and I think of buying it. His family were in great distress though we helped them on a little to get to the back country, where, I hear, they are doing pretty well again."

I will not trouble you with the moral of this story, but conclude by bidding you beware of discounts.

Journeying along one day, *apropos* of things in general he has his fling at "the universal Yankee nation," in the shape of the following

CHARACTER OF BROTHER JONATHAN.

The truth is, that mine honest, sanguine, and heels-over-head friend, brother Jonathan, is one of those people who are for eating their cake and having their cake, and reconciling all sorts of incongruities. He is for doing things in a great hurry, and would be free and hardy, with all the enervated refinements of slavery. Not content with the enjoyments necessary to happiness, and the essential characteristics of a nation destined to mighty things, the foolish lad would needs strut about in the gilded paraphernalia of pictures, palaces, and statues, that serve to amuse some nations into a forgetfulness of their chains. He is continually flaring away in the awkward second-hand finery of Europe, that gives him the appearance of a servile imitator, instead of coming out in his honest homespun, to challenge the respect of the world. The rogue often reminds me of a little, fat, greedy urchin, with an apple in each hand, and its mouth full of gingerbread, whining and fretting, because it can't appropriate to itself at the same time a pretty picture or lacquered image on the mantelpiece.

As our author himself observes, descriptions of scenery are not apt to give the reader much idea of the reality. I nevertheless bring up the rear of my extracts with one of the many spirited sketches of nature to be found in these volumes. It seems to me to bring the scene forcibly before the mind's eye.

### THE CAPHON ROCK.

From the summit of the highest point of this mass of rocks, there is a clear view of the valley of Caphon, or Cacapehon, as it is called in the maps. On the right of this valley, at its western boundary, the Potomac comes out from a break in the mountain, crosses it at the foot of another, in a line almost as straight as a canal, and loses itself again in the mountains at the eastern extremity of the valley. To the south is seen the river Caphon, winding and turning in every direction, so as to form the appearance of several little green islands; and at last, with a sort of affected reluctance, joining its waters with those of the Potomac, just before it breaks through the eastern mountain.

The valley is surrounded, on all sides, by high hills, beyond which, to the west, higher ones appear in continued succession, paler and paler, until they are lost in the heavens, by becoming confounded with the blue sky. Houses were dispersed at solitary distances, whose curling smoke, as it rose out of the trees, added to the peaceful character of the scene, and divested it of that melancholy loneliness, which affects us in contemplating those beautiful landscapes which have never yet been appropriated by man. After awhile, I descended the mountain to where the two rivers form a junction, and forded them both, for it was a very dry season, and the streams of this country were very low. I could see along the banks of the Potomac, where the logs were lodged, and in the crotches of trees, sedge and branches deposited by the waters, at least twenty-five feet above the present level of the current. You can form no idea how these mountain streams swell with the rains or the melting of the snows; or with what tremendous force and velocity they roll and roar along at such times.

In returning from the valley, I went to take a last look from the rock. It was becoming cloudy, or rather hazy, and little showers were falling in some parts, while others were glowing in the sun. The light and shade was disposed in endless variety, and the general haze of the atmosphere softened the objects appearing through its medium, as past scenes are mellowed and endeared by the slight obscurity thrown over them by the mists of memory.

# VII.

1818. [ÆT. 40.]

THE BACKWOODSMAN — LETTERS TO IRVING ABOUT — "CROAKER" ON — HALLECK ON — OUTLINE OF, AND EXTRACTS FROM.

The first hint of our author's next publication, THE BACKWOODSMAN, which was brought out in one volume by Moses Thomas, Philadelphia, in the summer or autumn of 1818, I find in the letter to Irving of April 5, 1818, previously quoted from: —

I have during the last winter employed as much of my time as I durst, considering my health, in sketching a poem which has been floating in my brain for years past, and have nearly completed it. The story is that of one of the early settlers on the Ohio, and the course of it enables me to sketch the scenery of various parts of the country, as well as to introduce the Indian character and manners. How it will succeed, without turbans and Eastern costume, which are used nowadays to disguise our old acquaintance, whom we scarcely recognize in their new dress, I cannot say. At all events it has given interest to a long winter, and kept me from sinking into utter lassitude and indifference, and so far it has not been written in vain.

The difficulty with this poetic effort is, that the author did not start with a definite idea of the effect he wanted to produce, or any due consideration of the means of bringing it about. He says, indeed, in his preface: "That the author may not be charged with having failed in what he did not attempt, it may be as well, perhaps, to state the extent of the design of the following poem. His object was to indicate to the youthful writers of his native country, the rich poetic resources with which it abounds, as well as to call their attention *home*, for the means of attaining to novelty of subject, if not to originality in style or sentiment. The story was merely assumed as affording an easy and natural way of introducing a greater variety of scenery, as well as more diversity of situation."

But this, I think, is hardly admissible as an apology for a total lack of any clear plot; and he surely asked too much of the public when he went on to declare: "Whether the writer shall ever attempt to complete his original intention in the construction of a regular plan, will principally depend on the reception given to this *experiment.*"

From a scheme so unpromising it may be divined that nothing like a complete poem of thirty-three hundred lines could be evolved. In fact there is no attempt at any thing of the sort, the manipulation of the work being incidentally illustrated in some lines occurring in the Sixth and last book. He is speaking of his "humble muse".

> She loves to linger through the livelong day
> Plucking each wild flower blooming on her way;
> To stop where'er she lists, and gaze around,
> Where winding stream, or verdant vale, is found;
> Chase the wild butterfly on vagrant wing,
> And haunt cool shades where merry warblers sing,
> Wasting long luscious hours in doing nought,
> Caught in the cobweb of some airy thought.

Perhaps it would not be unfair to apply the stronger

terms which our author uses in reference to himself in one of his "Letters from the South": — "But I am getting a bad habit of digressing in such a desperate manner, that sometimes I have hard work to find what I ought to be talking about. It seems with me as it fared with Achilles, of whom it was foretold, that if he ever left his native home he would never return. So, if I lose my subject, I seem fated never to light on it again; like the poor man in The Rambler, who strayed about in search of flowers, till he could neither find the place of his destination, nor that of his departure."

Again, Basil, the hero, is treated, not as an individual character, but simply as a type of the Emigrant, and as exemplifying in a general way the possible career of every such an one. To say truth, the thread of the story is insufficient to hold together the sketches of scenery and developments of opinion which make up almost the entire body of the work.

As might have been expected, the poem was a failure. In a letter to Irving, January 20, 1820, Mr. Paulding thus alludes to the fact.

My unfortunate poem has been over and over again attacked by the combined powers of wit and dullness, the former led by a wicked wag called *Croaker*, the latter by our old friend H., who I believe can't forgive me for beating him with his own weapons. Had I not been built of stubborn oak, seasoned in the school of poverty, like an old chimney-piece in a log house, I should sometimes have scratched my head a little to find if I had any brains. As it was, I consoled myself with the example of Milton, and appealed to posterity, which you know is like throwing a suit into the Court of Chancery, where, if the decision is made at all, it is after the death of the parties, who are never the worse off if it be against them.

The following paragraphs are interesting, as giving his theory, or at least his excuse.

Should I ever write poetry again, which I think I shall not do, (at least till my back is well again), I will certainly take your advice, as to abstaining from jesting, and taking time to revise and correct, although, to say the truth, it seems to me that uniform sweetness and sentiment is tiresome at last, and that a little occasional rugged carelessness is no blemish, when taken into view as part of a whole.

Joseph Rodman Drake, subsequently author of "The Culprit Fay", was the original "Croaker", and thus, (to give a single example), he croaks over our author, in the verses addressed "To John Minshull, Esq., Poet and Playwright, who formerly resided in Maiden-lane but now absent in England", published in The Evening Post, March 18, 1819.

"But hail to thee Paulding, the pride of the Backwood!
The poet of cabbages, log huts, and gin,
God forbid thou should'st get in the clutches of Blackwood,
Oh Lord! how the wits of Old England would grin:
In pathos — oh who could be flatter or funnier?
Were ever descriptions more vulgar and tame?
I wronged thee by Heaven! when I said there were none here
Could cope with great Minshull, thou peer of his fame!"

Fitz-Greene Halleck, ("Croaker Jr."), subsequently returned to the charge in the better-known lines in his poem of "Fanny", published in 1821.

"Homer was well enough; but would he ever
Have written, think ye, the Backwoodsman? never.

LXI.

"Alas! for Paulding—I regret to see
  In such a stanza one whose giant powers,
Seen in their native element, will be
  Known to a future age, the pride of ours.
There is none breathing who can better wield
  The battle axe of satire. On its field

LXII.

"The wreath he fought for he has bravely won,
  Long be its laurel green around his brow!
It is too true, I'm somewhat fond of fun
  And jesting; but for once I'm serious now.
Why is he sipping weak Castalian dews?
The muse has damned him—let him damn the muse."

Despite this general keel-hauling, our author seems to have had, at several periods, an idea of recasting The Backwoodsman; and, in pursuance of that purpose, altered in many instances forms of expression, and even entire pages. Unluckily he never attempted to give it greater coherence. Still, from the trouble he has taken in revising and almost rewriting it, I conclude he was attached to this belabored progeny. Indeed he says as much in 1852: "The Backwoodsman has always been a favorite work of mine."

The above statement will account for many deviations from the printed poem in the extracts I am about to make; for, with all its shortcomings, there occur pasages of genuine descriptive poetry, or original outlooks on things, which need no apology for being reproduced here.

The poem opens:—

  My homely theme is of a hardy swain,
Among the lowliest of the lowly train,
Who left his native fields, afar to roam,
Through Western wilds, in search of happier home.

Simple the lore I venture to rehearse,
For unfledged is the Muse in flights of verse;
Nor dares she wing her wild adventurous way
To that bright region of eternal day
Where dwell those awful greybeard bards sublime,
Victors o'er dark oblivion, death, and time;
Yet, haply in the woodland path she treads,
Some nameless wild flowers still may lift their heads,
Unknown to those immortal men of yore,
And never twined in any wreath before.
For if there there be, as frolic Fancy tells,
Hid in the unsunned depths of rocky dells,
Or in dumb forests where the prying day
Even at noontide never groped its way,
An unseen sprite, that wakens latent fires,
Warms the strong heart and mighty thought inspires,
Where are there glens more apt for his lone seat,
Where denser shades, where springs more cool and sweet?
Where are there clearer streams and grander floods?
Where broader prairies, where more massive woods?
Where is the land beneath the vaulted sky
That ought to lift the mystic torch more high,
To light the genius into quenchless flame,
And give its bards more fair, enduring, fame!

This fine introduction was in the original edition filled by the following, very characteristic of the author's mind and modes of thought.

Simple the tale I venture to rehearse,
For humble is the Muse, and weak her verse;
She hazards not, to sing in lofty lays,
Of steel-clad knights, renowned in other days
For glorious feats, that in this dastard time
Would on the gallows make them swing sublime;
Or tell of stately dames of royal birth,
That scorned communion with dull things of earth,
With fairies leagued, and dwarfs of goblin race,
Of uncouth limb, and most unseemly face —

Tremendous wights! that erst in nursery-"keep"
Were used to scare the froward babe to sleep.

But he goes on:—

Neglected Muse of this our Western clime,
How long in servile, imitative, rhyme,
Wilt thou thy stifled energies enchain,
And tread the worn-out path still o'er again!
How long repress the brave decisive flight!
How long be blind to all thy native light!

To these lines I find affixed, on a fragment of manuscript, this note:—"It should be recollected this was written some twenty years ago, before Bryant, Percival, Halleck, Drake, Brainerd, and others, had redeemed the land from this reproach." And again, on another copy of the page: "It should be recollected, this was written almost forty years ago." He continues:—

Does not the story of our early days
Teem with the spirit of eternal lays?
Can not those glorious exiles who first sought
The untracked forest world, and with them brought
Unconquered and unconquerable mind,
That cast no weak and wistful look behind,
Scorned every danger in their high career
And planted every future blessing here,
Prompt some undying genius to engage,
With all a poet's strong yet tempered rage,
Above their tombs that laurel wreath to wave
'Tis true they need not, and they still should have?
Can grey tradition, or historic page,
Can every legend of each parted age,
Present a theme so fraught with patriot fire,
The dull to stir, the eager to inspire,
As that immortal struggle which here gave
To Freedom life, to Tyranny a grave?
Does Greece or Rome display a nobler field,
Or any nation's utmost records yield

A richer harvest, than our native land,
To him who'd reap it with a master's hand?
Or Nature in her generous zeal bestow
More splendid scenes to make his bosom glow,
Than here with mild exuberance she strews,
To rouse the dozing spirit of the Muse?
  The Past, the Present, Future, all combine
To waken inspiration in each line;
And yet we turn to Europe's old Rag-fair,
To deck ourselves in cast-off finery there,
And, like the wretched prodigal of old
Whose plaintive story is in Scripture told,
The plenty of our Father's house resign,
To starve on offal, and to herd with swine.

This terrible onslaught I fancy due to my lord Byron, for whom and whose school our author cherished a profound disgust. Perhaps the prevalence of "Yellow covers" had a hand in it: for it is possible that era was upon us when these lines were written.

His poetic fury now takes a prophetic turn: —

Thrice fortunate who first shall wake the lyre
With home-bred feeling and with home-bred fire;
He need not envy any foreign bard
Whom fame's bright meed, or fortune's smiles, reward,
Secure, that wheresoe'er this empire rolls,
Over the West, or toward the firm-fixed poles,
While, haply, Europe's honors fade away
And set the glories of her better day,
Unnumbered millions shall his words rehearse,
And love the author of the happy verse.

Basil, the hero of the poem, is now introduced. A child of the Hudson, married on faith, he is obliged to labor day in and day out on another man's land, to support his family; but his spirit of independence revolts against the prospect of working always as a hired man.

Hence comes it that our poorest barefoot boy
Aspires to taste the proud and manly joy
That springs from holding in his own dear right
The soil he tills, the home he seeks at night.
For this he leaves his friends and youthful home
'Mid forest wilds and Indian haunts to roam.
Wide sweeps his axe, his rifle is at hand,
And lo !, he soons subdues a savage land.
Then as the waving harvest field he sees,
Like sunny ocean, rippling in the breeze,
And hears the lowing herd, the lambkin's bleat,
And snuffs the fragrance of the clover sweet,
His heart sits lightly on its rustic throne —
The flocks, the fields, the hearth-stone, all his own.

But there is no such luck for Basil at present. On the contrary, year by year, his family, his toils, his anxieties, increase. A severe winter brings on him the climax of misery in an attack of rheumatism which lays him helpless on his bed. He does not die, however, but suffers throughout the dreary season, with what distress of body and mind may be imagined, as he finds himself absolutely thrown on the charity of his not over-wealthy neighbors for the sustenance of his family. But the months pass; and spring arrives: and with her presence the author's imagination is warmed, and he breaks out:—

Who can resist the coaxing voice of Spring,
When flowers peep forth, and feathered minstrels sing?
Who that inhales her breath in fields or groves,
But thinks of the sweet lips of her he loves?
Who that partakes of her life-giving smile,
But dreams of her he loves the best the while?
If there be one amid her wealth can rove,
And feel no thrill of joy, no stir of love,
He is no honest son of mother Earth,
And shames the holy dame that gave him birth.

We are her children, and when forth she hies,
Dressed in her wedding suit of varied dyes,
Beshrew the churl that does not feel her charms,
And long to nestle in her blooming arms;
He has no heart, or such a heart as I
Would not possess for all beneath the sky.
  Oh! thus to sit upon the clovered brow
Of some full-bosomed hill as I do now,
And see the river wind its silvery way
Round jutting points with Spring's new verdure gay,
Its flowing waters flashing to its brim,
While flocks of little barks its surface skim
This way and that as wayward zephyrs blow,
Like buoyant swans, all white as virgin snow;
And hear, yet scarcely hear, the distant wave
The pebbled shore or rocky margin lave,
While over all the sun's last splendid rays
Gild the glad fields and make the forest blaze —
Gives me more pleasure than would all the spoils
Ambition ever gained with all her toils.
  Then, as I watch the slow-retiring day
Stealing in shadows silently away,
While other suns of paler face arise,
Trembling and sparkling in the nightly skies,
I think, so when the Sun of Righteousness
No more with his bright beams the world could bless,
He did not doom the earth in darkness drear
To mourn the close of his sublime career,
But left the apostolic band behind
With borrowed lustre still to bless mankind.
  I love to revel in soft solitude,
And call around me Memory's phantom brood,
By turning to the folded leaf, to look
For some old record in Time's sacred book
That brings to mind a train of gentle themes,
Dear, blameless, joys, and early cherished dreams,
And happy hours I never can forget,
Barbed with no pang of sorrow or regret —
Airy memorials that brighter seem
Contrasted with the mist through which they gleam,

E'en as the splendors of departing day
Amid the Western skies in flashes play,
Reflected in the clouds when day is past,
Each varying tint still lovelier than the last.
  Is it not wise to thrust this world aside,
And for a while in fancy's realm abide;
To chase some nimble tenant of the brain,
Some bright associate of the starry train,
And dream such ecstacies we needs must sigh,
When, at our waking, swift the raptures fly?
If mortals find not happiness in this,
Where shall they seek the bower of earthly bliss?

With spring Basil revives; but, though health returns, his anxieties for the future are not lessened, and he broods continually over his prospects. In this condition of mind, he hears rumors of the great WEST. Tales reach him of the cheapness and fertility of its soil; of the opening for enterprise there. His imagination is excited by the idea of this wonderful land:—

As rich as ever glowed beneath the sun;
As wide as mad ambition ever won;
As fair as ever tempted man to stray
From childhood's haunts unto the far-away;
Where miles on miles of grassy meads abound,
And endless streams pursue their endless round;
Where Nature all her youthful might puts forth
To make for man a still more glorious earth.

He sets himself to persuade his wife into the scheme of emigration, and with success. They make their preparations; secure a sturdy nag; pack their small stock of household goods in a little covered wagon; and are equal to any fortune. Of course there are some who blow cold on the undertaking, and tell dreadful stories to alarm the adventurers. But Basil remains firm.

He shook their outstretched hands, and bade them pray
That Heaven would speed him on his lonely way;
Then sought the aged tree beneath whose shade
Father and mother side by side were laid,
Bent o'er the grassy mounds that marked the spot
Haply by all but him long since forgot,
And prayed to live a life of honest fame,
And leave behind, like them, a spotless name.

This brings us to the end of Book the First. Book the Second finds the house closed, the emigrants upon the road. They start on a foggy morning, which however soon clears, just as they mount a rise from which they have a last view of their deserted home on one side, and a burst of landscape on the other. Any one familiar with the Highlands of the Hudson should be struck with the photographic correctness of this picture. Cultivation has altered the scene a little, but not materially.

In truth it was a landscape wildly gay
Before his pensive vision smiling lay —
A sea of rolling hills with forests crowned,
Whose green clothed every height for leagues around,
Save where some grey-beard cliff upreared its head
As if just rising from a leafy bed.
By its bald brow, which unwinged steps ne'er pressed,
Our native eagle builds his rugged nest;
Oft in the warfare of the whistling gales,
Amid the scampering clouds serenely sails,
With scarce a motion wins the loftiest sky,
And looks into the sun with steadfast eye.
Lonely and lofty, through the unmapped skies
With steady sweep his royal wings he plies,
Gaining new strength from every effort made,
By others feared, of nought on earth afraid.
Prophetic emblem of this giant sphere,
This cradled King of Kings, be his career!

Through these great hills in groups of grandeur piled
Majestic Hudson wound his way, and smiled;
And, as he swept each ridge's tide-worn base,
In the pure mirror of his morning face
A lovelier landscape caught the gazer's view,
Softer than Nature, yet to Nature true.
Beyond, on either side the river's bound,
Two lofty promontories darkly frowned,
Through which in times long past, as learned ones say,
The pent-up waters forced their wilful way;
Grimly they frowned, as menacing the wave
That stormed their bulwarks with its current brave,
And seemed to threaten from each battered brow
To crush the sloops that lay becalmed below,
Whose white sails, hanging idly at the mast,
In the still tide a deep reflexion cast.
The stately flood, like conqueror on his way
Through sullen realms subjected to his sway,
Smiled as in scorn of those he erst subdued,
The ragged cliff, proud hill, and barrier rude,
That now like quailing vassals stood aside,
And gave free passage to th' imperial tide;
While still beyond, half hazy to the eye,
The far-off Katskills kissed the farthest sky,
Mingled with that their waving line of blue,
And shut the world beyond from mortal view.

Tearing themselves from this prospect, they are fairly on their way, and presently we find them in "Jersey's pleasant land." Passing through Pennsylvania, they reach the summit of the Alleghanies.

Here, seated where the first and last bright ray
Of morn and evening on his forehead play,
By brightest omens of the future blessed,
Resides the genius of the growing West.
Throned halfway to the vast etherial skies,
His glorious inheritance he eyes,

Watches with equal care each sister state,
Holds fast the old, and clasps each new-born mate,
And joys, from every jealous feeling free,
In ALL the land's combined prosperity.

The emigrants had encamped upon the crest of the mountains.

Our Basil beat the lazy sun next day,
And bright and early had been on his way,
But that the world he saw e'en yesternight
Had faded, like a vision, from his sight.
One endless chaos spread before his eyes,
No vestige left of earth or of the skies;
A boundless nothingness reigned all around,
Unbroken by a movement or a sound.
As stark he stared upon the blank below,
The lively morning breeze began to blow,
The magic curtain swayed, was moved, was torn,
And bits of landscape danced into the morn.
As the light flecks of vapor were upreared
And off into the boundless ether steered,
A novel charm each passing instant brought,
As ever-varying forms his vision caught:
A dripping precipice, a solemn wood,
A deep-scored dell, a foaming mountain flood,
Each after each, with coy and cool delay,
Yielded itself to sight's alluring sway.
So when the wandering grandsire of our race
On Ararat had found a resting place,
At first a shoreless ocean weltered round,
With not a sign, save where he stood, of ground;
But, as the waters day by day drew back
Into the confines of their former track,
Gradual, the lofty hills, like islands, crept
Out of the waste, and into sunshine stepped;
Then the green hillocks and the meadows bright
Greeted in turn the patriarch's longing sight;
Until, at length, with all its parts complete,
Appeared the earth again in order meet.

Yet oft he looked, I ween, with anxious eye,
In lingering hope somewhere, perchance, to spy
Amid the silent scene some living thing
Crawling the earth, or moving on the wing.
But neither man nor beast nor bird was there;
Nothing that breathed of life on earth, in air.
'Twas a vast mansion tenantless and drear;
A garden, like a churchyard, void of cheer.
Sadly he turned from the oppressive waste,
And, with a heavy heart, he Westward faced.

Descending the mountains, our travellers, after narrowly escaping from a freshet, in course of time reach the Ohio. Here the close of the Second Book leaves them. The introduction to Book the Third insists on what may be called the theory or moral of the poem — independence, or more properly, self-dependence, of character. This is illustrated by the fact that Basil, who has anticipated years of absolute solitude in the wilds, encounters others bound on the same errand as himself. They join forces, and presently are found at the point of embarkation, Pittsburg, surrounded by the idlers of the neighborhood, who have collected to see them off.

A common, simple, scene! Yet view it well —
'Twill soon to grander outlines haply swell;
For here, as on a chart engraved, we see
Our people's fated course, and destiny.
So came our fathers Westward — volunteers,
Who left behind them doubts, and fronted fears;
Thus did they sever every early tie
To win the meed they sought, or failing, die;
And thus their hardy offspring still go on,
Doing as their progenitors have done —
Waking to life the dreary solitude,
Planting refinement in the forest rude,
Nor pausing in the glorious race they run
Toward where the ocean bathes the setting sun.

The emigrants, now nearing their goal, dare not land at close of day, for fear of Indians.

So through the livelong night they floated, slow,
And Night was gentle as the river's flow.
So still, so bright, so tranquil was her reign,
They scarcely cared that day should come again.
The moon, high wheeled the distant hills above,
Silvered the fleecy foliage of the grove,
That, as the wooing Zephyr on it stole,
Sighed out the greeting of its sylvan soul.
The queen of night sailed on with face unblurred;
The sleepy leaves no more in rapture stirred;
No deep-mouthed hound the hunter's haunt betrayed;
No light along the shore or waters played;
No laugh intruded on the drowsy ear,
Nor yet a sound of grief, nor yet of fear.
All, all was still on gliding barque and shore,
As if the earth had slept, to wake no more.

A voyage of three days and nights brings them to their destination. They break up their boats to form a temporary shelter, and begin on the business of a settlement. Amid their various labors they do not forget the worship of the Almighty, gathering upon every Sabbath for prayer and the singing of hymns in the open air. Though our emigrants do their best, and hurry to the utmost, the course of the seasons falters not. Summer wanes; the fall of the year approaches:—

The palsied aspen reared its yellow head;
The maple motley, and the oak its red;
While here and there, the gaudy ranks between,
Towered a tall and sombre evergreen;

. . . . . . . . . . .

And then the dappled cloak of Autumn fell,
And Winter roared through wood and winding dell.

Silent the river's soothing murmurs were,
And still the myriads of the peopled air;
The trees no more their whispered music played,
But howling blasts the shrinking ear dismayed;
Or if, at times, the season's icy breath
Died to a calm, it seemed the calm of death.

Apprehensive still more at this season, (like all frontier settlers from the beginning of our history), of attack by the Indians, they, at first, occasionally mistake at night the howl of the wolf for the war-whoop. But habit soon steels them against alarms. The occupations of the winter are indicated: Basil employs his leisure hours in imparting to his children the rudiments of education he had acquired at the road-side school, and in the evening, by the blazing hearth, expatiates on the Revolutionary men and times. Among the memorable characters we may be sure that the foremost, Washington, is not forgotten. But Basil does not confine his legends to the world-known of that era. He tells of the nameless men whom History ignores—how they left their homes, urged to the battle field not by the desire of fame but the sentiment of patriotism; how they suffered all manner of peril and hardship, cheerfully, constantly, and with a fidelity to their cause as conspicuous as their courage and endurance; how some came home at last, broken and crippled; and how some never came home at all.

Sometimes Basil and his family anticipate the pleasure of revisiting the old home, and telling their adventures to an admiring neighborhood. But years elapse while they discuss the scheme, the wilderness fills up, old acquaintances join them, and lo!, a world very like that of memory. The village flourishes; the inhabitants wax rich; the children grow up, brave, active, healthy, hearty, independent. What they miss the following lines declare:—

'Tis true—yet 'tis no pity that 'tis true—
Many fine things they neither felt nor knew.
Unlike the sons of Europe's happier clime,
They never died to music's melting chime,
Or groaned, as if in agonizing pain,
At some enervate, whining, sickly strain;
Nor would they sell their heritage of rights
For long processions, pomps, and pretty sights,
Or barter for a bauble, or a feast,
All that distinguishes the man from beast.
With them, alas! the fairest masterpiece
Of plundered Italy, or rifled Greece,
A chiselled wonder, miracle of paint,
A marble god-head, or a canvas saint,
Were poor amends for cities wrapped in flame,
A ruined land, and a dishonored name;
Nor would they mourn Apollo's exile more
Than Freedom turning downcast from their door.
Among them was no drivelling princely race
Who'd beggar half a state to buy a vase,
Or starve a province haply, to reclaim
From mother earth a lump without a name,
Some mutilated trunk decayed and worn,
Of head bereft, of arms and ankles shorn,
And fit for nought save puzzling learnéd brains,
And causing worlds of most laborious pains,
To guess if this same headless, limbless thing,
Were worthless demi-god or worthless king.

In Book the Fourth we have premonitions of war, and an Indian prophet appears upon the scene.

Far in a dismal glen whose deep recess
The sun could never penetrate to bless,
Beside a lone and melancholy stream
That never sparkled in the moon's pale beam,

Remote from all his copper-colored race,
A moody Indian made his biding place;
Here 'mid green carpets of perennial moss,
And solemn pines, that locked their arms across
Great sluggish pools, and with their gloomy shade
In brightest noon a dusky twilight made,
With hurrying steps, like maniac oft he trod,
And cursed the white-man, and the white-man's God.
Once the proud painted chief of warriors brave,
Whose bones now bleaching lay, without a grave,
A thousand red-men owned his savage sway,
Followed where'er he chose to lead the way,
Ranged the wide wilderness for many a mile,
And hailed him lord of cruelty and wile.
Now, like a girdled tree, discrowned he stood,
The only relic of a stately wood;
The last man of his tribe, he lived alone,
His name, his being, and his haunts, unknown.

Brooding over his people's wrongs, half madman half impostor, he presently begins to preach a crusade against the whites. Rambling from tribe to tribe, and discoursing with the phrenzied eloquence of a monomaniac, no wonder that he makes a deep impression on a race

Whose mind was like the forest that he roved,
Dark, gloomy, rayless, rugged, unimproved.

He is joined by a chief who uses him to forward designs of his own, and together they excite the passions of the tribes to the utmost. With a war-dance the Book closes.

Book the Fifth is devoted to the preparations of the Indians for war, and also brings to light a certain renegade white who is associated with their plans. We have this brief sketch of an Indian march:—

Now through the irksome forest's twilight gloom,
Where bees ne'er hum, or honeyed flowrets bloom,
By paths unmarked by all but Indian eyes,
By nameless streams in nameless wilds that rise,
Whose banks ne'er echoed to the fowler's gun,
Whose wave was never cheered by Summer sun,
With silent haste and quick elastic tread,
By day and night they on their errand sped,
While the light footsteps of that wily race
Scarce left behind distinguishable trace.

The prophet, preceding the main body, makes a reconnoissance to the vicinity of Basil's village. In the outskirts of the settlement he encounters a missionary to the Indian tribes. With him the prophet, considering that he is physically incompetent to fight, enters into a discussion, in the course of which he forcibly illustrates his own unhappy fate; but his wrath declines at length into prophetic sorrow, as he anticipates the day when the bones of his people shall be dug up—

To tell that there a gallant race of yore
Trod the free earth, but ne'er shall tread it more.

And so he vanishes.

Book the Sixth brings the threatened invasion. War with Great Britain sets in. Rumors thicken: more particularly, that the Indians are on the war-path, and committing all manner of atrocities. The people run to arms, and we have the undisciplined volunteers of the country assembled. Our author now observes that it is easy for a man conspicuous in the view of the world to risk all for reputation; but that in reality the men who never expect to be heard of, and sacrifice themselves for a sentiment or a principle, deserve more credit.

These are the warriors that my homely muse
For heroes of her lowly tale would choose,
And haply if this rough, unpolished, lay,
To future times could hope to find its way,
Gladly would I, with an immortal pen,
Record the glories of the nameless men.

Following out this train of thought, he celebrates THE PEOPLE as the sole dependence of a State in a great emergency.

Is it a fable — that in ancient time
The hardy Goths forsook their wintry clime,
Lured by the hope of plunder, or beguiled
By the fair fields in Italy that smiled,
And, like the locust flight that dusks the day,
O'erran the land with famine and dismay —
Is it a fable — that while lordly pride
Stood helplessly to view the carnage wide,
Or skulked away to some secure retreat,
Afraid the fierce barbarian horde to meet,
Or dirty refuge in its treasons sought,
And with its country its own safety bought,
The only men that strove against the flood
Were men without a drop of noble blood?
Probus for one, and Claudius truly brave,
And Diocletian, offspring of a slave!
These propped the falling empire of the world,
And bloody vengeance on the plunderer hurled;
Nor fell she quite, while peasants ruled in Rome:
'Twas the blood royal brought the ruin home.

Is it a fable — that in later day
When hosts of veterans were swept away,
And the proud phantom of this trembling earth
Played with the chains of kings as if in mirth,
The peasant's, and the peasant's arm alone,
Upheld the hopes of every tottering throne?
Is it a fable — that the *landwehr* rose,
A wall of hearts, his progress to oppose?

Is it a fable — that the Spaniard brought
A spirit to the cause for which he fought,
That could, and did, the lord of Europe foil,
Because he battled for his native soil?

No power on earth a country can subdue,
When a whole PEOPLE to themselves are true;
It may o'errun, may crimson it with slain,
May spoil its fields, but never can retain.

We now have the march, and the battle, the backwoodsmen remaining victors on the field. Having fulfilled the last duties to the dead, and rescued the frontier from fears of Indian depredation, they hasten home. Here we are reminded for a moment of one who has been for a long while kept in the background, namely Basil, who is presented in a green old age, enjoying all the rewards of a well-spent life. The whole country likewise is prosperous.

Again Peace showered her blessings o'er the land,
And Happiness and Freedom, hand in hand,
Went gayly 'round and knocked at every door,
Hailing the rich, and biding with the poor,
While wondering nations watched our bright career,
And looked, and longed to seek a refuge here
From all the countless pack of galling ills
That slaves still suffer when the tyrant wills.
And oh!, be such thy ever-during fate,
My native land!, still to be free as great!
Still to be dear to nations — doubly dear —
The people's hope, the tyrant's lasting fear;
Still to be cherished by the good and brave;
Still to be hated by the dastard slave
That turns in sickening envy from thy face,
The mirror that reflects his deep disgrace;
Still to be feared for thy far-beckoning smiles,
Alluring emigrants in countless files;
Still to be loved by all who joy to see
The race of man live happy, great, and free.

The following apostrophe closes the poem.

Yes! lone and spotless virgin of the West,
No tyrant pillows on thy swelling breast;
Thou bow'st before no despot's guilty throne,
But at God's footstool, and at His alone!
Genius of Freedom!, may the future raise
Chorus on chorus, hymning to thy praise!
Do thou the nations of the earth inspire
With the deep glow of thy celestial fire;
Teach them a sober way to break their chains;
Wipe from thy sacred brow those bloody stains
That hasty zealots sprinkled madly there,
And show thyself to them, as pure as fair!
Then may those nations freed fresh chaplets bring,
And to their Western sister praises sing —
Thy FIRST-BORN still, however born the rest,
The dearest still to thy maternal breast!

# VIII.

1818–1819. [ÆT. 40–41.]

MARRIAGE — SECOND SERIES OF SALMAGUNDI — EVERT A. DUYCKINCK ON — LETTER TO IRVING ABOUT — ALLUSION TO, IN "FANNY" — LETTER FROM IRVING — A WARNING TO BIOGRAPHERS — THE CHURCHYARD.

ON the 15th of November, 1818, Mr. Paulding married Gertrude, daughter of Peter Kemble, a retired merchant of New-York, and sister of his friend Gouverneur Kemble. Of this connexion it is enough to say, once for all, that he was as fortunate in the choice of a wife as he declares himself to have been in the character of his mother.

In 1819 our author made a hazardous experiment — the attempt to renew an eccentric success, in a SECOND SERIES OF SALMAGUNDI. The first number was issued by Moses Thomas, May 30, 1819; the concluding one, August 19, 1820.

In a preface to the latest edition of the first series, Mr. Evert A. Duyckinck says: "Some ten years or more after the conclusion of Salmagundi, Paulding ventured alone upon a second series. Washington Irving was in Europe, and the muse of Pindar Cockloft was silent. It was a dangerous undertaking, for the very essence of a Salmagundi is the combination of divers ingredients — a product of many minds. . . . Yet it contains many delightful pages."

It does not on the whole, however, compare favorably. We miss that light and audacious gayety which makes up so much of the charm of the first series. The Indian Chief is but an indifferent substitute for Mustapha Rub-a-dub Keli Khan, and Will Wizard and Anthony Evergreen leave too much of the burden of the scheme on the shoulders of their old associate, Launcelot Langstaff. But there are fine papers in it, and the Cockloft characters are reinspired in a much more fortunate manner than might have been expected, considering, as Mr. Irving remarks, that they "had grown to a very troublesome old age during the interval." Very likely some of these articles were conceived, and perhaps sketched, before the first series was so summarily "bitten off."

In a letter to Irving, of January 20, 1820, the same in which "The Backwoodsman" is referred to, Mr. Paulding writes in reference to the publication we are considering: —

I must now make two or three explanations concerning myself, and proceedings. Hearing last winter from Wm. Irving that you had finally declined coming home, and finding my leisure time a little heavy, I set to work, and prepared several numbers of a continuation of our old joint production. At that time, and subsequently, until Gouv[r] Kemble brought your first number [of The Sketch-Book] down to Washington with him, I was entirely ignorant that you contemplated any thing of the kind. But for an accidental delay, my first No. would have got the start of yours. As it happened however, it had the appearance of taking the field against you, a thing which neither my head nor heart will sanction. I believe my work has not done you any harm in the way of rivalship, for it has been soundly abused by many persons, and compared with the first part with many degrading expressions. It has sold tolerably, but I shall discontinue it shortly, as I begin to grow tired, and I believe the public has got the start of me. It was owing to Moses that I did not commence an entire new work.

It must have had a certain run of fashion, as I gather from a stanza of "Fanny", where Halleck speaks of his heroine's tastes:—

CXVIII.

"And though by no means a *bas bleu*, she had
For literature a most becoming passion;
Had skimmed the latest novels, good and bad,
And read the Croakers, when they were in fashion;
And Doctor Chalmers' sermons, of a Sunday;
And Woodsworth's Cabinet, and the new Salmagundi."

Mr. Paulding's letter continues:—

In reading over your last edition of Knickerbocker, after some years during which I had not looked into it, I was struck with several enormous plagiarisms I had unconsciously committed upon you. The public may not, but you who know me I hope will, give me credit when I assure you I was not aware of the offence. Indeed my memory is of that vague kind, that half the time I can't distinguish between my own ideas and those I have got from books. These I believe are all the sins I can at present charge myself with on the score of apparent rivalry, or plagiarism, against my old friend.

. . . . . . . . . .

I thank you for your kind and affectionate wishes and remembrances. I need not tell you that Gertrude makes such a wife as she made a sister and daughter, and that I feel and know her value. We are now living in decent competency in one of *The Seven Buildings*, a present from Mr. Kemble, and as yet I have managed to keep the wolf from the door, as well as to escape the curse of Heaven — servility to the great ones about me.

The Seven Buildings, of which perhaps the reader might get a magnificent impression from the sounding title, were a row of small three-story brick houses on Pennsylvania Avenue, not far from the Presidential mansion. I again quote from the letter: —

The only man I ever yet envied was yourself, and when I tell you this, in God's name let us hear no more complaints on the score of fortune and future prospects. With youth, health, talents, and reputation — with all the noble means of pursuing noble ends still within your power, let me entreat you to contemplate yourself and future fortunes through a brighter medium. I am not good at preaching, but I wish you would let me hear from you now and then, for almost everybody I meet asks me about you, and I am ashamed to confess my ignorance. It looks as if we were no longer friends.

If I were not afraid of being even with you by exciting your envy, I would tell you what a pretty boy is sitting in his mother's lap just before me, who I dare swear is a fine fellow, though I am his father. Gertrude desires to be affectionately remembered to you, and thinks with me you had better come home. Remember me to my old friend the Doctor, [Peter Irving] under whose auspices I made my first campaign, quill in hand, in the Morning Chronicle. Would to God you were both here, and settled around us, for I want nothing that I know of, so much as a little circle of old friends, to talk of old times with.

Farewell, and believe me your friend,

J. K. PAULDING.

The answer to the above, dated London, May 27th, 1820, is one of three letters, all that have been preserved of this side of the correspondence. I give a couple of extracts.

"You have taken the trouble to make some explanations as to your literary concerns which were quite unnecessary. I have no idea of rivalship or competition in our writings, and never could have suspected you of any thing of the kind. I have no feeling toward you than that of the old fellowship of the pen with which we started together, heaven knows how carelessly and vagrantly; and am only solicitous that you should maintain your stand in Literature."

. . . . . . . . . . .

"And now, my dear James, with a full heart I take my leave of you. Let me hear from you just when it is convenient; no matter how long or how short the letter, nor think any apologies necessary for delays, only let me hear from you. I may suffer time to elapse myself, being unsettled, and often perplexed and occupied; but believe me always the same in my feelings, however irregular in my conduct, and that no new acquaintances that a traveller makes in his casual sojournings are apt to wear out the recollections of his early friends. Give my love to Gertrude, who I have no doubt is a perfect pattern for wives, and when your boy grows large enough to understand tough stories, tell him some of our early frolics, that he may have some kind of an acquaintance with me against we meet.

Affectionately your friend,

W. IRVING."

What the particular imitations were, into which our author had been betrayed by his fallacious memory, he does not mention. Perhaps the first one of the Letters from the South is a case.

But I revert to the Second Series of Salmagundi. The introduction closes with this graceful allusion to one of his coadjutors in the First.

"The reader will not fail of hearing, in good time, all about the worthy COCKLOFT family; the learned JEREMY, and the young ladies, who are still young in spite of the lapse of ten years and more. Above a dozen years are past since we first introduced these excellent souls to our readers, and in that time many a gentle tie has been broken, and many friends separated, some of them for ever. Among those we most loved and admired, we have to regret the long absence of one, who was aye the delight of his friends; and who, if he were with us, would add such charms of wit and gayety to this little work, that the young and the aged would pore over it with equal delight."

Mr. Paulding had a profound contempt for those *ante-mortem* biographies intended to make somebodies out of nobodies. To a friend who had inquired of himself about himself he wrote in 1852: —

"That my literary and personal history is not more generally known, is partly owing to my never having been what may be called a fashionable writer, and partly to my own somewhat peculiar notions, or perhaps I may say peculiar disposition. . . . and though frequently applied to for information on this subject, with a view to its publication, [I] have always declined, either because I did not deem it worth communicating, or from an opinion I have always entertained, that publishing a man's life before his death was little better than a fraud on Posterity, by attempting to forestall its decision."

He hits off this foible of our people in the ensuing paper, which may be styled

### A WARNING TO BIOGRAPHERS.

I insert the following letter for no other reason whatever, than because it exactly makes up the pages requisite to complete this number, a matter which our publisher has most especially at heart, as his sagacious brethren generally buy books by the square foot, as I am informed.

TO LAUNCELOT LANGSTAFF, ESQ.

"SIR,

"I AM induced to address this communication to your Elbow Chair, rather with a view to relieve myself by complaining, and warn others from following my example, than in the hope that your advice or assistance will be of the least service.

"You will be pleased to understand, sir, that I was employed, a few years since, to write the life of a distinguished personage, who, besides being either president or member of a vast number of societies, was sole proprietor of two newspapers, which were employed day and night inventing new proofs of his extraordinary merits. Having thus, as it were, a bladder under each arm, he managed to float down the stream of popularity with very considerable reputation, and in the opinion of his most particular friends, was fairly entitled to a biography.

"My instructions being to make him out a first-rate great man, and as good as he was great, I went to work in the usual manner, and gathered together all the cardinal virtues, which I mixed up with several handfuls of the most distinguishing characteristics of our most illustrious ancient and modern statesmen, heroes, and philosophers. These I stirred well together, and having let them ferment through about twenty octavo pages, the heterogeneous mass produced, when it came to subside, one of the most perfect modern great men you ever saw in all your life. So complete was it in all its parts, that I actually came near being the dupe of my own cleverness, and could scarcely refrain from falling down and worshipping the idol of my own creation. Well, indeed, may we biographers call these great people 'our heroes' in speaking of them, since, if the honest truth were told, they are as much of our own creation as the imaginary champions of romances and fairy tales.

"My employer, however, was delighted, and turned my great man to considerable profit. The biography had a run, and the people were not only charmed at possessing so distinguished a fellow-citizen, but astonished at not having known it before. They forthwith elected him to an office of great trust and profit, as a reward for his extraordinary merits, as well as extraordinary modesty in keeping them so long from public view. All this, I am bold to say, arose from my not having weighed, and discriminated, and balanced, and hesitated, between weaknesses and great qualities, as certain biographers do, thereby puzzling their readers, and leaving them in great doubt whether most to admire or contemn.

"Perceiving the astonishing success of this new system of superlative biography, several people, ambitious of the like distinction, applied to me for a character, and I was in a fair way of getting into a profitable business, when a most untoward accident happened, which put an end to the whole affair. The great man whom I had put in a way of making a fortune by means of his biography, and whom I had decked with every talent, and every virtue under heaven, took occasion all at once to turn out, not only a very great blockhead, but a very great rogue. By this means, he not only disgraced himself, but his biographer also, by destroying his reputation for veracity, and falling from the high elevation to which I had raised him by dint of great puffing and exertion. The most melancholy part of the business, however, was, that it put a stop to the growth of a number of most promising candidates for immortality that I had taken in hand. These I was in a fair way of making each one greater than his predecessor, whom I had just before proved the greatest man of his time, by a method peculiar to myself, and which I take pride in having brought to the utmost possible perfection.

" In short, worthy sir, my business was quite ruined by the unlucky backslidings of my hero, while the country was irretrievably injured in its glory, by the loss of several great personages whose fame I had brought to considerable maturity, and who will now, most likely, never be heard of more. For the sake of my own character for truthfulness, I am determined in future never to become sponsor for the reputation of any great man, until he is as dead as Julius Cæsar, and consequently utterly incapable of bringing his biographer to shame, by belying his good word through some unseemly misbehaviour. By this method I shall obviate the possibility of my hero turning out a fool or a knave, after I have pledged myself to the world and to posterity in favour of his worth and abilities.

"In pursuance of this inflexible determination, I have lately declined immortalizing a number of living worthies, simply because they could not produce sureties for their future good behaviour; and I do hereby publicly announce my resolution never to become responsible for a living great man, most earnestly recommending this example to my brother labourers in the fertile field of biography, both in Europe and America. It is for their especial benefit and caution that I have made this matter public, earnestly hoping, as I do, that in future they will not commit themselves to the world in favour of great men, who may possibly, in the natural course of events, turn out arrant ninnies or swindlers before they die.

"I am, Mr. Langstaff, your sincere friend,

"MAURICE M'LEAD."

This recalls to mind a certain great work on "Distinguished Americans" which I have somewhere seen, in which Clay, Jackson, Webster, and men of that note, are allowed about three quarters of a page apiece, and the originator of the publication something like half a volume.

Mr. Paulding was fond of contemplating his country as the asylum of the poor and persecuted of the earth, and in his writings often recurred to the theme. In the following paper he gives a pathetic illustration of the subject. "Bayard's farm" was East of Broadway, about on the line of Canal Street.

### THE CHURCHYARD.

ONE of the most endearing aspects in which this country presents itself to my view, is that of a place of refuge for the indigent and oppressed of every corner of the earth. Whatever may be their habits manners, language, religion, or sufferings, it is to this happy country they look as a haven of rest, where industry is the passport to competence; where the earnings of the poor do not pass into the coffers of the rich, or the strong-box of government; and where they can pursue the path which, in their opinion, leads to eternal happiness, without forfeiting any of their civil rights.

The experience of every day proves that the eyes of that portion of the civilized world with which books and business have connected us, are fixed upon this country. The rich and noble begin to look toward it as a refuge from the indiscriminate vengeance of revolutions often brought about by an obstinate refusal of reform, when reform might have at least delayed, if not warded off, the catastrophe — while the poorer classes long for the enjoyment of its generous plenty, and contemplate it at a distance, as the wanderers of Israel did the land of Canaan flowing with milk and honey. No doubt this latter class often, perhaps always, over-rate the advantages held out by this country; but still we do not find that experience deters them from remaining. Few ever return. Like the adventurer of the days of enchantment and elfin influence, once within the magic circle of freedom, they remain willing sojourners; and if they sometimes cast a remembering thought toward the land of their birth, it is, perhaps, to wish some dear friends, and dearer relatives, were here to share with them the blessings of a chastened liberty.

In rambling over various parts of our country, and visiting the busy crowded towns, it is a curious subject of reflection, as well as a source of honest satisfaction, to mark the various physiognomies, and the peculiarities of manner and dialect, which point out the natives of far distant climes, who all flock hither as to a common centre, in search of the great objects of man's pursuits — freedom and happiness. The blue-eyed laborious German — the saving Hollander — the calculating Scot, and the uncalculating Hibernian — the Englishman grumbling and eating — the Welshman with his long breeches, and the Welshwoman with her short petticoats — are dispersed through every town, or gathered together in little knots in the western land of promise. Wherever they are, industry and economy make them flourish, and obedience to the laws secures them all the privileges accorded to the most distinguished citizen.

Whatever evils the deep-thinking politician, or the politician who believes he thinks deeply, may anticipate from the extraordinary mixture of human tempers and physiognomies which this country presents, I, for my part, have little doubt that it will, in the end, produce all the advantages derived from crossing the breed in other animals. We find that all old stocks, whose members are continually marrying their cousins and second cousins to keep estates in the family, degenerate into a sort of libel upon the human race; and, if I might be allowed the conjecture, I would give it as my opinion, that the orang-outang and the Hottentot, are the progeny of some of those exceedingly ancient families supposed to be extinct, but which gradually lost their rank in the scale of human dignity, by a too great care in marrying among themselves in order to keep the blood pure and the estate in the family. But let the future take care of itself; it is sufficient for me, that this propensity of our fellow-creatures to come among us from the uttermost ends of the earth, if not a proof of the superior plenty and happiness we enjoy, is at least a demonstration of the good opinion entertained toward us by these strangers. Let us, therefore, be proud of our country and its institutions; and, above all, let us endeavour to justify their good opinion, not only by a becoming hospitality, but by cherishing those laws, and preserving those habits, which have made us an object of trembling interest to the lovers of rational freedom all over the world, and our country the home of the stranger and the sanctuary of the oppressed.

I was led into these reflections from having by chance strolled into the burying-ground of the Catholic church, now standing on what, within my memory, was called Bayard's farm. I remember it was in consequence of my being one of a party of boys that robbed an orchard on this very spot, that I felt the first pricks of that monitor, whose struggles are so powerful at first, but grow weaker and weaker, like the receding thunder, as we advance in life, and at last are awakened to new and terrible energy, by the approach of death. I distinctly remember that my struggles were very painful while there was danger of our theft being found out, but gradually subsided with my apprehensions of temporal punishment, and were quite forgot by the time this fear was over. We at that time gambolled over the green grass teeming with insect life, ourselves the very imps of youthful hilarity, on the spot where now repose the mouldering bones of hundreds of strangers from almost every corner of the peopled earth. Such are the curious and rapid mutations of our country. In a few years the desert is in some places changed into the abode of thousands of living men; in others the rural field, prolific of flowers and fruits, is converted into a charnel-house for thousands of the dead.

The crosses at the top of the tombstones marked out the sleeping crowd as having belonged to the ancient Catholic church; and the legends engraven on them, told that almost all were born in foreign lands. They had torn asunder the ties of country and the ligaments of kindred affection, and, forced by hard necessity, had come hither, as it seemed, only to die. They had, no doubt, promised to write home, and let their friends know how they sped; and their friends had in like manner promised to write to them. But these letters had probably never been received by the wanderers, whose destiny had carried them into every part of this extensive country. They remained without the sweet solace of news from home, and died without knowing whether they preceded their old friends or relatives, or had left them behind to wonder at their long silence. That this occurs continually, no one that sees the notices of the different post-offices can doubt. We there find letters advertised in great numbers for names, so evidently foreign, as not to be mistaken. They are directed to the ports whither these wanderers were bound; but before they arrive, the dispersion from the ark in which they floated over the waves has taken place — the emigrants have gone, no one knows whither, in search of a resting-place or of employment, and the letter never comes to hand.

Hence it often happens, that the relations who come out afterward, in search of them or of happiness, go to the churchyards to inquire of the gravestones the fate of their lost ones. It is at least some little assurance of their being alive, if they are not found among the tombs; and it is for this reason that the poor Irish especially, if they cannot afford a stone to tell their names and whence they came, erect a wooden slab over the dead, to serve at least as a frail guide to those who may come to inquire their fate. Any one who goes into the burying-place of one of these Catholic churches on a Sabbath day, cannot fail of seeing a number of men, women, and children, wandering about, and consulting the gravestones for news of those who have preceded them to this new world, and many of them got the start to the world to come. There is something affecting in such a sight, and sometimes, instead of attending a sermon, I go to the tombs of the Catholic church, and there receive a lesson of the uncertainty of life, as well as the vanity of human hopes and worldly pursuits.

Indulging in these feelings and reflections one Sunday afternoon, I at last found myself the only person left in the burial-place, except an old man who lingered behind, and was standing in front of a wooden slab at the head of a new-made grave. He might have passed for a statue, only his costume was not classical, and his attitude too much like nature; at any rate, he seemed immovable, and the first impression on my mind was, that some bodily infirmity, or sudden indisposition, prevented his retiring. I am a shy sort of person, and never address a stranger without some particular reason. When I do, I am very apt to say something rather ridiculous, or to make some observation exceedingly far-fetched and outré. It was so on this occasion. I felt a sympathy for this old figure, and not knowing exactly what to say, walked up to him, and very abruptly asked "what he was looking for?" The figure then raised his eyes as if he was offended at this intrusion, but seeing an old man, and an oldfashioned man too, before him, who, I will venture to say, does not look as if he could be impertinent, answered, after some little hesitation, "I was looking for a lost son, and have just now found him." Not knowing exactly what to say, I uttered a sort of bungling congratulation. "What makes the discovery more precious," continued the old man, "he was my only son — my only child — the only relation I had in the world." By this time I felt extremely awkward, and cast an inquiring look about, as if to ask where the young man was. He seemed to understand me, and pointing to the grave, answered — "There."

# IX.

1819–1820. [Æt. 41–42.]

SECOND SERIES OF SALMAGUNDI CONTINUED — AN ECCENTRIC SAGE — HIC FINIS FANDI — EARLY RECOLLECTIONS OF JAMES K. PAULDING.

Here is a richly-toned study of a happy, if whimsical, old man. Many of the touches are derived from the father of his friend Brevoort, and his establishment, which, by the way, was situated not very far from the location of the present Grace Church. The article is simply "From my elbow chair", but, for the sake of a heading, I call it

## AN ECCENTRIC SAGE.

That man is, in my opinion, truly fortunate, who, amid the frivolous pursuits, artificial enjoyments, and heartless follies which allure him on every side, preserves a taste for the pure and simple pleasures of a country life. Whether he devotes himself to the cultivation of those productions which are necessary to the existence of his fellow-creatures, or amuses his leisure hours in watching the progress of his flowers, or beautifying the little world where centre all his enjoyments, still to him the beneficent Creator has been most bountiful, by giving a source of innocent happiness, awakened by the contemplation of rural objects everywhere spread over the face of nature, and fed by the purest springs of moral and intellectual feeling.

From my very boyhood, it has been my peculiar happiness to share the friendship and affection of a worthy gentleman, whose gentle virtues and singular turn of mind will furnish me with a happy illustration of the foregoing observations. He inherited from nature a mind of uncommon strength, as well as singular benevolence of heart; but owing to various circumstances, to his living much within the boundaries of his own territories, and exercising unlimited authority therein, his strength of mind and goodness of disposition have branched out into sundry peculiarities, all characteristic of the best feelings, however whimsically displayed.

His ancestors were among the first Christian settlers of this fair and prosperous isle, and, unlike most of their worthy contemporaries, preserved their lands entire, although often tempted by the mighty speculators of the times to sell them, and become paupers in the third generation. My old friend inherited the whole, free from bond, note, or mortgage, and has retained them to the present time; when, in consequence of the near approach of the city, they have become a valuable estate. I question, however, whether this immense increase of wealth makes him amends for the vexations the inroad of the town occasions him. Numerous are the border wars, the watchings and inventions, to which he is obliged to resort, in order to protect his subjects from the raids of the moss-troopers of Greenwich, the Bowery, and Kip's Bay; and I have great doubts whether any of the renowned commanders of ancient or modern times ever devised more excellent stratagems to circumvent their enemies. Truth obliges me to confess, however, that not one of them ever succeeded, except in a single instance, where he caught a fellow in his fowl-house by means of a contrivance of such singular excellence, that, in going to secure the culprit, my old friend was himself caught in the same trap. Being thus unintentionally placed in bad company, he made the best of his situation by entering into conversation with his neighbour, who gave such an affecting account of the distresses of his family, that the old gentleman became an accomplice in robbing his own henroost, and actually bestowed two of his fattest pullets upon the rogue. He denies this story, but I give the reader my word it is true.

One of the most amusing peculiarities of my excellent friend is an extravagant fondness for the whole animal creation. His old mansion is a kind of ark, inhabited by almost every variety of the feathered race, from the voluble and various mock-bird, to the solemn owl. His poultry-yard also abounds in a vast number of different kinds of domestic animals and fowls, all of which he cherishes with a sort of parental affection, and among which he administers justice with the sagacity and uprightness of a Marshall. Such, indeed, is the mildness, yet vigour of his administration, that I have often looked upon him in the light of a mighty potentate, exercising an affectionate and patriarchal sway over his numerous and partycoloured subjects, and have more than once been tempted to hold him up as an example to the present race of kings, being fully persuaded, that the same equitable system of legislation extended over the human race, would produce a degree of happiness among my fellow-creatures, to which they are almost everywhere strangers. It is quite impossible for me to afford myself space for a full development of all the little arts of state policy practised in the government of his animal kingdom. The reader must be content with a brief account of some of the leading features, which will, however, be amply sufficient to show the excellence of his system.

Like all wise rulers, his great object is to preserve peace and union among his subjects at home, and guard his frontiers from the incursions of enemies. Early in the morning, you will see him walk forth like one of the patriarchs of olden time. The moment he appears, his subjects come running and flying from every direction to welcome his approach, and give the merry morning salutation. The poultry flutter about his feet, or perch familiarly upon his shoulder, knowing by experience the good monarch will not harm a feather of their speckled wings. The pigeons too, of which he has a great variety, fan-tails, pouters, tumblers, and letter-carriers, the moment they see him, descend from the air, or from the roofs of the out-buildings, hovering and fluttering their congratulations; the turkeys run gobbling toward him, the ducks and geese come waddling up with toes turned inward, while half a dozen dogs of various generations, but all of one family, approach, wagging their tails, and leaping up to his honest old heart.

All this is pleasant enough. It is like going about among the people, and receiving addresses of congratulation, such as grateful hearts bestow on those who govern wisely and justly. But it is inconceivable what difficulties my old friend has to encounter, and what exertions he is obliged to make to keep the peace among his motley subjects, when he administers their breakfast. I remember at one time there was a tall boasting gander, of the Chinese breed, who occasioned him a vast deal of trouble by reason of his quarrelsome, overbearing disposition, which kept the whole kingdom in a state of utter confusion and ferment. He was at length decreed a triangular yoke, which not only mortified his pride, but also impeded the progress of his further enormities. On another occasion there was a lordly turkey-cock, whom my old friend dubbed the noble lord in the red ribbon, and who, like a notable bully, stalked over the common people without ceremony, creating great confusion, and sometimes trampling on the little chickens. I shall never forget the exultation of the old gentleman when a favourite game chicken of the Delancey breed attacked the bully one morning, and gave him such a sound drubbing that he always kept the peace afterward. The gray-haired monarch, like another Bonaparte, immediately erected one of his barnyards into an independent kingdom, which he assigned to this valiant champion, together with a seraglio of half a dozen of his plump pullets. There is a wise-looking owl, which has been attached to the court of the old gentleman for nearly twenty years past, and whom he calls his minister of police. His functions consist in the particular superintendence of the kingdom at night, when he prowls about like a trusty watchman, detecting the rats and weasels in their depredations, and putting martial law in force against them. On one occasion, however, he was caught in the fact of eating a favourite pup spaniel, and, in consequence of this abuse of power, was for some time confined to a hollow apple-tree, like a disgraced Spanish minister in the tower of Segovia.

One fine morning last spring I walked out to pay a visit to this exemplary monarch, and found him in one of his best humours. He shook my hand with great glee, exclaiming at the same time, "They are come — they are come!" — "What, your grandsons from school?" replied I. "No — no — the martins — don't you hear the little rogues twittering on the box yonder?" Honest, pure soul — thought I — happy, thrice happy, in the virtuous simplicity, which can banquet on such cheap and innocent gratifications! Just then a tumbler pigeon flew high in the air, and, according to the singular instinct of that curious bird, poised itself for a moment, and throwing a somerset backward, descended again to the infinite delight of the monarch, who talked of bestowing a new coop on the occasion, and rewarded the feat with a handful of grain, of which the rest of his courtiers, according to custom, managed to get the best share. I am of opinion that my friend enjoyed this feat with much greater zest, than if he had seen the clown at the circus exhibit those wonderful evolutions, which a discerning public rewarded, not long since, with a benefit of twelve hundred dollars.

We now went in to breakfast, where the good man entertained me with a long account of the wars between the pigeons and martins, the Guelphs and Ghibellines of his commonwealth, who alternately turned each other out of house and home. The injuries inflicted on the swallows by the martins, were also another fruitful source of difficulty. "Plague take them," said he, in the tone of a fond parent, affecting to find fault with a favoured urchin who quarrels with his school-fellows—"Plague take them. I believe they would master my whole territory, if it were not for a little wren, who is a perfect Bonaparte, and whom I shall be obliged to send to St. Helena if he don't keep the peace. There is no telling you what trouble I have with these three conflicting powers, the pigeons, the martins, and the little wren, who seems a match for all together."

When breakfast was over, after examining his aviary, turning the eggs of his canary-birds' nests, feeding the young orphans, (for whose safety a sort of stronghold, faced with wire, is constructed at one end of the room), and playing a few tunes on the organ for their instruction, we sallied forth to inspect the farmyard, as well as the more remote frontiers. As the most perfect ruler that ever existed always has a secret corner of his heart in which is cherished some weak partiality, that every now and then discloses itself in an undue favouritism, so am I obliged to confess that I have more than once detected the old gentleman in this grievous fault. His pigeons are undoubtedly his chief courtiers, and it is in respect to them that the cares of sovereignty lie heaviest on his mind. These birds partake more than others of the foibles and caprices of human beings, and the old gentleman assured me, with much gravity, that he has known the domestic happiness of a worthy family entirely destroyed by a neighbouring rival having its coop repaired and embellished. This occasioned jealousies, discontents, and heart-burnings, which displayed themselves in the males' fighting, and the females' scolding, whenever they met each other.

He moreover complained to me, that very often a young rake-hell of a pouter (the dandies of the dove-cot) will obstinately refuse to unite in the bands of matrimony with a plump heiress he has specially selected, and, in spite of his efforts, persevere in a course of wicked debauchery, to the utter confounding of his species and ruin of his constitution. Every day the behaviour of some one of these unworthy favourites brings my worthy friend into fresh trouble. Sometimes the children disobey their parents, by venturing out into the temptations of a bad world before they are properly fledged, and, falling to the ground, become a prey to cats, children, and other arch enemies that are always on the watch to entrap helpless innocence. At other times, he is put to his wits' ends in attempting to reform some wicked polygamist, who, in open defiance of the laws, persists in taking to himself half a dozen wives, and as many concubines. In a word, it is my opinion, that my friend displays more of the policy of a wise magistrate, more of the uprightness of an inflexible judge, and more of the temper of a true philosopher, in keeping peace among the quarrelsome, pacifying the rebellious, reforming the profligate, providing for the orphans, affiancing the widows, and chastising the bachelors, than any one single member of the holy alliance, or indeed all of them together. By this excellent mode of recreation, he not only procures to himself a rich and abundant source of happiness, but exemplifies at the same time as complete a system of morals and laws, as ever came from the brain of a Solon or a Lycurgus.

I must not omit to mention, before I conclude this

paper, that the old gentleman, by a course of experiments upon his pigeons, has become a complete convert to the doctrines of the great Isaac Bickerstaff. He assures me that he can produce at pleasure, (that is, provided they will only follow his directions), pigeons of the most whimsical and opposite colours, and breed a fan-tail with any given number of feathers in his tail, not exceeding thirty-eight, which is the *ne-plus-ultra* of nature's efforts.

After exhibiting to me a pair of choice trumpeter pigeons, he exemplified his doctrine by a history of their birth and lineage.

"Not six months ago," said he, "I got possession of that rare and beautiful bird," — pointing to the male — "but being the only one of its kind in the country, I was quite in despair, lest I should not be able to increase the stock. In this dilemma, how do you think I managed matters? i' faith, I immediately married him to a beautiful *Capuchin lady*, she being the nearest to him in affinity. The first brood was doubtful; the second gave me the liveliest hopes; and the third promised to crown my wishes, had it not been for a *black carrier*, who sat just facing her during the sympathetic period, and turned the young ones at least ten shades darker than the mother. The fourth experiment was of course lost, in merely restoring the natural colour they had forfeited by the preceding one, and in the prosecution of the fifth, I was overtaken by a great misfortune. A strutting young libertine of a pouter captivated the affections of the lady, who consented to an elopement. All the consequences of such an imprudent step naturally followed. But to bring the affair to a conclusion, the sixth generation completely rewarded my cares, and gave me full assurance of the truth of my theory."

In such converse we continued our walks over the ample domains of this worthy potentate. The same peculiar humour that governs the economy of his farmyard and pigeon-house, displays itself in his system of gardening and husbandry. He is always indulging himself in curious experiments in grafting and planting, and is a firm believer in the fanciful system of Darwin. Affinities and antipathies are carefully consulted in the disposition of his plants and vines, and he is particularly attentive in preventing all kinds of vegetable debauchery, by planting his melons, cucumbers, &c., at such a distance as to render every kind of criminal intercourse quite impossible. With a liberality truly admirable, he sows an acre of millet-seed every year, by way of voluntary alms to the wild birds of the air, who, though not his subjects, annually resort to his domains in flocks that veil the clouds, with all the punctuality of pensioned courtiers or soup-house paupers. It is expected, however, that they will keep terms, and refrain from all depredations on the rest of the kingdom; otherwise they may be pretty certain of being shot, with a gun at least twelve feet long, which never yet failed in committing great slaughter.

After traversing many well-cultivated fields, we at length ascended a pretty high hill, commanding an extensive and variegated prospect of smiling meadows and waving woods, putting forth their spring verdure in gay profusion. The scene naturally called up agreeable or tender associations, and the good old man insensibly glided into a train of long past yet happy recollections. Every field was pointed out as the theatre of some frolicsome exploit of buxom boyhood—here he had caught a mockbird, which sung so loud that his mother kept him in a dark room for fear of disturbing the children; there he had shot a covey of quails: and yonder, said he, under that old stump, once a spreading oak, I used to sit of an evening, with one who was my mistress in youth, my wife in manhood, my staff in age, and who is now an angel in Heaven.

As I walked home that evening, and saw the busy crowds of the city panting in tides and eddies in all directions, and pursuing pleasure, through every avenue of pain, at the expense of ease and comfort, often at the sacrifice of health, fortune, and fame, the simple and amiable eccentricities of my old friend gradually assumed the airs of sober wisdom; and I could not help acknowledging to myself, that he was not only the happiest of old men, but one of the most rational I had ever known.

In the last article of this series our author has something to say of the original fictitious trio of reformers critics and men about town. The account is professedly written by Anthony Evergreen. The note refers, as I assume, to "The Legend of Sleepy Hollow."

### HIC FINIS FANDI.

THE reader who, with a patience worthy of a greater reward than any in our power to bestow, has thus far resolutely accompanied us to the present issue of our labours, must have noticed that almost all the fatigues of conducting the work have fallen upon our worthy principal, Launcelot Langstaff. Although the secret has hitherto been carefully concealed, lest it might throw a gloom over the public mind, and increase the depression of the times, it can now no longer be concealed. The health of the old gentleman sunk under the task, and for some time he had been gradually declining into a state that called forth all the anxieties of his friends, who foresaw that his course was soon to be brought to a close.

In conducting the second series of this work he fared indeed like the undertakers of most of our periodical papers, who set out with the promise of assistance from a vast many literary gentlemen, who never contribute a single line. He was wont to observe, that from the increasing indolence of his worthy copesmates, many people began to suspect, that notwithstanding the great show of men he affected to muster in his outset, he was in reality pretty much in the predicament of some of our excellent brevet officers, who scamper about on the Fourth of July as if the enemy was at their heels, and make a great figure, without having so much as a little bandy-legged drummer under their command.

In justice to myself and honest William Wizard, I will endeavour, now that we are about to bid a final farewell to the public, to account for the little agency we two have had in conducting the latter part of this work. However careless men may be in preserving a good name during their lives, all are ambitious of a little praise after death, and aspire at least to the honours of an epitaph.

For myself, I confess to the world that I have lately discovered I begin to grow old, which is generally one of the last lessons of a bachelor's life, and, like the recovery of a madman's wits, indicates that he has not long to live. I have therefore been lately endeavouring to make preparations for the final catastrophe by looking out for a wife, that I may have somebody to close my eyes when I am dead, and to hold me up as an example to her second husband. Should I succeed in my attempts, I mean to behave so kindly to my wife, that though an old man (I confess it), she shall not fail to remember me with gratitude, if not with love. For this desertion of the most ancient order of bachelors I have no other apology to make than that, although the single state may be pleasant enough through the spring and summer of life, the autumn and the winter are melancholy seasons when there is none near and dear to us to make the fireside look cheerful.

The occasion of *Will Wizard's* obstinate silence is also a love affair, which has for a long while past occasioned infinite merriment to those in the secret. It is now more than ten years since he began to exhibit demonstrations of a preference for Miss Barbara Cockloft. This predilection he displayed in various ways altogether peculiar to himself, but most especially by sitting with his chin resting on one end of the sofa, gazing at her as she sat at the other, for whole hours together, without uttering a single word. At other times he would sit beside her, snipping little bits of riband or muslin with her scissors; and when he felt himself sufficiently imboldened, would insist upon threading her needle, with a wink which, though nobody could comprehend, he considered particularly significant. Having pursued this method of courtship some six or eight years, he began to look upon her as actually engaged to marry him, although he had never talked of love in her presence; and grew intolerably jealous of several spruce old bachelors who visited at the house occasionally, none of whom, I verily believe, had a thought of interfering with his happy prospects. I remember some years since presenting her with a rose, a piece of oldfashioned gallantry I hold in great respect, which so affronted *Will* that he called me Mr. Evergreen for a week afterward, and took every opportunity of sneering at the gallantries of old bachelors.

About six months ago he wrought himself up to a declaration, being thereunto stimulated by the late almost total stagnation of commerce, which left him entirely out of employment. Being too modest either to declare himself *viva voce*, or even to deliver the letter in which he had poured forth his whole soul with genuine Eastern pathos, he concluded to send it by one of the carrier pigeons which belonged to the old gentleman whose system of rural economy we commemorated in a former number. Accordingly he tied the letter round the bird's neck after the manner he had seen practised in the East, and sent her on this important errand of love.

The pigeon, unconscious of the dignity of her embassy, instead of bending her course directly to Cockloft Hall, as she ought to have done, gambolled about in airy circles for a while, and at length dropped the letter where it was found by an old lady walking in her garden, who forthwith called a tea-party on the occasion. I don't know how it was, but though every one present disclaimed opening the letter or knowing any thing of its contents, the secret transpired, and, in the natural course of events, came to the ears of Mrs. Cockloft. The old lady forthwith categorically demanded an explanation of her daughter, who first fainted away, and then confessed her secret. Will was immediately sent for; and after receiving a severe reprimand for thus secretly tampering with the affections of a young and inexperienced girl, was formally acknowledged as the future son-in-law.

Never was there such a bustle at the hall as the disclosure, and the preparations for this marriage, occasioned. Such an event had not taken place in the family of Cockloft in all its branches for thirty years, and it was determined that it should be remembered at least thirty years more. Every thing was conducted in a style of sixty years ago, before the fashion came up of crying at weddings and laughing at funerals. The old demijohn of wine, which had been set aside on Miss Barbara's birthday to be drunk at her wedding, and which everybody had long despaired of tasting, was now drained of its sparkling freight, and every thing above stairs, as well as every thing below, shared in the liberal festivity. Limbs that had not capered, and hearts that had not leaped with joy, for many a year, now waxed merry in the sprightly revelry; nor did the bride faint, or the bridegroom look as if he was just going to be hanged, as is usual on such occasions. One thing I must not omit to notice on this occasion, as it was considered as a clear indication that Miss Cockloft the elder would never be married. The demijohn of wine which had in like manner been set apart for her wedding-day was discovered to be entirely empty, without any person being able to give any account of the matter.

But alas! reader, the toe of the grave-digger is on the heel of the dancing-man! That very night, when the sound of gayety had ceased in the old hall, and sleep hovered over all the house, the good Launcelot, having perhaps tasked his almost worn-out spirits too hardly in order to do honour to the nuptials, was smitten with the arrow of death; which, after rankling about his heart a few days, carried him at last to his long home. His death was such as might naturally have been expected from the innocence of his life, and the mingled strength and careless eccentricity of his character. He gave little keepsakes to all his old friends, and devised every thing away that he had in the world but a plain gold ring, which he had worn ever since I first knew him, and which he desired might go with him to his grave. At his decease the newspapers forgot to record the old story, that "a great man had fallen in Israel," neither did the whole world weep for his loss. But there were left behind him a few old friends who must soon follow, but who, while they live, will not forget their ancient comrade.

Should any stranger ever be inclined to visit his grave, he may find it by the description which follows. He lies buried in the graveyard of a neighbouring church,* which would hardly be perceived

* The reader may perhaps see some resemblance between the scene and characters here described, and a sketch by our old associate Geoffrey Crayon, in a late number. It is hardly worth while to alter this now, as it was done some time before the publication of the other. It may remain as a memorial that our early associations had much in common.

through the groves of old locust-trees which shadow it on every side, were it not for the little white steeple that peeps over the tops. On the right, at a little distance, and near enough to be associated with the building, is a forest of silver pines; to the left, and just at the extremity of the burial-ground, runs a brawling brook, whose high rocky sides are covered with a growth of hemlock-trees, that would make a stranger totally unconscious of the neighbourhood of the stream, were not its murmurings heard beneath. A short distance below, the brook is crossed by a dam, which makes a beautiful little pond nearly in front of the church, whose waters are like crystal, reflecting the rocks and trees that hang over its steep and rugged banks.

A number of old trees half decayed, fit emblems of man and all the productions of nature over which his beneficent Maker gave him dominion, are dispersed at random among the tomb-stones, where are recorded the virtues of half a dozen generations of men, whose faults, if they had any, are long since forgotten. Some of these memorials are carved in wood; others engraved on freestone; while here and there a stately white marble rears its head high above the humble things around, often mistaken for a sheeted ghost by the skittish rustic whose hard fate it is to pass by the churchyard at night. But by far the greater number of tenants of these silent mansions sleep without any memorial, and nothing marks the spot where they rest but a little mound, covered with grass and briers, or a little hollow in the earth, where it has sunk in consequence of the decay of their "narrow house." I remember the last time Launcelot and

I visited this spot together, one mild summer twilight. He stopped at one of these undistinguished mounds, and, planting his cane upon the ground, addressed me with a smile half serious, half gay, as follows: —

"Would you believe it, my old friend, in this spot repose the remains of the first man — I don't mean Adam — but the first man that ever inflicted upon me the discipline of the birchen twig. It is almost sixty years since I saw him deposited in this very grave. I remember it almost as if it were but yesterday; for it was the first time I ever witnessed this last scene of life's drama, and it made a lasting impression. His name was Tobit, and he was reckoned the most expert flogger for fifty miles round. That he deserved the character he had obtained I can bear testimony. I remember I wore a red coat at that day, which not only occasioned me many a severe battle with certain Whig turkey-cocks, but likewise cost me many a sound flagellation from the professor of birch. I never robbed an orchard, or made one in a moss-trooping expedition, that my red coat did not betray and bring me to condign punishment. Tobit used once or twice a day to leave his school, and pay a visit to a pretty black-eyed widow that lived at no great distance, at which times he would delegate the charge of keeping order upon one of his flock. If the regent did his duty to his master by telling tales, he of course got the ill-will of his playmates; if he played the honest fellow, and said nothing, he got well flogged for his pains; for the secret was pretty sure to be discovered one way or another. It was by acting occasionally in this responsible situation that I first took a distaste to places of honour, which I still preserve. He had been pinned to this same spot more than forty years; and was heard to boast, not long before his death, that there was not a man in the whole neighborhood that he had not flogged at least half a dozen times. Yet here he lies, at least all that is left of him, without a memorial, a pregnant instance of human ingratitude. If I live, I am determined to erect a stone over his grave, if it be only that the memory of his dexterity in flourishing the birch may not be lost to posterity.

"But see here" — continued he, passing on a little farther to a high grave-stone, purporting to be erected to the memory of a man of many titles — "Here lies a most notable hero, who commanded a company of militia during the old war, and, as I remember, wore a cocked hat in consequence, all his life afterward. He used to come into the village where I boarded when at the academy, mounted on his war-horse, which possessed the singular instinct of carrying his master home safe without his knowing any thing of the matter. On these occasions the whole village was in an uproar; for the first sortie he made was generally into the tavern on horseback, as he scorned to enter it in any other manner. Here, after carousing pretty lustily, telling the story of his having once put a whole troop of *yagers* to flight with his own hand, and treating every one that came in his way, he would mount his horse, and ride up the steps into the long piazza of a worthy townsman, who, as the revolutionary hero affirmed, was a great tory during the war. Here he would prance back and forth, vapouring and braving, until his antagonist was fain to turn out and accompany him to the inn, where they never failed to quarrel during the rest of the evening. The warrior was a large, burly fellow, full of sound and fury, who always waxed wroth in proportion as his adversary grew cool. The other, on the contrary, was a tall, rawboned, shrewd man, who knew the captain's cue exactly, and had a perfect command of his own temper, which gave him great advantages. He would alternately irritate and soothe him, to the infinite amusement of the village loungers; and, when tired of the sport, conclude with telling the story of the captain's once hiding behind the chimney when he thought the British were coming. By the time he had got fairly through the story the captain was on horseback, defying his adversary to mortal combat; but, after parading some time, he generally put himself under the safe conduct of his charger, who soberly trotted home with his valiant master."

In this way the old gentleman amused himself by revealing his early rural recollections, until we came to a tomb over which certain shrubbery had been planted, which indicated something more than ordinary. "Here," said he, with a countenance more sad than usual, "here are deposited the remains of a mother and her little twins, who died within four-and-twenty hours of each other. The mother was my only sister; a noble woman, whose mind and person were equally lovely. The twins were so much alike that I never could distinguish the one from the other, and even the quick searching eye of an affectionate mother was often at a loss. One of them wore a pink, the other a blue ribbon, in order that they might be known apart. One spark of life seemed to animate them, and it was extinguished almost at the same moment. One of those sore throats which sometimes almost depopulate country neighborhoods swept away the children and their mother, who all rest here together, their fate commemorated in this simple epitaph:—

"'*They were lovely and pleasant in their lives, and in their deaths they were not divided.*'

"I believe," continued he, "I could give the story of all the human race, their lives and deaths, were I to traverse the whole of this little refuge of mortality, and sketch the history of each of the tenants of these silent mansions. But the cowbell is silent, the dew begins to fall heavily, and if Mrs. Cockloft were to hear yon whippoorwill, she would think one or other of us would certainly die before long. If it should be my lot to go first," added he, smiling, "bury me beside those innocents. I hope I may not disgrace their society, either now or hereafter."

I recollected his wish, and it was complied with. His epitaph is not yet written. The reader may make one to please himself, provided he does not venture to insinuate that the old gentleman ought to have died some ten years ago.

ANTHONY EVERGREEN.

The preceding article is full of recollections of Mr. Paulding's early life. The military hero is not a creation of fancy. There is a reminiscence of those days as related by my father, which occurs to my memory, and which seems as if it might have been connected with him and his tormentor. At any rate I will assume that it was. It appears then that one of the expedients of the enemy, to annoy the Captain, consisted in the use of uncommon and turgid words.

"Well, Captain," would he remark, "this is a pluvious afternoon, eh?"

*Captain.* "What the —— do you mean by 'pluvious'!"

*Adversary.* "Oh, you dont understand English — wet, dampy, dewy."

*Captain.* "A—a—h!"

When he had excited the poor giant to a pitch of fury, he would observe: "Never mind, Captain, there have been worse men than you in the world." As the personage addressed brightened up under the insidious light of this questionable compliment, he would add: — "But then they were hanged."

The red jacket of "Launcelot Langstaff" was indeed our author's own, and is connected with a little incident, which, though sufficiently commonplace, is not without a shade of pathos, due to its associations. It was to his childish mind the first intimation of altered position, and, as he declares, the recollection of it, even late in life, always affected him "almost to tears", as bringing back to him vividly the mother to whose unvarying kindness he so often bears testimony. After observing that, until the ruin of his father, the children had been brought up in some style, he continues: —

"When however my father was carried to jail, and he was finally divested of his all, it became necessary to cut our coat according to our cloth, and accordingly a severe retrenchment took place. The circumstance that dwells most deeply and affectingly on my memory at this distant period, is my mother's calling me in from play, to exchange my red coat and its accompaniments for a suit of homespun linen. I opposed this proceeding with all my might, until my mother soothed me into acquiescence, by assuring me the new suit was much handsomer and far more comfortable than the old, and I went to play again fully satisfied."

But, of these slight glimpses of a condition of things long passed away, enough. That customs and means were so different from the present must be the excuse for their having been given at all.

# X.

1821–1822. [Æt. 43–44.]

BENJAMIN FRANKLIN IN HADES — A SKETCH OF OLD ENGLAND, BY A NEW ENGLAND MAN — REVIEWED IN "THE QUARTERLY" — THE ROYAL, AND THE PRESIDENTIAL, HOUSEHOLD.

During the latter half of 1820, and the whole of 1821, Mr. Paulding seems to have kept himself in the background; but the subjoined sketch occurs in an article furnished to The National Intelligencer of January 20th, 1821, over the words "*Parvus Homo*", which indicate his contributions to that paper. Our author is giving an account of a supposed visit to Hades.

BENJAMIN FRANKLIN.

Our Franklin happily passes his time, in pleasing sobriety, with the illustrious sages and philosophers of all nations and ages. Though uniformly cheerful, he seldom or never laughs; and, with all the engaging simplicity of a child, he pours forth the matured and comprehensive wisdom of experience. Uniting the essence of wit, quickness of thought and facility of combination, with that brevity which is its appropriate garb, he charms without effort and teaches without appearing the master. It is delightful to see him in simple dress and simple language, like one of the primitive instructors of mankind, condensing some fine moral in the compass of a single sentence, or illustrating some glorious precept by a happy allegory that embodies, and gives life and being to, the truth. The weight of wisdom and benignity united with good temper and unaffected manners, was never more strikingly exemplified than in the influence of this immortal Printer upon the country to which he was a benefactor, and the age to which he was an ornament.

In 1822, Mr. Paulding came before the public with A SKETCH OF OLD ENGLAND, BY A NEW ENGLAND MAN, published in two volumes by Charles Wiley, New York. It is written in the shape of letters purporting to have come from one in England to his brother in New York; but the coloring is not well preserved. The gist of the work is a comparison between matters and things in England and in this country, of course very much to the prejudice of the former. It had the fortune to provoke a review in "The Quarterly" for January, 1824, seemingly from the pen of Mr. John Murray himself, which is a clever enough series of thrusts at points where our author had certainly laid himself open to attack. It is not as acrimonious as many of its congeners in The Quarterly Review, but we have, as usual when treating of any thing American at that day, a specimen of the tomahawk style. The reviewer, with great acumen, doubts "whether the volumes are not a mere compilation from radical newspapers, treasonable pamphlets, blasphemous libels, vulgar jest books, and all that species of ribald literature." Which is pretty well for one fling.

I confine myself to a single extract from this work.

It refers to a class of subjects which always excited our author's spleen. Doubtless his banter was frightful indeed in the eyes of the loyal English publisher.

THE ROYAL, AND THE PRESIDENTIAL, HOUSEHOLD.

The preparations for the king's coronation, and the consequent marshalling of the household troops, together with the various claims to services of one kind or other on the occasion, naturally turned my attention to the subject, and caused me to compare the state of his majesty with that of our worthy president.

In making some little researches into these matters, it is inconceivable what a nest of officials I have routed out of his majesty's chambers, wardrobe, cellars, kitchen, scullery, stables, and dog-kennels. All these are more or less privileged persons; most of them paid for doing nothing, and all living at the expense of the people. To me it was really amusing to note the uncouth names of some of these offices, and the pitiful functions of others, that are filled by some of the highest nobility of the kingdom. It is in these, as well as in more important particulars, that the radical, essential, and irreconcilable difference between this people and government, and ours, is clearly indicated. Our people would laugh ready to split their sides, or, if they did not laugh, they would groan in spirit, to see these men, to whom they had been accustomed to look up with reverence or respect, deriving dignity, importance, and wealth, from the performance of the most menial offices, such as the lowest white man among them would not deign to discharge for the highest. Indeed, the whole arrangement of the court here would be irresistibly ridiculous, were the farce not turned into a tragedy by the additional burthens and privations the people are obliged to sustain to support this mummery. As our good people are, however, happily exempt from such degrading impositions, they are free to make themselves merry on the occasion. I will assist you as far as I can, by entering into the details.

The first of these important personages is the Lord High Steward of the king's household, formerly the great master of the king's household, whose province it is to superintend the state of his majesty's chambers, kitchens, &c., and to whom all officers and servants of the king's house, except those of the chapel, chambers, and stable, are subject. His dignity, state, and honour, are said to be exceedingly great, for he attends bare-headed upon the king, and swears the members of parliament. His salary and emoluments are probably two hundred times greater than those of the High Steward of the President of the United States, whose functions are pretty similar, except that he does not administer the oath to members of congress, and is not, I believe, called lord.

The second great officer of the household troops is the Lord Chamberlain, who, it is to be remembered, is different from the Lord *Great* Chamberlain of England. To the former belongs the superintendence of all the offices of the king's chamber, except the precincts of the king's bedchamber, which territory belongs to another great man, called the Groom of the Stole. All above stairs, to the very garret, is subject to his control. He is also overseer of the wardrobes, beds, tents, revels, music, comedians, hunting, messengers, trumpeters, drummers, artisans, handicraftsmen, physicians, apothecaries, surgeons, barbers, and chaplains. In this capacity of Master of the Revels and Comedians it is, that he exercises the prerogative of licensing plays. The present Lord Chamberlain is said to be a capital judge of Pantomime. The Lord *Great* Chamberlain is still greater than he, being entitled to livery and lodging at court, besides other mighty privileges. On the day of the coronation, before the king rises from bed, the Lord Great Chamberlain is privileged to bring him his shirt, coif, and wearing apparel, for which he is entitled to all the king's night clothes, and the bed and bedclothes, as a fee. Then he carries the coif, gloves, and linen, at the coronation; the sword, the scabbard, the royal robe and crown, with privilege to undress and attire the king. For these great services he receives forty ells of crimson velvet for a robe. Lastly, he serves the king on that day, before and after dinner, with water to wash his hands, and has the basin and towel for his pains. Only to see the vast difference between a king, "by the grace of God," and a President, by the will of the people! The persons, whose functions approach nearest to these mighty lords, in the President's establishment, are, or at least were, when when I was last at Washington, two clever black fellows, named Pompey and Paul, if I recollect right, whose services did not cost the nation a farthing. Our worthy President, it is true, is respected and beloved by all the people; wherever he goes he is received with acclamations, and he was never shot at in his whole life, except by the enemies of his country in battle. But for all this, there is not a freeman of a white colour, and in decent circumstances, born and bred in our country, that would not feel himself degraded by the performance of such menial services. These offices are at present filled in England by a marquis and a baroness, the latter by hereditary descent, who, I hope, for the sake of decency, did not insist on her claim of undressing the king at the coronation.

After the Great Chamberlain cometh the Master of the Horse, *Comes Stabuli.* This *great* officer, as he is called, hath now the ordering and superintendence of the king's stables, horses, footmen, grooms, farriers, coachmen, smiths, saddlers, &c. Besides all this, he, and he only, — think of that, brother! — has the privilege of making use of any horses, pages, or footmen, belonging to the king's stables. Another of his great privileges, is that of riding next behind the king, leading the king's horse of state. The person at present exercising these high functions is a duke, the descendant of the greatest of the Grahams of Scotland. The President's coachman is the person most nearly resembling the Master of the Horse, and receives, I suppose, about fifteen or twenty dollars a month for his services.

Under one or other of these three mighty officers, all, or nearly all, the subordinate ones are marshalled, and an army of them there are, I assure you, numerous as the drones of the hive, and, like them, for the most part, living by the labours of others. There be "land rats and water rats;" Treasurers of the Household; Comptrollers; Cofferers; Masters of the Household; Clerks of Green Cloth; Clerks Comptrollers; Gentlemen of the Privy Chamber; Gentlemen Pensioners; Gentlemen Cup-bearers; Gentlemen Carvers; Gentlemen Sewers; Gentlemen Ushers; Gentlemen Grooms of the Bedchamber; "all honourable men," I assure you; and, what is of more consequence, all well paid by the people.

Next come the Pages of the Presence Chamber; Grooms of the Great Chamber; Pages of the Bedchamber and Backstairs; Officers of the removing Wardrobe; standing Wardrobe keepers; Laundresses of the Body Linen; Sergeants at Arms; Messengers of the Great Chamber; Clerks of the Checque to the Messengers in Ordinary; all of them, too, "honourable men," or women, and most of them having deputies, who have their deputies, &c. &c., *ad infinitum.* In the rear of these, march "four and twenty fiddlers all in a row," under the command of the Grand Master of the Music. Next come the Sergeant Trumpeters; Court Drummers; Masters of the King's Tennis Court; locksmiths; card-makers; embroiderers; cabinet-makers; operators of the teeth; oar-makers; harpsichord-makers; sergeant-skinners; distillers; pinmakers; perfumers; strewers of herbs; apothecaries; rat-killers; mole-catchers; necessary women; and yeomen of the mouth—all very honourable persons, that serve the king, and are well paid by the people.

I have not done yet. I must not forget the Master Cooks, those important personages—nor the people of his majesty's bakehouse, pantry, buttery, cellar, spicery, confectionery, ewry; the scourers, turnbroachers, doorkeepers, soil-carriers, of the king's privy kitchen, the queen's privy kitchen, the household kitchen, larder, scalding house, pastry, scullery, and woodyard; nor the harbingers, the porters of the gate, the bread-bearers, wine porters, table deckers, purveyors, and pankeepers; not one of whom would ever forgive me for not making honourable mention of their several dignities, as servants of the king. A vast number of these offices are of the most frivolous kind, as you may well believe, from the nature of the functions ascribed to them.

Here too, as in every other department of the government, we see the same care taken to instil and preserve a sense of dependence and inferiority, distinct from every moral, mental, or physical qualification, and derived from the king's pleasure alone. One grade of officers of the court is not allowed to approach nearer to the king's person than a certain room, beyond which a superior order of beings, gifted with superior privileges, inhabit or officiate. In short, from those who are permitted to perform menial offices about the king's person, to those who only come within the outskirts of the court, there is a regular gradation of inferiority. The great man, who hands the king his shirt, looks down upon the little man, who is only admitted into the king's presence; while the great man, who is allowed to come inside of a certain door, considers the little man, that waits on the other side, vastly and radically his inferior. The divinity of a courtier is the king; and whoever can get nearest to him, partakes, in exactly the like proportion, of the divine nature of majesty.

# XI.

1823. [ÆT. 45.]

KONINGSMARKE, THE LONG FINNE — LETTER TO IRVING ABOUT — GOVERNOR PIPER — THE GOVERNOR'S "PALACE."

KONINGSMARKE, THE LONG FINNE, "a story of the New World", comes next in the order of Mr. Paulding's publications. It was issued in two volumes by Charles Wiley, New York, in the summer or autumn of 1823. The title page bears this mysterious legend: —

"This affair being taken into consideration, it was adjudged that Koningsmarke, commonly called the Long Finne, deserved to die; yet, in regard that many concerned in the affair being simple and ignorant people, it was thought fit to order that the Long Finne should be severely . . . . . . . . . . — *Fragment of minutes of Council in New York.*"

This novel is a sort of compromise between such an unaffected story as our author would have been likely to write without any disturbing influences, and a desire to quiz the romantic school introduced and upheld by the genius of Walter Scott. Bombie of the Frizzled Head, an old negress, is an evident parody of "Norna of the fitful head"; but the parodist occasionally forgets himself, and she becomes in reality a boding and impressive creature. The work is divided into Books, each with an initial chapter after the manner of Fielding. These are, for the most part, devoted to ironical praises of the *modus operandi* of "the Great Unknown".

The thread of the story is simple in the extreme. Koningsmarke is a youth born in Finland during the wars of Gustavus Adolphus, and left penniless by the death of his father, a military adventurer. Finding his way to the New World, he seeks the Swedish colony on the Delaware, and there falls in with the family of the Heer Piper, also a Fin, and now Governor. Arrested for having in his possession certain interdicted coins, he is thrust into a jail, which, shortly after, burns up, and he escapes at the last moment. He saves a life or two, that of the Governor's daughter, for one, and of course the young folk fall in love. Bombie of the Frizzled Head, however, becomes the marplot of their affections, and indulges in mysterious denunciations which have the effect of making the lovers very miserable. The Governor gets into trouble with his Indian neighbors, who attack and destroy the village which is his capital, and carry Koningsmarke and his lady love into captivity. They are, however, at last, ransomed by the Quakers of Coaquanock, now Philadelphia, and return in safety. Just at this point of the story the English of New York seize the colony in the name of their king, and Koningsmarke is kidnapped by their fleet. The next we hear of him he is about to be publicly whipped and sold into slavery, on a false charge of rebellion against the crown of England. He is saved, in the nick of time, by the interposition of Governor Piper and his daughter, and all ends happily.

On the whole, our author's acknowledgment in the

course of the work is not amiss: — "To confess the honest truth, we are, as has most likely been discovered ere this, rather new in the trade of novel-writing, having been partly induced to enter upon it, as people engage in the tobacco or grocery line, from seeing others prosper mightily in the business."

As usual heretofore, we find some account of the composition of this work in the correspondence with Irving. The author writes, New York, March 20th, 1824: —

The work of mine you mention having read with pleasure, was written for no earthly purpose but to pass the leisure hours of about six weeks that I was left alone at Washington, Gertrude and the children being on a visit to New York. My stay in this city being limited, in order to have the opportunity of correcting the sheets, I commenced the printing before the book was finished. In the interim I got the intermitting fever, as I mentioned; and the latter part was written during the intervals between the attacks of that amusing disorder. No doubt you have observed symptoms of the intermittent in various parts of the book. My motives for "tilting" as you term it, at some of the fashionable English writers, are altogether national, and devoid of any personal feeling. We Americans are treated so scurvily by the English press that my feelings often rise against this persevering ill-nature, and I am prompted to retaliate. Whatever may be its effect abroad, at home it has its influence in maintaining some little independence of taste and judgment. However, I learn from all quarters that Sir Walter is a fine liberal fellow, and his being your friend, shall in the future, as indeed it ought to have been in the past, render him sacred to me. As the gnat said to the eagle, "I'll spare him hereafter."

I select sufficient matter from these volumes to outline the character of the Heer Piper, the best in the book. Filled always with a grand prescience of the imperial progress of this country, the small importance of the great authorities of a petty colony tickled our author's fancy amazingly. On the first introduction of the magnate, he accordingly hits him off in an amusing style.

GOVERNOR PIPER.

"Peter Piper picked a peck of pickled peppers,
Where is the peck of pickled peppers Peter Piper picked?"

THE curious traveller along the western bank of the Delaware river will hardly fail to notice some few scattered remains, such as parts of old walls, and fragments of chimneys, which indicate where once stood the famous fort and town of Elsingburgh, one of the earliest settlements of the Swedes in this country. The precise spot these ruins occupy we shall not point out, since it is our present intention to give such an accurate description, that it cannot be mistaken by a reader of common sagacity.

At the time this history commences, that is to say, somewhere about the middle of the sixteenth century, a period of very remote antiquity considering the extreme juvenility of our country, this important little post was governed by the Heer Peter Piper, a short thickset person, of German parentage, whose dress, rain or shine, week days or Sundays, in peace or war, in winter and summer, was a suit of olive-coloured velvet, ornamented with ebony buttons. A picture still preserved in the Piper family, represents him with a round, and somewhat full face, a good deal wrinkled; sturdy short legs, thin at the ankles, and redundant at the calves; square-toed shoes, and square buckles of a yellowish hue, but whether of gold or brass is impossible to decide at this remote period. We would give the world, that is to say, all that part of it which is at present in our possession, namely, a magnificent castle in the air, to be able to satisfy the doubts of our readers in respect to the problem whether the Heer Peter Piper wore a cocked hat. But as the painter, with an unpardonable negligence, and a total disregard to posterity, has chosen to represent him bareheaded, we can only say, that his poll was ordinarily covered with a thick crop of hair that curled rather crabbedly about his forehead and ears. It hath been aptly remarked by close observers of human nature, that this species of petulant curl is almost the invariable concomitant of an irritable, testy, impatient temper, which, as it were, crisps and writhes about in emulation of the twisted locks.

Certain it is that, whatever exceptions may occur to the general rule, the Heer Piper was not one of them, he being, as the course of our history will fully substantiate, an exceeding little tyrant, that fell into mortal passions about nothing, broke his nose over every straw that lay in his way, and was seldom to be found in any sort of good humour, except when he had sworn vengeance at every soul that excited his wrath. Indeed, to say truth, he was one of those blustering little bodies, who differ entirely from those who are said to be no heroes to their valet-de-chambre, since it was said of him that he was a hero to nobody but his servants and dependents, whom he bullied exceedingly. The good people of Elsingburgh called him, behind his back, Pepper Pot Peter, in double allusion to the fiery nature of his talk and his fondness for the dish known among our ancestors by that name, and remarkable for its high seasoning. The distich placed at the head of this chapter, was made upon the Heer Peter, by a wag of the day, who excelled in alliterative poetry, and of whom we shall say more anon, if we do not forget it in the multiplicity of adventures we intend to incorporate into this true history. But as we mean to leave a good part of our work for the imagination of the reader to supply to the best of his abilities, we will let the character of Governor Piper develop itself in his future conduct, and proceed with our story.

One sultry afternoon in the month of July, the Heer Peter having finished his dinner by one o'clock, was sitting in his great arm chair, under the shade of a noble elm, (the stump of which is still to be seen, and being hollow, serves for a notable pig sty), smoking his pipe as was his custom, and ruminating in a luxurious state of imbecility between sleeping and waking. The river in front spread out into an expansive lake, smooth and bright as a looking glass; the leaves hung almost lifeless on the trees, for there was not a breath of air stirring; the cattle stood in the water, lashing the flies lazily with their tails; the turkeys sought the shade with their bills wide open, gasping for breath; and all nature, animate as well as inanimate, displayed that lassitude which is the consequence of excessive heat.

The Heer sat with his eyes closed, and we will not swear that he was not at this precise moment fast asleep, although the smoke of his pipe continued to ascend at regular intervals, in a perpendicular column, insomuch that it was affirmed by Wolfgang Langfanger and some of his friends and counsellors, that the Heer Peter did sometimes smoke instinctively, as a man breathes, in his sleep. However this may be, whether sleeping or waking, the Governor was suddenly roused by the intrusion of one Lob Dotterel, a constable and busybody, who considered himself, in virtue of his office, at full liberty to poke his proboscis into every hole and corner, and to pry into the secret as well as public actions of every soul in the village. It is astonishing what a triumph it was to Lob Dotterel, to catch any body tripping; he considered it a proof of his vigilance and sagacity. And here, lest the reader should do Master Dotterel wrong, in supposing that the prospect of bribes or fees stimulated him to activity, we will aver it as our belief, that he was governed by no such sordid motive, but acted upon an instinct similar to that of a well-bred pointer dog, who is ever seen wagging his tail with great delight when he brings in game, although he neither expects to be rewarded, nor to share in the spoil, — at least so far as we have been able to penetrate his motives of action.

Master Dotterel was backed, on the occasion aforesaid, by one Restore Gosling, and Master Oldale, keeper of the Indian Queen, the most fashionable, not to say the only, tavern, in the village of Elsingburgh. These three worthies had in custody a tall, straight, light-complexioned, blue-eyed youth, who signified his contempt for the accusation, whatever it might be, the constable, Master Restore Gosling, Master Oldale, and the Heer Peter himself, by rubbing his chin on either side with his thumb and fingers, and whistling Yankee Doodle, or any other tune that doth not involve a horrible anachronism.

There are three things a real genuine great man cannot bear; to wit: — to do business after dinner — to be disturbed in his meditations — or to suspect that the little people below him do not think him so great a person as he is inclined to think himself. All these causes combined to put the Heer Peter in a bad humour, insomuch that he privately communed with himself that he would tickle this whistling, chin-scraping stripling.

"Well, culprit," cried the Heer, with a formidable aspect of authority — "Well, culprit, what is your crime? I can see with half an eye you're no better than you should be."

"That's no more than may be said of most people, I believe," returned the youth, with great composure.

"Answer me, sirrah," quoth the Heer, "what is thy crime, I say?"

"Ask these gentlemen," said the other.

"What — eh! you can't confess, hey! an old offender, I warrant me. I'll tickle you before I've done with you. What's thy name — whence came you — and whither art thou going, culprit?"

"My name," replied the fair tall youth, "is Koningsmarke, surnamed the Long Finne; I came from the Hoarkill, and I am going to jail, I presume, if I may augur aught from your Excellency's look, and the hard names you are pleased to bestow on me."

Nothing is so provoking to the majesty of a great man as the self-possession of a little one. The Heer Peter Piper began to suspect that the Long Finne did not stand in sufficient awe of his dignity and authority, a suspicion than which nothing could put him in a greater passion. He addressed Master Dotterel, and demanded to know for what offence the culprit was brought before him, in a tone which Lob perfectly understood as encouragement not to suppress any part of the prisoner's guilt. Lob hereupon referred the Heer to Master Oldale, who referred him to Restore Gosling, who had laid the information. This apparent disposition to shift the *onus probandi* caused additional wrath in the Governor, who began to tremble lest the Long Finne might give him the slip, and escape the consequences of his contempt of authority. He thundered forth a command to Gosling to state *all* he knew against the culprit; laying hard emphasis on the word "all."

Master Gosling, after divers scratches of the head, such as my Lord Byron indulgeth in when he writeth poetry, gathered himself together, and said as follows — not deposed, for the Heer held it an undue indulgence to prisoners to put the witnesses against them to their Bible oath — Master Gosling stated, that he had seen the young man, who called himself Koningsmarke, or the Long Finne, take out of his pocket a handful of Mark Newby's halfpence, or, as they were commonly called, *Pat's* halfpence, which every body knew were prohibited being brought into the dominions of Sweden, under penalty of confiscation of the money; one half to the informer, and the other half to his Sacred Majesty, the King of Sweden, Denmark, Norway, and the Goths.

"Ho, ho!" exclaimed the Heer, rubbing his hands; "this looks like conspiracy and plot, with a vengeance. I should not be surprised if the Pope and the d——l were at the bottom of this." And here we will remind the reader that this was about the time that the manufacturing of plots, Popish and Presbyterian, Meal Tub and Rye House, flourished so luxuriantly, under the fruitful invention of Shaftesbury, Oates, Tongue, Dugdale, Bedlow, and others. Now the Heer Peter always took pattern after the old countries, insomuch that whenever a plot came out in England, or elsewhere, he forthwith got up another at Elsingburgh, as nearly like it as possible. In one word, he imitated all the pranks, freaks and fooleries of royalty, as an ape does those of a man. At the period, too, which this history is about to commemorate, there were terrible jealousies and heart-burnings betwixt the representatives of royalty in the adjoining or neighbouring colonies of New-Jersey, Pennsylvania, Maryland, New-York, and Connecticut. The different monarchs of Europe had not only given away with astonishing liberality what did not belong to them, in this new world, but given it away over and over again to different persons, so that it was next to impossible either to settle the boundaries of the various grants, or to ascertain who was the real proprietor of the soil. As to the Indians, they were out of the question. Now, though these tracts were, ninety-nine parts in a hundred, a perfect wilderness, and the number of inhabitants as one to a hundred square miles, yet did these potentates, and especially their governors, feel great solicitude lest they should be stinted for elbow-room. They were, consequently, always bickering about boundaries, and disputing every inch of wilderness most manfully, by protest and proclamation.

The Heer Piper governed a territory by right of discovery, grant, possession, and what not, something larger than Sweden, and which, at the period of this history, contained exactly (by census) three hundred and sixty-eight souls, exclusive of Indians. It is therefore little to be wondered at, if, being as he was, a long-headed man, metaphorically speaking, he should begin to look out in time for the comfort of the immense population, which he foresaw must speedily be pressed for room. His jealousy was of course continually squinting at his neighbours, most especially the Quakers at Coaquanock, and the Roman Catholics, who about this time settled at St. Mary's under Leonard Calvert. He therefore pricked up his ears, and smelt a plot, at the very sound of Mark Newby's halfpence, a coin then circulating in West Jersey and Coaquanock, and forthwith set down the Long Finne as an emissary from the Quakers, who, he swore, although they would not fight, had various ways of getting possession of his territories, much more effectual than by arms. Moreover, he abhorred them because they would not pull off their hats to the representative of Gustavus Adolphus, and, as he affirmed, were a people who always expected manners from others, although they gave none themselves. In addition to these causes of disgust, it was rumoured, that his Excellency the Heer, being once riding out near Coaquanock, met a Quaker driving a great wagon, who refusing to turn either to the right or to the left, caused Peter Piper in attempting to pass to be precipitated into a slough. Let me tell the reader, that trifles less than these have more than once set mankind together by the ears, and caused the rivers of the earth to run red with blood.

Under the influence of these statesmanlike views, jealousies, and antipathies, the Heer viewed the possession of such a quantity of Mark Newby's halfpence as a suspicious circumstance, and indeed had little doubt, in his own mind, that the Long Finne had come into the settlement to seduce it from its allegiance to the great Gustavus, by actual bribery. The reader may smile at the idea of corrupting a community with halfpence, now that paper money is so plenty that dollars fly about like may-flies in the spring, and that it sometimes actually takes a hundred of these to purchase a man's conscience. But we will make bold to tell him, his smile only betrays an utter ignorance of the simplicity of those times, when a penny was deemed equal to six white and four black wampum; and a tract of land, larger than a German principality, was at one time purchased for sixty tobacco-boxes, one hundred and twenty pipes, one hundred Jew's-harps, and a quantity of red paint. It hath been shrewdly observed, that the value of money regulates the consciences of men, as it does every other article of trade, so that the suspicion of Governor Piper was not quite so ridiculous as many uninformed readers may be inclined to suppose at first sight. This explanation we afford gratuitously, hinting, at the same time, that as it is no part of our plan to make things appear probable, or actions consistent, we shall not often display a similar disposition to account for what happens.

"Long Finne," said the Heer, after considerable cogitation — "Long Finne, thou art found guilty of suspicion of traitorous designs against the authority of his sacred majesty, Gustavus Adolphus of Sweden, and in order that thou mayest have time and opportunity to clear up thy character, we sentence thee to be imprisoned till thine innocence is demonstrated, or thou shalt confess thy guilt."

By this time half the village, at least, was collected, as is usual on these occasions, when they flock to see a criminal, as porpoises gather about a wounded mate, not to succour, but to worry him. The whole assembly were struck with astonishment at the wisdom of Governor Piper's decision, which they looked upon as dictated by blind Justice herself. Not so the Long Finne, who, like most unreasonable persons, that are seldom satisfied with law or equity when it goes against them, seemed inclined to remonstrate. But the Heer, whose maxim it was to punish first and pity afterward, forthwith commanded him to be quiet, quoting his favourite saying, "Sirrah, if we both talk at once, how are we to understand one another?"

As they were taking him from the presence of the Governor to convey him to prison, the tall, fair youth, turned his eye mildly, yet significantly, toward the Heer, and pronounced in a low voice the words, "Caspar Steinmets." "What! who! whose name did you utter?" exclaimed his excellency in great agitation—

"Caspar Steinmets"—repeated the youth.

"What of him?"—rejoined the Heer.

"I am his nephew"—answered the Long Finne. "The friend of your youth would be little obliged to you, could he see you hurrying the son of his bosom to a prison, because he possessed a handful of Mark Newby's halfpence."

"Pish!" cried the Heer—"I never heard that old Caspar Steinmets had a nephew, and I don't believe a word of it."

"He had a sister, who married a gentleman of Finland, called Colonel Koningsmarke, against the wishes of her friends. She was discarded, and her name never mentioned. On the death of both my parents, my uncle adopted me, but he died also, not long after you sailed for the new world.—Look, sir, do you know this picture?"

"Blood of my heart," exclaimed the Heer, contemplating the miniature, "but this is old Caspar Steinmets, sure enough! Ah! honest, jolly old Caspar! many a time have thou and I drunk, fought, and raked together, in bonny Finland! But for all that, culprit, thou shalt not escape justice, until thou hast accounted to me for the possession of this picture, which hath marvellously the appearance of stolen goods."

"Stolen goods, sir!" interrupted the fair youth, passionately; but, as if recollecting himself, he relapsed into an air of unconquerable serenity, and began to whistle in an under tone.

"Ay, marry, stolen goods! I shall forthwith commit thee to prison, and retain this trinket till thou provest property, and payest all charges. Take him away, master constable."

The youth seemed about to remonstrate, but again, as if suddenly recollecting himself, remained silent, shrugged his shoulders, and quietly submitted to be conducted to the prison, followed by the crowd, which usually, on such occasions, volunteers as an honourable escort to heroes of the bridewell and quarter sessions. But nothing could equal the triumph of Lob

Dotterel, who looked upon the establishing of a man's innocence as lessening the importance of a constable, who, he affirmed, acquired dignity and consequence in exact proportion to the crimes of mankind.

Having despatched this weighty business, the Heer Piper knocked the ashes out of his pipe, and returned to the gubernatorial mansion, with the full resolution of communicating the whole affair to the Chancellor Oxenstiern.

Pepper-pot though he be in one aspect, he is elsewhere described as having "a certain mellowness about him that caused his heart to curvet and caper at the sight of human happiness."

Nor does he lack courage. When his village is nearly lost, he is urged by Koningsmarke to save himself. "'*Der Teufel*,' quoth the Heer, 'go thou — I must be the last man that deserts his post; — away.'"

He comes closer to our hearts after his daughter has been carried off by the savages.

"All this while the poor Heer remained without a hope, without a comforter, his mind ever running on the blue-eyed maiden he had, peradventure, lost for ever. The judgment which, according to aunt Edith's theory, had fallen upon his head, for the punishment of his sinful delights in contemplating the mild virtues and gentle, unobtrusive charms of his duteous, affectionate daughter, seemed only to bind him more closely to the earth, for he could think of nought but her. His sole employment was in doing nothing, although he was incapable of sitting still more than a minute at a time. Like Bombie of the Frizzled Head, he wandered and wandered about, almost without purpose, or even consciousness, until some sound, some object, some nothing as it would seem, struck upon one of those chords by which every thing that is beautiful or sweet in nature is connected with the memory of those we love, and have lost. Then his trembling lip, and wan, wet eye, bore testimony, that the light still continued to burn, though the lamp which held it seemed quite broken to pieces."

And the re-union of father and child is told in a touching manner.

"As the Heer thus indulged himself in melancholy ponderings, his attention was called off by a distant noise, that came to his ear like the shouts of joyful exultation. He listened, but again all was silent. What can it mean, thought he. But the thought was only momentary, and he sunk into his usual train of dark and dismal contemplation. Again the shout was repeated, still nearer, by the limber tongues of the village train, whose unladen spirits were ever ready to seize occasions for noise and jollity. Nearer, and still nearer, came the rout, until at length the attention of the Heer was roused by something which struck upon his heart like a repetition of Christina's name. He started up, and, hurrying with faltering steps to the window, beheld, a little way off, a crowd of people, in the midst of which seemed to be a tall, stately figure, mounted on horseback, with something that looked like a woman seated behind him. The blurring of his aged eyes would not permit him to distinguish any more. Yet — and the hope glanced upon his heart like lightning — yet, if it should be *she*, returning at last to his arms! As the eye, when long accustomed to darkness, shuts close its lids at the slightest gleam of light, so does the mortal spirit, weakened by age, long suffering, melancholy thoughts, and dark forebodings, become overpowered by the first ray of hope that glances into its gloomy recesses. It often happens, too, that the ardent desire to realize a darling hope, is checked by an apprehension that certainty, instead of leading to fruition, will only lead to disappointment. To minds naturally weak, or weakened by long suffering, uncertainty is less painful than to know the worst.

"From one or both of these causes, the good Heer, instead of going forth to learn the truth, returned trembling to his chair, and there sat waiting, almost in a state of insensibility, the approach of the crowd.

"'My father! where, where is he?' exclaimed a voice that went to the innermost soul of the old man, who sat riveted to his seat, without the power of speech or motion. A moment after, a figure rushed in, and, falling at his feet, kissed his hands, and wept upon them.

"'My father, hast thou forgotten Christina,—or, Oh! heavenly powers! perhaps he has forgotten himself! Speak to me, dear father, or kiss me, or press my hand—Oh, do something to show thou rememberest and lovest thy child.'

"The Heer pressed her hand, in token that he had not forgotten his daughter, but it was some minutes before he became sufficiently recovered to take her to his bosom, weep over, and bless her. When he did, the scene was so moving, that the spectators shed tears of sympathy; and even the dry and parched cheeks of Shadrach Moneypenny exhibited indications of moisture."

After sorrow, comes a quiet evening to his life.

"The worthy Heer Piper lived happily to a patriarchal old age, and though he sometimes sighed over the recollection of his departed glories, it was but a momentary feeling, which the duteous attentions of his daughter and the smiles of his grandchildren soon soothed away. He seldom went from home, except once a year to visit his good friend William Penn, and the worthy Shadrach Moneypenny, with whom he had many a bout concerning the wearing of hats, the propriety of making bows, and the moving of the spirit. But, so far from making any impression on the dry soil of Shadrach, it was observed that whenever he saw the Heer approaching he would adjust his beaver with most determined emphasis, and give it a smart rap on the crown, as if in defiance of his old antagonist.

"But the Heer and his daughter could never agree on the subject of rural economy. Christina was for planting flowers and ornamental shrubs, and beautifying all around; while the Heer had a most pestilent propensity for the useful, and valued a patch of cabbages above a bed of tulips of a thousand dyes. Christina at length succeeded so far as to make him promise to pay some little attention to appearances, and cultivate a few favorite flowers; which engagement he conscientiously kept, by setting out a notable bed of cauliflowers."

As I have devoted considerable space to the Governor, I shall give a little to his official residence, or "palace, as he called it, videlicet, a two-story brick house, with a steep roof, covered with fiery red tiles, lapping over each other like the scales of a drum fish. The bricks which composed the walls of the palace were of the same dusky hue of red, so that the whole had the appearance of a vast oven, just heated for a batch of bread. Agreeably to the fashion of the times, the house was of little depth, the windows of the same room opening to both front and rear; but then it made up in length what it wanted in depth, and when not taken in profile, had a very imposing appearance."

So much for the Heer Piper. The other characters in the book are neatly sketched, but room to introduce them is wanting.

# XII.

1823–1825. [ÆT. 45–47.]

NAVY AGENT FOR NEW YORK — GEORGE L. STORER — LETTER TO IRVING — JOHN BULL IN AMERICA; OR, THE NEW MUNCHAUSEN — LETTERS TO IRVING ABOUT — WELL RECEIVED IN ENGLAND — G. KEMBLE'S SETTLEMENT AT COLD SPRING — ANADOSTAN — LOST!

NOT long after the publication of "Koningsmarke" Mr. Paulding removed from Washington to New York. This change of residence was caused by the death of his father-in-law, Mr. Kemble, in July, 1823. He resigned the position of Secretary of the Board of Navy Commissioners, November 8th, 1823, and was appointed Navy Agent for New York by President Monroe, January 8th, 1824.

Mr. Paulding found Mr. George L. Storer already in the office. Him he retained as chief clerk, and was most fortunate in securing his services. Together for fourteen years, he proved an associate most desirable in every respect, who relieved his principal from all the detail of the Agency.

On the 20th of March, 1824, Paulding writes to Irving, from New York; — a long letter, detailing these changes, and other matters. I make brief extracts, prefacing them with the remark that the "Mount Kemble" referred to was a property in New Jersey that had long been in the family of his wife, and that the "brother William" mentioned is the one who first procured him employment in the city.

You have heard of my transfer to New York, and all I shall say of it is that the situation is specially agreeable on account of there being little to do in it, whereby I am afforded good time for scribbling, which has become a most incurable habit with me, absolutely necessary to kill time. It is also agreeable, on the score of being the free unsolicited gift of the President, who was closely besieged by fifty-three candidates. I had resigned my situation at Washington previous to this appointment, with a view to settle at Mount Kemble.

In the division of the estate, the old house, which we have so often haunted, in Whitehall Street, has fallen to my share. Here I have set up my tent, and if living in a great house constitutes a great man after the fashion of New York, a great man am I, at your service. I fear however, I shall never realize your forebodings in regard to the honours of an association with the Rutgers, the Willets, and the Gelstons, or arrive at the apotheosis of the Cocked Hat. My brother William is already Brigadier-General and Mayor of the city, and these are sufficient glories for one family. Still I can't help hoping with you that we shall yet hang our hats on the next peg before we die. . . . .

When you look at the length of this letter, [eight closely-written pages] and call to mind that all our family are either constantly or occasionally sojourners in the Castle of Indolence, you will estimate it accordingly. It is needless for me to say that I rejoice in the reputation you have so justly acquired, and that I anticipate the period, when, having realized all the pleasure reputation can give, you will turn toward home, hang up your hat among us, and astonish our ears with a thousand stories of the littleness of greatness. You must not put this off, by the way, till we are both too old to anticipate the propriety of a few honest, frisky, old-fashioned jollifications.

JOHN BULL IN AMERICA; OR, THE NEW MUNCHAUSEN, was the next publication of Mr. Paulding, brought out in 1825 in one volume by Charles Wiley, New York. This is a broad caricature, if that be possible, of the early type of British traveller in the United States. He had hitherto defended his country seriously from this sort of man; he now took up the more effectual weapon of ridicule. This work will be included in the republication about to be made. The following detail to Irving, gives the melancholy circumstances under which it was written, and furnishes another illustration of the mysterious workings of the human mind.

New York, 31st Augt. 1825.

We have had a heavy hand laid upon us about three months ago in the loss of that little boy, who, I think, I once told you we had named after our brother William Irving, and who, after lingering almost eight months in some inscrutable disorder which baffled all remedies, died at last, with an eye as bright, and a mind as clear, as the day he was taken ill. . . . It was in the midst of these anxieties I wrote the little book which perhaps you have seen, and which the world little suspects was the product of a season of gloomy anticipation — of intervals of watching and nursing our poor boy.

Believe me, my dear Washington, I have thus opened my heart to you, because I felt that though long absent from, and distant from, each other, with little communication and less profession, there was that in your recollections of the past which would induce you always to feel an interest in my history. Once therefore, for the first and last time, I have given you my feelings on the subject of the only calamity I have ever for a moment sunk under. I am relieved by the disclosure — and have said to you all I ever mean to say on the subject.

The letter closes with some family notices.

In the course of last winter I lost my good old father, who

died ninety years old. . . . My mother is still living in health and comfort at Tarrytown. Our worthy Uncle John is waxing old and infirm, and no more aspires to buxom widows, or blooming maidens. Yet he still admires a pretty girl.

This John Paulding, uncle of his namesake the captor of André, as well as of our author, was the original of the fine sketch in the first series of Salmagundi, entitled "Mine Uncle John."

"John Bull in America" is alluded to in the next letter to Irving, under date of September 3d, 1825.

I am glad you were amused with the squib against the Quarterly. You know under what circumstances it was written, and I have only to add in excuse for its crudities, that it was actually begun and finished in three weeks' time. As a mere temporary thing, I did not in truth think it worth while to take any pains with its revisal; and circumstances occurred that tore my mind from all such matters. That it should be well received in England is what I never anticipated, and is one of the absolute eccentricities of John Bull, I think.

This letter concludes: —

Remember me affectionately to the Doctor, who I hope will soon be quite well. I hope yet to see you and him enjoying the same hospitalities in this house you were accustomed to do, when it was inhabited by a much better man than myself. I would get tipsy on the occasion, though it cost me a week's headache.

Farewell my dear Washington — though you are not building houses like Brevoort, or villages like unto Gouv, you are building what will last longer than either. God bless you.

The allusion to Kemble has in view a settlement he had made in the spring of 1817, at Coldspring, Putnam County, New York, where he originated iron works now grown into a very large establishment.

This year, 1825, the poetic impulse was aroused in our author again. The following verses are no doubt a reminiscence of his life at Washington.

ANADOSTAN.

There is a little grassy isle
That parts Potomac's ample tide,
Where nature wears her gayest smile,
And nature's choicest sweets abide.

On either side, and all around,
The weltering wave is seen to flow,
Noiseless, or, if you hear a sound,
'Tis but a murmur, soft and low.

With the thick groves the gentle flood
Playing at hide and seek appears,
Now glittering through the waving wood,
Now lost as one its margin nears.

It seems as nought but holy rest
Could find a home in that fair spot;
It seems as mortal might be blessed,
If there were cast his happy lot.

There's not a sound that greets the ear
But lulls the worn and weary soul;
There's not a sight that meets us here
But calms the breast where passions roll.

The great trees, nodding to and fro
In stately conclaves not a few,
Whisper as secretly and slow
As bashful lovers ever do.

The wild birds sing their roundelay,
For no rude sportsman spoils their glee,
And, all the live-long summer day,
Delight the ear with minstrelsy.

And careless up and down they fly,
Nor heed the stranger passing near;
For undisturbed they cleave the sky,
And undisturbed their young they rear.

And oh! how sweet the roses bloom,
And sweet the ruddy clover spreads;
And, springing from earth's fruitful womb,
How thick the violets lift their heads!

And, when the sun's last splendors beam
Upon the light clouds in the West,
The glassy surface of the stream
What ever changing tints invest!

At first a gorgeous red prevails;
And next, a glowing purple hue;
To feebler gleams the glory pales;
Then comes a deep, fast-fading, blue.

Then idles in the pensive hour,
When Twilight, wrapped in robe of gray,
Steals softly from her secret bower,
And shuts the gates of parting day.

Then hies the fire-fly gayly out,
And trims his lamp at evening's fall,
To light the little rabble rout
Of Fairies to their nightly ball.

The tinkling bell, the plashing oar,
The buzzing of the insect throng,
The laugh that echoes from the shore,
The unseen thrush's vesper song —

Combined with the mild influence
Of sober Evening's matron sway,
'Gainst worldly wish give strong defence,
And chase all sinful thought away.

At such an hour I long to rove
Along the paths of that fair isle,
With those who simple nature love,
Those who, like Nature, know no guile.

And I, at such an hour *have* roved
Along the paths of that fair isle,
With one who simple nature loved,
One who, like Nature, knew no guile;

With one whose eye of modest blue
Beamed ever with a radiance bright
That seemed to something inward due,
A fountain of celestial light;

With one whose voice was sweeter far,
As I one eve enjoyed it there,
Than all the singing birds there are,
Or all the sounds that soothe the air;

With one whose lips outblushed the rose,
And forth a fresher perfume breathed
Than e'er the rose at evening close
To dewy stars of night bequeathed;

With one whose bosom was more pure
Than the pure stream that wandered by;
In its own innocence secure,
And safe, were basest evil nigh.

When faintly beamed the setting sun
Along the paths of that fair isle,
*Once* I have strayed with such an one,
And heard her gayly talk the while.

And when I count the earthly hours
That I shall cherish most of all,
That walk in Anadostan's bowers
Will be the first that I recall.

The following stanzas I have selected from a longer poem. Several of them put one strongly in mind of Thomson, by the way a favorite author with Mr. Paulding. Neither this nor the preceding poem, as I believe, has ever been in print before.

## LOST!

Once on a time a traveller wound his way
Far in the West, that world of boundless plains,
And endless rivers that meandering stray
Through the wild warrior-Indian's lone domains,
Where Nature in despotic vigor reigns,
The freshness of her power undefiled
By mortal man in search of petty gains,
Unmarred by frippery Art, sublimely wild,
Unrivalled and supreme, Creation's giant child.

Tracking the prairie, he had left afar
Turbid Missouri's rash and headstrong tide,
That ever with its neighbor Earth at war
Resistless tears its way in foaming pride,
Rending her breast to atoms far and wide,
To scatter them at random to and fro,
Just as its rage, or accident, may guide;
Capricious in its rude relentless flow,
Robbing a world above, to form a world below.

'Twas Autumn, and the dim and hazy air
Diffused a double softness o'er the scene,
That made the landscape more obscurely fair,
And waked seducing indolence I ween,
And caused him pause each lagging step between;
Far as he gazed o'er all the boundless space
That mocked his vision though his eye was keen,
On every hand dame Nature showed a face
Of most contented calm, and soft, bewitching, grace.

Here drowsy-headed Silence held her breath,
And Echo lay entranced in heavy sleep;
The quiet and solemnity of Death
Eternal watch and ward appeared to keep,
And palpably upon the air to creep;
And naught rebelled against the strong duress;
No insect shrill was heard, or murmur deep;
In truth, it was a stillness to oppress —
Unbroken, dreary, sole, and utter, loneliness.

And not a trace of man here could he glean,
Though eagerly he cast his wearied eyes
O'er the mysterious paradise of green;
But saw, instead, far off, weird phantoms rise,
Dancing against the mirror of the skies; —
City, and tower, and frowning battlement;
And lengthened lines of men in martial guise;
And thousand unsubstantial figments, blent
In dizzy Fancy's wayward wild divertisement.

The skies their dark-blue banner broad unfurled,
Watched by the sleepless sentinels of night,
While all the upper and the lower world
Blended in one pale harmony of light,
Might fill the Soul with music, to that height
Which bards declare was reached in olden time
When all those heavenly orbs serenely bright
Joined in one solemn, soul-subduing chime,
Uplifting praise unto their Architect sublime.

But not for him was joy by night or day,
Though all the joys of sight and sound should meet;
Cold in his heart a grim suspicion lay;
"I'm on the trail — *the trail!*" — would he repeat,
And, for awhile, his growing fear would cheat,
And make himself a self-deceiving boast;
But not for long endured the poor deceit;
Upon a sea of doubt and terror tost,
That most tremendous horror came upon him — LOST!

# XIII.

1826. [ÆT. 48.]

THE MERRY TALES OF THE THREE WISE MEN OF GOTHAM — INTRODUCTORY DISSERTATION — THE FIRST PHILOSOPHER — THE SECOND PHILOSOPHER — THE THIRD PHILOSOPHER — PANEGYRIC ON THE COMMON LAW — DEATH AND BURIAL OF DOCTOR GALLGOTHA — CATASTROPHE OF THE BOWL.

IN 1826 appeared THE MERRY TALES OF THE THREE WISE MEN OF GOTHAM, a volume published by G. & C. Carvill, New York.

The title page bears a motto from Mother Goose's Melodies: —

> "Three wise men of Gotham
> Went to sea in a bowl;
> If the bowl had been stronger,
> My tales had been longer."

Mr. Harmony, Mr. Quominus, and Dr. Spurrem, tell their stories, under the titles of — The Man Machine; or The Pupil of "Circumstances"; The Perfection of Reason; and, The Perfection of Science: which are, respectively, satires on Mr. Owen's theories of Human Perfectibility, the Common Law, and Phrenology.

The "Introductory Dissertation" is a good sample of our author's grave irony and humor.

## INTRODUCTORY DISSERTATION.

Although most of the celebrated cities of antiquity have been described with such accuracy, and their situations pointed out with so much precision, that there is little difficulty in at least making a tolerable guess at their remains; yet are there two most remarkable exceptions. To this day no one has succeeded in establishing beyond question where Babylon once stood, and still less have the most indefatigable inquiries even led to a reasonable conjecture as to the site of the little less renowned city of Gotham. No circumstance can furnish a higher proof of the superiority of the works of the head over those of the hands, than that the fame of these two great cities should have been preserved in books long after every other certain vestige of their existence had perished from the face of the earth.

History, sacred and profane, alone preserves the remembrance of Babylon; and of Gotham we possess scarcely any other memorial than the immortal lines to be found in the titlepage of this work. And this example furnishes a striking proof of the importance of heroes, poets, and philosophers, in cities and states. How many of these have been utterly forgotten in the lapse of time, merely for want of some great man to rescue them from oblivion! How many of the most insignificant have, on the contrary, become renowned solely in consequence of having been the birthplace or residence of some illustrious citizen! Who would ever have heard of Stagira but for the nativity of Aristotle? Who would have remembered half the cities that contended for the honour of being the birthplace of Homer, had it not been for that illustrious rivalry? Who would not go ten miles out of the way to avoid Arpinum, but for the glory of Cicero? And who, finally, would ever have dreamed of the existence of such a city as Gotham, had it not been for the unparalleled distinction of having possessed three sages at one and the same time?—a circumstance which places her far above all the cities of ancient Greece. They had their single wise men; and all that the force of ancient genius seems to have been capable of was to produce one of these at a time. In short, a thousand proofs are extant to show that the memory of illustrious men is among the strongest of those everlasting links which bind together the different ages and nations of the earth; and that were it not for these indestructible landmarks of time, we should scarcely have any thing to remind us that we have been preceded by hundreds of generations.

These reflections may serve to place in a more striking point of view the ingratitude of mankind, in so often neglecting or persecuting those profound sages and philosophers, who not only confer upon them while living the most substantial benefits, but carry the renown of their birthplace to the latest posterity. The virtues, talents, and glorious services of illustrious men of every nation constitute their best inheritance, their most rational source of pride and exultation, and it has often happened that the renown of a people, like that of the Thebans, began and ended with a single man. Yet how often we find nations either entirely indifferent to their best benefactors, or persecuting them with all the barbarous rigours of religious, political, or philosophical intolerance! Not to mention the numerous instances recorded of ancient times, we shall find, even in the most enlightened ages, humanized by the mild and forgiving precepts of Christianity, these examples, if possible still more numerous and flagrant. Galileo is a hackneyed instance; but it is not so generally known that Newton was charged by bigotry and ignorance with holding opinions at war with orthodoxy, and Locke expelled from that reverend bedlam Oxford by political intolerance. Among the most illustrious reformers, as well as the most enlightened of reasoners, Melancthon, Erasmus, and even Theodore Beza, were suspected and denounced, because they did not keep pace with the rampant zealots of the times, who would willingly have warmed them at the stake. In short, it would seem to be among the inflexible dispensations of Providence, that no selfish motive should ever operate upon the great benefactors of mankind, in their glorious endeavours, since all they can rationally anticipate as their reward in this world is to pass their lives amid persecutions and slanders, among a race of ungrateful beings, who never become sensible of their ingratitude or their obligations till it is too late to make reparation.

Owing to this waywardness of mankind it has happened, that now, when a disposition prevails to do justice to the illustrious dead, for want of a sufficient number of distinguished persons to employ the pens of the innumerable biographers that stand ready, pen in hand, to strip the unfortunates before they are cold, and lay their foibles open to the world, they are fain to bestow their labours on persons whose greatest merit is their insignificance. Owing to this, I say, it has happened that not only the precise place occupied by the famous city of Gotham, but likewise the era in which her three sages flourished, cannot now be ascertained. All that can be done is to grope in the obscurity of vague conjecture, and then leave the matter more obscure than before. It may be, however, worth while to pass in review the different opinions heretofore advanced upon this important point.

Some will have it that Gotham was the ancient capital of the Goths, of whom, we thank our stars, King Roderick was the last, according to Mr. Southey. Others, on the contrary, have maintained with great zeal that Gotham is a corruption of Gotha, the seat of a northern university, where they philosophize pretty deeply, and study metaphysics. A third class of inquirers affirm that such a city never existed, because they have not been able to find any traces of its existence, which in our opinion is the poorest reason in the world. The four lines of our titlepage furnish better proof of its existence than all the fragments of Carthage, or stately ruins of Thebes and Palmyra. Antiquaries ought to blush for such frivolous doubts! They are utterly unworthy of the strong faith which should ever animate this class of explorers.

Among the vast variety of opinions upon this point, that which identifies Gotham with the famous city of Gottingen, which is the seat of a university founded by the renowned Baron Munchausen, is not the least plausible at first sight. There are numerous examples, not only of cities but of empires, whose names, being ill adapted to poetry, have been changed into others more musical and harmonious. In short, almost all countries have a prosaic and a poetical name — Gallia, Iberia, Ausonia, Hesperia, Albion, Hibernia, Columbia, and a hundred others, will at once occur to the general reader. It will readily be conceded by all unprejudiced persons that Gottingen is neither sonorous, musical, nor poetical; and therefore, without any great violation of probability, we may suppose a poet of a delicate ear would soften it down to Gotham, a name wonderfully adapted to poetry. But there is a still stronger presumption in favour of this opinion. At Gottingen, as we are credibly informed, the professors actually adventure upon animal magnetism, phrenology, and such dangerous sciences, which would seem to justify a shrewd suspicion that they would not be a whit too good to venture out to sea in a large bowl, well ballasted with punch, such as whilom used to be placed upon the smoking board of a jolly New-Netherlander, by four stout menials on New-year's Eve, ere the dire irruption of liqueurs, and other outlandish poisons. Nor would this adventure have appeared so rash as might seem at first sight, since we have been assured by a person of great experience in nautical affairs and punch-drinking, that there is a natural antipathy between salt-water and punch, insomuch that being once half-seas over, he fell into the ocean with a bowl of punch in his hands, and floated several hours, quietly sipping, until he was taken up again. Not a single drop of sea-water had polluted his beverage all this while. He declares a punch-bowl is far preferable to a life-boat, and a skin well lined with toddy a thousand times superior to a cork jacket. These facts are sufficient to put to the blush all those who conceive it any imputation upon our Three Wise Men, that they should venture to sea in a bowl.

But there is one opinion put forth by certain English writers, who, if they could bring it about, would not leave the rest of the world a single philosopher, which we are inclined to treat with infinite contempt. We mean the absurd notion, that Gotham is actually a town in Northamptonshire, or rather a rotten borough, which, although destitute of inhabitants, returns three members, who are generally called the Wise Men of Gotham, because they instinctively vote with the ministry, agreeably to the instructions of their constituents. It is said that this place was remarkable for goats in the time of William the Conqueror, and that the people used to ride them instead of horses, which, in the opinion of some, gave rise to their being called the Wise Men, or, according to the opinion of others, the Mad Men of Gotham. A great Oxford antiquary, of whom it has been said that he remembered whatever others forgot, and forgot whatever other people remembered, speaks of the "Merry Tales of the Mad Men of Gotham," a work in great repute in his time, when the kindest name given to a philosopher was that of a madman, a phrase which often saved him from the stake or the block. This work was long supposed to be extinct, but at length came to light not long since, at Mr. Bindley's sale, and was bought by a young American traveller for a trifle, owing to the deplorable ignorance of two munificent noblemen, who little suspected that it was the only copy in the known world.

It is this work which is now presented to the reader, divested of its antique garb, that it may be more extensively circulated and understood, and restored to its genuine title of the "Merry Tales of the Three Wise Men of Gotham." It was thought inhuman to hoard up the treasure, and keep all this huge bundle of knowledge to ourselves, after the manner of certain great lovers of literature, who think a book is like a mistress, of no value if her beauties are enjoyed by another. But to return to our subject.

Though we have adopted the work as genuine, we are by no means inclined to humour the English writers in their claim to this illustrious city. They are welcome to London and Liverpool, and even to Oxford and Cambridge, with all our heart. But as to the renowned city of Gotham, we will not yield a single hair of its head to England or any other country. We are willing to let the matter rest as it is, so that every nation may have an equal claim, but our disinterestedness will go no further. All we will concede is, that Gotham, like some glorious philosophers and benefactors of the human race, is a city belonging to the whole civilized world, the emporium of arts, the head-quarters of philosophy, and the illustrious seat of the perfection of reason. Whether in the New or the Old World is of little consequence, since such is its glory and renown that there is quite enough of it to satisfy half a dozen worlds. Leaving this part of our inquiry to take care of itself, we will proceed to discuss other equally important matters.

It cannot be sufficiently lamented by those who rightly consider the forgetting of any thing a great misfortune, whether it was worth remembering or not, that such a culpable carelessness and indifference prevailed in early times in respect to the little peculiarities and private particulars which no doubt distinguished the great men of those days. It is melancholy to think how much we read, and how little we know, of the great writers of antiquity. The race of "d——d good-natured" biographers, who in the present age so amply furnish all these interesting minutiæ, was unknown at that time, at least none of their works have come down to us. It is owing in a great measure to this circumstance, that the great men of antiquity preserve a sort of prescriptive superiority over the moderns; not that they were really wiser, or more virtuous or brave, but because there were no prying, curious, industrious, pains-taking persons, who noted their foibles, set down their folly for wisdom, and made use of the intimacy they had obtained by cringing sycophancy to furnish themselves with materials to shame them with posterity.

Thus it is that the ancients tower above the moderns, because of the former we scarcely know any thing but what is great, and the greatness of the latter is overshadowed by littlenesses. Their virtues and vices, their wisdom and folly, their magnanimity and meanness, their strength and their weakness, are so mixed up, and withal so impartially dwelt upon by the faithful biographer, that we approach the most illustrious sage with the familiarity of a pert valet, by long service become acquainted with all the foibles and secrets of his master. We become, as it were, quite relieved from that sense of degrading inferiority inspired by the naked simplicity of ancient virtue, as handed down to us by writers so neglectful of their duty as one-half the time to forget whether their heroes had in reality any vices to bring them down to the level of humanity.

Still more is it to be regretted that the noble ambition of collecting those works which derive their peculiar value from having been long since forgotten, did not originate somewhat earlier, and before so many valuable relics, so much invaluable information, had been irretrievably lost. Follies and weaknesses that might have been dignified by the examples of illustrious men are become degraded by being supposed to appertain exclusively to the vulgar; and the mousing gossips of literature cheated of all chance of pulling to pieces the character of an ancient worthy.

This blamable neglect in recording the littlenesses, and preserving memorials of the vices, of great persons, can perhaps best be accounted for and excused on the supposition that a great portion of the now illustrious sages of antiquity had not their merits brought to light until long after they were dead, when the only memorials of their having once existed were their immortal works. Conquerors, heroes, and fashionable bards, receive the admiration of their cotemporaries, and reap their harvest while living; but sages and virtuous men must, for the most part, content themselves with being venerated in their ashes, and rewarded in a future world. The difference between the mere vulgar idol of a fashionable mob and the retired votary of wisdom, genius, and virtue is, that the one is remembered while living and forgot when dead, while the other emerges to light and immortality at the moment he ceases to live. It is then that the literary "resurrection-men" for the first time discover that he is worth disinterring, and that they set about disturbing his ashes, and raking up, with pious industry, the memory of all those little, frivolous, and impertinent particulars, the knowledge of which answers little purpose but that of adding to our contempt for poor human nature. Thus it is that the longer the time which elapses after the death of great men before mankind discover they were really great, the more fortunate for their lasting reputation. They revive with greater lustre, when all the little clouds and shadows which dimmed their glories are passed away, and appear in the imperishable brightness of their own immortal productions. Of Homer, Shakspeare, and the few names that occupy the summit of the temple of Fame, how little do we know; while everybody knows all about the lesser lights, that will twinkle for a little while in the darkness which surrounds them, and then go out for ever. The "Great Unknown" has, we are credibly informed, not less than six industrious "resurrection-men," watching day and night only for the breath to be fairly out of his body, to make an example of him. Nay, so impatient are they for his decease, that it is currently rumoured on this side the water, they have it in serious contemplation to make away with him the first convenient opportunity, in their apprehension that he will cheat them of his biography by unluckily outliving them all. We earnestly advise him not to go out at night, nor wander in solitary places; or at least, if he will, to wear a coat-of-mail, and take every reasonable precaution. It would be twice unfortunate, to be first made away with in cold blood, and afterward murdered in a biography. The best way, we think, and we advise him to it forthwith, will be to write his own life, after the manner of certain persecuted worthies, who, in order to disappoint the mob of a public spectacle, fairly hang themselves up the night before execution. Be this as it may, it is without doubt owing in a great measure to the fact that our Three Wise

Men were of the class of the immortals who live only in after-ages, that their fame has lain thus long, as it were, in abeyance, while so many insignificant persons have been handed down with honour, not indeed from generation to generation, but from the reviewer to the magazines, and from the magazines to the newspapers.

A still greater uncertainty obtains in respect to the precise era in which our sages flourished than exists in relation to the place of their nativity. In the original black-letter copy, neither the date of the publication nor the name of the printer is preserved, so that we are left entirely in the dark as to these interesting particulars. Neither can any thing decisive be inferred from the nature of the topics discussed, or the events alluded to, in the course of the work, since nothing is more certain than that the opinions as well as the events of the world, like the world itself, are perpetually moving in a circle. Revolving years, as they bring about a return of the same seasons, and the same fashions in dress, reproduce at the same time similar errors of the vulgar and absurdities of the wise. Old errors are pretty sure to return, after having been absent long enough to be forgotten, under a new name, and with a new face. They are like spaniels; we cannot beat them from us. Thus it is, in like manner, with the theories and inventions which are daily passed upon us for original, but which, for the most part, will be found to be nothing more than the revivals of old and exploded fashions, which the world had worn till it was tired, and then thrown by among the lumber of antiquity, for some new rattle, that had its day, and then followed its predecessor, quietly into a temporary oblivion. To argue then that the following work is modern, because it treats of topics fashionable at the present day, is in effect to deny, what is certainly true, that one age is a mere edition of another, with some alterations, but the contents substantially the same. It tickles human vanity to tell us that we are wiser than our fathers; and it is one of those propositions which is likely to pass without contradiction, from the circumstance that all those most interested in denying it are dead and gone. But if the grave could speak, and the churchyards vote upon the question, we living boasters would be in a most pitiful minority. That the knowledge of mankind is not always progressive, and one age inevitably wiser than another, is exemplified most miserably in the history of the world. It is only to cast our eyes toward the country of Homer, of Aristotle, and of Socrates, to behold millions of living testimonies to prove that the mind of man, like the crab, moves backward and forward with equal facility, and that ages of knowledge seem naturally succeeded by ages of ignorance. Man cannot do or know every thing at once; and it is not altogether improbable, that in proportion as a succeeding age adds to the knowledge of a preceding one, it makes way for its acquisitions by displacing something equally important. Men may forget as well as learn; and, without doubt, many, very many, wise and virtuous habits and practices have been from time to time elbowed out of the world, to make room for outlandish and pestilent novelties. He, therefore, who should take upon him to pronounce this work a production of the present age, merely on the authority of the topics it discusses, would very probably decide that the elderly gentlemen about town are all young, because some of them dress like dandies, dance cotillons, and aspire to the possession of youthful belles.

Some may suppose that the names of the Three Wise Men might possibly lead to detection. But we feel bound in candour to confess that these are of our own invention. Such is the innate modesty of true wisdom, that not one of this illustrious trio ever took occasion to disclose his name to any living person, so far as we have been able to discover. Certain it is, that if they did, the author or compiler, whose name is equally unknown, has either wilfully or ignorantly omitted it through the whole course of the work, leaving blanks, which we thought proper to fill up to the best of our judgment, as the frequent omissions had an unpleasant effect on the eye of the reader.

The circumstance of their going to sea in a bowl we are rather inclined to consider as allegorical; or perhaps it may be a poetic license. At all events, whether it be so or not, it indicates in the most striking manner the opinion entertained by the poet of their daring intrepidity, in thus venturing out upon the most unstable of all elements in so frail a bark. It shows a contempt of danger, when encountered in search of knowledge, far above that of Belzoni, Park, Hornemann, or any martyr to Egyptian mummies, incognita African rivers, or north-west passages. A love of knowledge so elevated above all fear of consequences, places them on a level with that distinguished phrenologist of Edinburgh, who is reported to have knocked out his own brains, for the purpose of demonstrating the truth of his favourite science.

Having now, as we presume to flatter ourselves, sufficiently established to the satisfaction of the reader the three points we set out to prove, to wit, that neither the birthplace, the era, nor the names, of the Three Wise Men of Gotham can now ever be known, we shall put an end to our inquiry.

It may be proper to add that there is neither introduction nor preface to the originals of these tales; no explanation of the particular circumstances which brought our Three Wise Men together; nor of the occasion which prompted them to relate their stories to each other. We may reasonably, however, suppose that it was done to while away the tedium of a long voyage; and that upon some placid summer morning, while the wave was calm, the sky serene, the sea-birds skimming over-head, and the dolphins playing beside them, the Man Machine, being politely requested by his companions, began, as will be seen in the following pages.

*New-Amsterdam, February,* 1826.

The story of the first philosopher begins:—

"I was born, began the first Wise Man of Gotham, in a country that I consider unworthy of my nativity, and for that reason I shall do all in my power to deprive it of the honour, by not mentioning its name. I am, moreover, descended from a family, which must necessarily be of great antiquity, since, like all old things, it has long since fallen into decay. My father had little or no money, but was blessed with the poor man's wealth, a fruitful wife and great store of children. Of these I am the eldest; but at the period I shall commence my story, we were all too young to take care of ourselves, until the fortunate discovery was made by some great philanthropist, that little children, of six or seven years old, could labour a dozen or fourteen hours a day, without stinting their minds, ruining their health, or destroying their morals. This improvement in the great science of PRODUCTIVE LABOUR, delighted my father—it was shifting the *onus*, as the lawyers say, from his own shoulders to that of his children. He forthwith bound us all over to a cotton manufactory, where we stood upon our legs three times as long as a member of Congress, that is to say, fourteen hours a day, and, among eight of us, managed to earn a guinea a week. The old gentleman, for gentleman he became from the moment he discovered his little flock could maintain him—thought he had opened a mine. He left off working, and took to drinking and studying the mysteries of political economy and productive labour. He soon became an adept in this glorious science, and at length arrived at the happy conclusion, that the whole moral, physical, political, and religious organization of society resolved itself into making the most of human labour; just as we use that of our horses, oxen, asses, and other beasts of burthen."

The story of the second philosopher begins:—

"My brother Harmony (said Mr. Quominus, the second Wise Man of Gotham), has fallen a sacrifice to the perfectibility of man; I, on the contrary, am a martyr to the Perfection of Reason. I was born in a country where they have sufficient wisdom to make their own laws, but not quite enough, as it would seem, to understand them afterward. In order to remedy this inconvenience they resorted to a method equally singular and original. They enlisted the wise men of other nations in their behalf; and justly considering that it was quite a sufficient effort of human wisdom for one country to make its own laws, they determined to resort to another for their interpretation. Accordingly, they made a vast number of laws, believing they could not have too much of a good thing, and then sent beyond sea to get them explained. In a couple of hundred years, these explanations, being all carefully recorded in books, amounted to upward of three thousand volumes of goodly size, each containing upon an average, one hundred contradictory interpretations of different wise men. Such a mass of wisdom, and such a variety of opinions, supported by such unanswerable arguments, never got together under the same roof in this world. Some very aged persons, who had lived long enough to get about half through this invaluable collection, discovered that it was like the sermon that suited any text, and the text that suited any sermon — for every man could find in it a decision, or at least an opinion, to suit his purpose. A system so supported on all sides by all sorts of opinions, certainly merited the honour of being called a science; and such a science as certainly deserved a respectable name. It was accordingly aptly denominated THE PERFECTION OF REASON, because it furnished every man, whatever his opinions might be, with reasons in support of them.

"In addition to this great requisite of every perfect system, namely, that it should suit everybody — this accumulation of contradictory opinions, it was affirmed, possessed another irresistible claim to the dignified appellation it had obtained. It cannot be denied, said the admirers of this science, that although the laws are expressly devised to settle such disputes, or conflicting claims, as might otherwise occasion a resort to force, still it is never the intention of a wise legislator, that people should actually appeal to them for this purpose. They are merely to be held up *in terrorem*, or rather like buoys, to float on the surface of society, for the purpose of warning mankind of the shoals and quicksands below. In this point of view, then, it is apparent, that the more intricate and inconsistent the laws, and the more various and contradictory their interpretations, the greater delay and expense there will be found in settling appeals to them, and consequently the number of law-suits will be greatly diminished. Thus, when the laws become perfectly unintelligible they are absolutely perfect, for then nobody in their senses will go to law, and the science will do its duty after the manner of a scarecrow, which frightens the birds from the corn, merely by flourishing its rattle. Thus you see, that no other name than that of THE PERFECTION OF REASON could possibly have suited this excellent science.

"In addition to the singular happiness of being born in a country governed according to the perfection of reason, I was brought up under an uncle, (my father dying when I was quite a child), who adored the law, and might be said never to have had any other mistress. He was a bachelor, of competent estate, but rather indifferent education — he was better fed than taught; and when I say he could read, and write, and cipher a little, I go as far as strict biographical veracity will warrant. He was without a profession, rich, and unmarried. Such a man has but one chance for happiness in this world — he must get unto himself a hobby, and ride away as if the sheriff were at his heels. To trace a man's hobby to its first cause is like searching for the source of the Niger. Yet I think I can account for that of my uncle. He had gained possession of a large part of his property by a law-suit, and ever after considered law to be the perfection of reason, while the honest gentleman who lost the estate held it in utter abhorrence. The suit lasted nineteen years, at the expiration of which there was found a great flaw in the defendant's title. He had no more money, and no man ever successfully appealed to the perfection of reason with an empty pocket.

" From this time it was my uncle's great delight to attend the courts, where, as he used to affirm with surprising satisfaction, they sometimes nearly argued his head off his shoulders, and so confounded his notions of the distinctions between right and wrong, that he could hardly tell the difference until he went home and looked over the ten commandments."

The story of the third philosopher begins: —

" My brother Harmony, (began the third Wise Man of Gotham), has, it seems, been shipwrecked in pursuit of the Perfectibility of Man; and my brother Quominus has fallen a victim to the Perfection of Reason, or the Wisdom of Ages, I can hardly tell which — I, on the contrary, am the martyr of Science.

I was born and educated in the most scientific, literary, and philosophical city of the world — for the women were all blues and the men metaphysicians. In truth, I may say, with perfect veracity, there were so many people running after science, that there were not sciences enough for them to run after. The business was overdone; the game was exhausted, as in countries too thickly settled and too much cultivated; and nothing was left for them but the invention of new sciences, to give them employment. Besides, such had been the unwearied industry, the deep sagacity with which they had pursued the old sciences, that they had driven them from their most secret recesses; detected all their arcana; exposed their occult mysteries; and, in fact, pulled them by the ears, as it were, out of every hole and corner where they had intrenched themselves for ages. Strangers, who were allured to the city by the fame of its learning, observed with astonishment, that the women could call every thing by its scientific name, and that even the poor children talked nearly as wisely as the very best of them. Learning, science, and philosophy were becoming vulgar, insomuch that several people of the highest rank and fashion began to study ignorance, and actually sent their children to school to unlearn every thing. It was high time, therefore, for the lovers of science to begin to look about them; for the writers and lecturers upon the old gray-beard mathematics, philosophy, astronomy, and the like, instead of an audience of pretty fashionables with nodding plumes, were content to confine their instructions to classes of rusty students, who actually came for no other purpose than to learn. The fashionable young ladies began to yawn at conversaziones, where they met to relax themselves with political economy and metaphysics; and a universal alarm prevailed, when a great heiress, who was considered the bulwark of the blues, backslided, and married a regular dandy with a thin waist and no learning.

"It was high time to get up something new for these people, and as the natives of our isle are more apt to improve upon the inventions of others than to invent themselves, I was selected by a coterie of philosophers, and sent out into the world to discover a new plaything for these grown-up children of knowledge. I travelled, and travelled, and travelled, as the story-books say, over divers countries that have neither latitude nor longitude; I visited all the colleges, scientific institutions, and bedlams; sought out the most learned and adventurous philosophers of Christendom: consulted the pundits of India, the chingfoos of China, the dervises of Turkey, and the jugglers of the Flathead Indians of the Missouri. In short, I ransacked the uttermost ends of the earth, and was returning disconsolate, through Germany, to my native city, with a firm conviction that there was nothing new under the sun, when an unexpected adventure befell me on the eve of a long day's journey."

Incidentally, we have, in "The Perfection of Rea son", this opening of a judge's charge, being his panegyric on the Common Law:—

"Gentlemen of the Jury: I cannot sufficiently congratulate both myself and you, that we are here deliberating and deciding under the purest and most perfect system of laws with which any people were ever blessed; a system combining the wisdom of our ancestors with that of our own—a system happily characterized by the sages of the law, as the result of the experience of ages, and the perfection of reason. I speak, gentlemen, of the common law—which is, I will venture to say — I can hardly say what it is — sometimes it is one thing, sometimes another — sometimes it is founded upon a rule, and sometimes upon exceptions to a rule — sometimes it is defined, and sometimes it is not defined — sometimes it is the product of ages of darkness, illustrated and explained by the wisdom of ages of light — and sometimes it is the offspring of ages of light, mellowed down, as it were, into an agreeable twilight, by the obscurities of ages of darkness. It is, in fact, gentlemen, a chaos of wisdom and experience, out of which issues beauty and order, as did the fair creations of this harmonious universe. Even its inconsistencies and diversities may be justly said to contribute to its unequalled perfection. As in a concert, the different instruments as played by different persons, and the different voices attuned to different pitches, men, women, and children, counter, tenor, treble, and bass, all conduce to the nicest and most accurate harmony; so do the dissenting opinions of various judges and jurists administer to the harmony, beauty, and perfection of the common law.

"Another excellence peculiar to the common law is its capacity of adapting itself to times, changes, and circumstances, without any other violence than an occasional departure from common sense — a species of instinct which the law holds in little respect. Hence we find it in one age one thing, in another age another thing; in the mouth of one judge it speaks one opinion, in that of another judge another opinion, according to the variations produced by time, the difference of climate, the wind, the fashion, and other modifying circumstances. Hence too — and this is another peculiar excellence of the law—let a man's case be apparently ever so bad, it is ten to one but he can find, somewhere or another, a decision of some court or judge that makes in his favour. This is what is meant by the law looking with equal eyes on all persons, and presuming every man to be innocent till he is found guilty. The common law has, in fact, all the qualities of the famous pair of enchanted seven-league boots, which, it is recorded, fitted everybody, great and small, from little Hop-o'-my-thumb to the great giant Blunderbore."

In "The Perfection of Science" occurs the following account of the death and burial of Doctor Gallgotha.

"While we were debating whither to frame our course, and just as I had almost brought the doctor to consent to accompanying me to the city of my nativity, the good old man fell sick, or rather the fabric of nature sunk under him, and the lamp which had illuminated it began to twinkle so faintly in its socket that it was plain the oil was quite spent.

"He took to his bed, from whence he never rose again. I was going to send for a physician. 'No,' said he, with a languid smile, 'I will die a Christian, but not a martyr. It is cruel to torture age with unavailing remedies. Besides, I have not money to pay a doctor, and it would mortify my pride to be killed for nothing.'

"I have a satisfaction, even at this distance of time, in the recollection that I attended him faithfully to the last, supplied his wants and administered to his infirmities, as if he had been my father. About four o'clock one morning, a little before the dawning of the day, and just at the period of time when nature seems to be in her last and profoundest repose, preparatory to waking — the doctor, after lying perfectly still for upward of an hour, suddenly raised himself on his elbow — and with an eye clear and bright surveyed the room all around with a slow and measured turn of the head. For a moment his eye rested upon me — but he did not speak. He then sunk easily upon his pillow — I put my face close to his — he breathed into it once — and there was a long pause. He is gone, said I — no, he breathed again, and there was another still longer pause. It is all over now, said I; but he respired yet once again — and that was the last — I waited, but he breathed no more.

"They would not let me bury him in a churchyard, because, as the confessor maintained, he was no Christian, and therefore was not entitled to Christian charity and forgiveness after he was dead. But I buried the old philosopher where the grass grew as green, the flowers bloomed as gay, and the birds warbled as sweetly, as if the spot had been blessed by the confessor himself."

The volume closes with a dispute in the bowl, which leads to personal violence, and a catastrophe.

"I have seen people keep their temper when the argument was against them, but I never knew even a philosopher that could stand two to one against him in a laugh. Dr. Spurrem lifted up a stout ivory-headed cane with intent, as I believe, to let it fall on the cerebral development of the Pupil of Circumstances; but that expert Spinning Jenny warded off the blow with his cocked hat, which was unfortunately knocked overboard, and the cane lighted directly on the combative organ of the Perfection of Reason. Each of the Wise Men now started up for the purpose of defending his person, or his theory; and in the confusion the jolly Bowl, being left without a cockswain, imperceptibly drifted into the eddying circles of a great whirlpool — beyond doubt the Mælstrom of Norway. Here, after whirling round and round for some time, it unluckily struck against the head of the Man Machine, who was dodging to avoid a second application of the ivory-headed cane. The concussion of these two hard bodies proved fatal to the bowl, which parted exactly in two pieces, just as it floated to the centre of the vortex, in which the whole party was suddenly engulfed. The last vestige of them seen was the tip of the ivory-headed cane, which the doctor seemed still flourishing in vindication of the infallible science.

"What became of these renowned philosophers is not precisely known. The most probable, and at the same time, the most consoling opinion is, that this tremendous vortex was one of the great avenues to the newly discovered CONCENTRIC SPHERES; and that, consequently, there is a possibility at least that our illustrious trio may have found in some other world what they vainly sought in this."

# XIV.

1828–1832. [ÆT. 50–54.]

THE NEW MIRROR FOR TRAVELLERS — THE OLD MAN'S CAROUSAL — TALES OF THE GOOD WOMAN — CHRONICLES OF THE CITY OF GOTHAM — THE LION OF THE WEST — LETTER FROM DAVID CROCKETT — LETTER TO IRVING — THE DUTCHMAN'S FIRESIDE — WESTWARD HO!

THE NEW MIRROR FOR TRAVELLERS; AND GUIDE TO THE SPRINGS, "By an Amateur", was published in one volume in 1828, by G. & C. Carvill, New York. It is a quiz of the fashions and manners of that day, and will be included in the republication about to be made.

To somewhere about this period, as I suppose, we may refer the following lines, which are to be found in "The Poets and Poetry of America" published in 1842 under the editorship of Rufus W. Griswold. They are noticeable, not only for their vigor, but as being almost the sole example of morbid feeling in any thing that Mr. Paulding has left behind him.

THE OLD MAN'S CAROUSAL.

Drink! drink! to whom shall we drink?
To friend or a mistress? Come, let me think!
To those who are absent, or those who are here?
To the dead that we loved, or the living still dear?
Alas! when I look, I find none of the last!
The present is barren — let's drink to the past.

Come! here's to the girl with a voice sweet and low,
The eye all of fire and the bosom of snow,
Who erewhile in the days of my youth that are fled,
Once slept on my bosom, and pillowed my head!
Would you know where to find such a delicate prize?
Go seek in yon church-yard, for there she lies.

And here's to the friend, the one friend of my youth,
With a head full of genius, a heart full of truth,
Who travelled with me in the sunshine of life,
And stood by my side in its peace and its strife!
Would you know where to seek a blessing so rare?
Go drag the lone sea, you may find him there.

And here's to a brace of twin cherubs of mine,
With hearts like their mother's, as pure as this wine,
Who came but to see the first act of the play,
Grew tired of the scene, and then both went away.
Would you know where this brace of bright cherubs have hied?
Go seek them in heaven, for there they abide.

A bumper, my boys! to a gray-headed pair,
Who watched o'er my childhood with tenderest care;
God bless them, and keep them, and may they look down
On the head of their son, without tear, sigh, or frown!
Would you know whom I drink to? go seek 'mid the dead,
You will find both their names on the stone at their head.

And here's — but, alas! the good wine is no more,
The bottle is emptied of all its bright store;
Like those we have toasted, its spirit has fled,
And nothing is left of the light that it shed.
Then, a bumper of tears, boys! the banquet here ends,
With a health to our dead, since we've no living friends.

TALES OF THE GOOD WOMAN appeared in 1829; and CHRONICLES OF THE CITY OF GOTHAM in 1830; each in one volume, and published by G. & C. & H. Carvill, New York. They contain several of our author's best stories, such as "Dyspepsy" and "The Politician", which, with some others, will form a volume of the forthcoming select edition of his works.

Sometime in the year 1830 Mr. James H. Hackett, the Falstaff of this century, and then known as a rising American comedian, offered a prize of three hundred dollars for "an original comedy whereof an American should be the leading character." For this prize he induced Mr. Paulding to compete, suggesting, as I learn from himself, the title of drama and hero; viz:, "The Lion of the West", and "Nimrod Wildfire." The drama was pronounced by the committee, composed of William Cullen Bryant, Fitz-Greene Halleck and Prosper M. Wetmore, the best offered for their consideration.

Before its production on the stage, (in 1831), I suppose that something of its character had leaked out, and that it had been by newspaper paragraphists trumpeted abroad as a take-off of David Crockett, then a member of the house of Representatives. At any rate it is evident from the following letter that about this time Mr. Paulding had written to that well-known personage, disclaiming any intention of the kind. The answer goes far to prove, that, though the Colonel may not have been perfect in his spelling or in the drill of the drawing room, he had the ring of the true metal in him.

TO J. K. PAULDING.

"WASHINGTON CITY. 22nd Decr. 1830.

Sir your letter of the 15 Inst was handed to mo this day by my friend Mr. Wilde — the newspaper publications to which you refer I have never seen; and if I had I should not have taken the reference to myself in exclusion of many who fill offices and who are as untaught as I am. I thank you however for your civility in assuring me that you had no reference to my peculiarites. The frankness of your letter induces me to say a declaration from you to that effect was not necessary to convince me that you were incapable of wounding the feelings of a strainger and unlettered man who had never injured you — your charecter for letters and as a gentleman is not altogather unknown to me.

I have the honour with
great respects &c —
DAVID CROCKETT."

As for the drama, I have found no traces of the original. Without doubt it was simply what Mr. Hackett styles it, "a vivid initial sketch." It was manipulated by Mr. J. A. Stone, an actor, the author of "Metamora," and, as a melodrama in four acts, was produced successfully by Mr. Hackett in all the larger cities of the Union. Subsequently, during his professional visit to England in the winter of 1832–3, it was re-adapted by Mr. Bayle Bernard, and, under the style of "A Kentuckian's trip to New York in 1815," "was produced at Covent Garden theatre, London, April 1833, made a hit, had a run of several weeks there and of about six weeks more thereafter at the Haymarket theatre."

Mr. Hackett goes on to say: "I have repeatedly acted the character in that drama in every principal city of the U. States with applause, and in every theatrical engagement I made for twenty years following; and it did not fail to amuse occasionally of later years, though most of its jokes had lost their point by the changes of time place and circumstances."

There must have been a certain force and freshness in the part, for it to have sustained itself so long. And such I gather to be the fact from the following quotation from The London Times, sent to me by Mr. Hackett. The critic is referring to the character of Nimrod Wildfire. "It is a pleasing one. He may be compared to an open-hearted, childish, giant, whom any one might deceive but none could daunt. His whimsical extravagance of speech arises from a mere exuberance of animal spirits; and his ignorance of the conventional restraints of society he overbalances by a heart that would scorn to do a mean or dishonest action."

Mr. Paulding was probably brought a good deal into connexion with theatrical folk about this time, and wrote, October 19th, 1831, to Irving, in reference to John Howard Payne, with whom his friend had been somewhat concerned in dramatic work. The "King Stephen" mentioned is Price, then (I think) manager of the Park theatre in New York.

We are trying to get up a benefit for John Payne here against his return, but King Stephen demurs, and says John is not worthy of it, being a borrower of money without paying, like many other honest gentlemen. The monarch has signalized his return to his ancient dominion by divers tyrannical and pragmatical capers, and has already injured the popularity of the theatre not a little. He is aiming at a system of economy, which you know is unpopular in all governments. The only person that as yet has been able to control the tyrant, as the story goes, is an old virago who scrubs the lobby, and, it is said, the other day made him retreat rather faster than became a gouty potentate. . . . I think Stephen will require a few protocols and non-interventions to keep him on his throne.

It does not appear that Mr. Paulding made any effort to follow up his dramatic success, if such it can fairly be called. He had little turn that way, and the appearance in this same year, 1831, of THE DUTCHMAN'S FIRESIDE, which made its mark at once, would naturally have reverted his mind into the old channels. This novel was published in two volumes by J. & J. Harper, New York. Republished in England, and translated into the French and Dutch languages, it has ever since maintained its favor with the public. Deservedly the most popular of our author's works, it will form part of the forthcoming reprint.

In 1832 appeared WESTWARD HO!, in two volumes, published by J. & J. Harper, New York. This novel is the story of a family of Virginia, broken down by prodigality in their old home, who remove with the wreck of their fortunes to Kentucky while it is yet a wilderness, and become wealthy again through the natural progress of the country.

The whole of the opening sketch of the magnifico of "The Old Dominion", and his establishment — his sixteenth cousin, his darkeys, his merchant — is capital in tone and handling. I have room but for the race which ruins him outright, and its immediate results.

Colonel Cuthbert Dangerfield is introduced, at first as deeply in debt, and gloomy in consequence.

"All at once, however, he seemed to rally again. A notice appeared in the public papers, under the signature of a noted gentleman-sportsman, offering to run his imported gray mare Lady Molly Magpie, four mile heats, at the next fall meeting, against all Virginia, for any sum from one to twenty thousand pounds, old currency. Colonel Dangerfield pricked up his ears; he had a famous horse yclept Barebones, who had long reigned lord of the Virginia course, and won him so much money, that he might have paid the Scotch merchant if he had not lost it all in betting on bay fillies, bright sorrels, and three year olds of his own breeding, all of whom had the misfortune to bolt, break down, or be distanced, to his great astonishment and mortification. He determined to accept the challenge, after which, as is usual with all wise men when they have made up their minds, he went to consult his wife on the matter."

In due time we have

THE RACE.

Time rolled on — the decisive hour approached — the worthy Mr. Littlejohn for once gathered himself together, cast aside the *vis inertiæ* with a mighty effort, and became a most indefatigable attendant on his illustrious friend Barebones, who was petted as never quadruped was petted before or since, except it might peradventure be a prize ox, a Teeswater bull, or a royal ram from the Rambouillet flock during the raging of the merino mania. It was now the charming month of October, when the earth and its foliage, the sky, its sun and stars, are so often shaded with a thin misty veil, that, while it obscures the face of nature, at the same time renders it more touchingly beautiful. All Virginia was in motion, from the alluvial to the primitive formation, from Chesapeake Bay to the Blue Ridge. The high-mettled cavaliers of the "Ancient Dominion" mounted their high-mettled steeds, anticipated the next year's crop of tobacco, and came with pockets richly lined; and many an ample estate long after rued the racing of that day. Nor must we omit to record that Mrs. Dangerfield took occasion to remind the Colonel, that, as it was possible he might lose his bet of twenty thousand pounds, his honour required that he should be prepared to pay on the spot. He accordingly once more wrote to his old friend the Scotch merchant, offering to give him a deed of trust for his whole estate if he would advance the sum of forty thousand pounds. The proposal was accepted, the deed executed, and the inheritance of six generations became subject to the disposition of a stranger.

At length the day arrived big with the fate of Lady Molly Magpie and Barebones, of Allen of Claremont and Dangerfield of Powhatan — and a glorious day it was. Previous to its arrival, Barebones had been escorted, with a dignity becoming the high destinies connected with his speed and bottom, to the neighbourhood of the racecourse. The colonel and Mr. Littlejohn rode on either side, while Barebones, richly caparisoned with a gorgeous blanket, and looking through a pair of holes, like an old gentleman through his spectacles, was led by uncle Pompey, or Pompey Ducklegs, as he was most irreverently nicknamed by the young ebonies, on the score of a pair of little bandy drumsticks, by the aid of which he waddled along after the fashion of that amphibious bird. Pompey claimed and received this post of honour by virtue of having once had the felicity of belonging to Lord Dunmore, the last royal governor of Old Virginia. He considered himself as a branch of the aristocracy, often boasted that he was one of the few gentlemen left in the Ancient Dominion, and never failed to lay all the blame of bad crops on the revolution. When he recollected that Molly Magpie was an "imported" horse, and a lady besides, his mind misgave him sorely, for he could scarcely bring himself to believe it possible that any animal foaled on this side the Atlantic had a chance of success against one so high bred and highly descended. "Dem *rebel* horse no bottom," thought Pompey. Close behind Pompey the Great rode Pompey the Little, his grandson, to whom the conduct of Barebones was to be intrusted in the coming contest between the houses of Claremont and Powhatan. He was dressed in a sky-blue jacket, red cap, and pantaloons of the same colour; and his black face presented a beautiful contrast to the ivory teeth which he ever and anon displayed in rows the brightest beauty in the land might have envied, as he recalled to mind the promise of his master, that, if he won the race, he would give him his freedom and a hundred a year for life. As thus they walked their horses slowly and majestically along, Pompey the Great would ever and anon turn round, shake his fist at Pompey the Little, and exclaim, "You young racksal, you no win dis here race, you disgrace you family—mind, I say so."

The race was to take place precisely at one o'clock, but long before the hour arrived the course was thronged with thousands of people in carriages, on horseback, and on foot, of all grades, sizes, ages, and colours. The day was delightful, the air inspiring, and the scene beautiful and lively beyond description. The racecourse was on an elevated table-land, which commanded a view of the city of Richmond, its imposing capitol (perhaps the most finely situated building in the United States), the turbulent rapids of the majestic river foaming and pelting its way among the rocks and islands fast anchored in the waves, and its quiet course beyond. It was a landscape which of itself might occupy the attention for hours. But the animation of the course rendered a long abstraction quite impossible. Gallant equipages every moment arriving, in which the pride of Virginia, her wives and daughters, displayed their fair and delicate countenances, — full-blooded horses champing the bit impatiently, and pawing the ground as if anxious to contest the prize of the day, or scouring the plain in all directions, like the winged Arabs of the desert, communicated indescribable gayety and interest to the scene. But the gayest of the gay, the happiest of the happy, the noisiest of the noisy, were the gentlemen of colour, young and old, to whom this was a holyday sanctioned by long prescription. Such a mortal display of ivory and crooked legs, such ecstatic gambols, such triumphant buffoonery, such inspiring shouts, such inimitable bursts of laughter, never were seen or heard among the grave, reflecting progeny of freedom; and the spectator might have been tempted to ask himself, "If these are not happy, at least at the present moment, where is happiness to be found?"

At twelve the champions appeared, and all was hushed. The knowing ones followed Barebones and Molly Magpie around the course, scanning them with a keen and critical eye, and making up their minds to bet on one or the other. The coloured rout thronged along the way, looking as wise as their betters, and giving their opinions in prophetic whispers, or climbed the trees and fences to witness the coming trial. Allen of Claremont and Dangerfield of Powhatan met and saluted each other with the dignified courtesy of two knights of chivalry on the eve of a joust in honour of their respective ladies; and it was singular to observe with what a degree of interest and almost sublimity the ownership of two such famous horses and the large sums at stake invested these two gallant cavaliers. The crowd followed them whithersoever they went, and where they were was the centre of attraction.

Tap—tap—tap! went the drum for the second time—the judges ascended the stand of judgment—the horses were brought to the starting pole champing and foaming, as if partaking in the feelings of their masters, and equally anxious for the event of the struggle. For our part we have no doubt that race horses are perfectly aware of the object for which they are contesting, and share in the triumph of victory. The judges were now standing with stop watches counting the minutes, and a breathless silence preceded the last tap of the drum. It was a scene of almost unequalled excitement, and in spite of all that may be said in disparagement of the sport, we neither blame those that encourage, nor those who partake in, its enjoyment, with due moderation.

Tap—tap—tap! went the drum for the third time. The riders were mounted, and the yellow cap and green vest of Allen of Claremont appeared side by side with the red cap and blue vest of Dangerfield of Powhatan. As Pompey the Great lifted Pompey the Little to the saddle, he repeated for the last time,

"Now you dem racksal, you no win dis race, you disgrace to you family."

The signal was given, and the two noble animals went off with a bound, as if they had suddenly been gifted with the wings of the wind. Now Molly Magpie, being the lighter and weaker of the two, gained upon Barebones, as they came to a little descending ground; and anon Barebones shot ahead, as they rose upon the ascent. The first two rounds continued thus alternately in favour of one or the other, the little red cap and the yellow appeared perched in the air, and the riders seemed hardly to touch the horses they rode. A dead and breathless silence held captive the crowd, and Allen and Dangerfield might be seen, each on a little eminence in the centre of the field, watching the struggle with a steady countenance and calm determined eye. The third round, Barebones decidedly took the lead: first a head, then a neck, then a whole body appeared in advance, and by the time they arrived at the goal, Barebones was computed to be ten lengths ahead of Molly Magpie. The assembled multitude shouted "Victory! Hurrah for Barebones!", and as for old Pompey, he scarcely waited for little red cap to be weighed after the heat, when he hugged him in his arms, and pronounced him an honour to his family.

The second heat was contested with equal obstinacy, but not with the like result; Molly Magpie came in ahead of Barebones, and the knowing ones began to hedge. Just at the moment of starting for the third and last heat, Allen of Claremont exclaimed, in a loud voice,

"Twenty thousand more on the gray mare!"

The temptation was irresistible.

"Done!" cried Dangerfield.

"Done!" cried Allen; and at that instant the horses started to decide the fortunes of the house of Powhatan. For the whole of the rounds you might have covered them both with a blanket, and nobody knew which had won, until the judges, after some consultation, decided in favour of Molly Magpie, by half a head. The same voices that had shouted and huzzaed for Barebones now shouted and huzzaed for Molly Magpie — such is the instability of popular applause; and it is recorded that Pompey the Great fought that day six pitched battles with certain gentlemen of colour, who belonged to the faction of the gray mare. Yet for all this he could not help saying to himself, "Eh! dem I spect so; dem rumpublican horse he no hold candle to tudder."

Dangerfield dined with the sporting club; toasted the winning horse, laughed his laugh, joked his joke, and received the compliments of many a sympathizing cavalier on the speed and bottom of Barebones, the conqueror of a hundred fields, with an air of careless self possession, that might have aspired to the honours of philosophy had the occasion been more worthy. He felt that he was a ruined man, but he was determined no one should penetrate his feelings, most especially Allen of Claremont.

"If it is inconvenient to you, colonel," said Allen.

"O, not in the least," said Dangerfield; and the debt was paid on the spot.

"Will you sell Barebones?"

"No, sir," replied the other, and abruptly turned away.

The next morning, the procession which set out with such exulting anticipations, returned home downcast and dejected, with the exception of the Colonel, who was determined to present a dignified front to Mrs. Dangerfield. Mr. Littlejohn, who had not uttered a single word since the loss of the race, rode carelessly on, scarcely holding his bridle which hung loosely on his horse's mane, and now and then casting his eye with a look of commiseration on his benefactor; old Pompey did nothing but shake his fist at little Pompey; and even Barebones seemed conscious of his defeat, for he slouched along with his head depressed, and had hardly spirit to brush away the flies with his tail.

The result of this disaster is a determination to emigrate to Kentucky, "the dark and bloody ground", and make a fresh start in life. Dangerfield notifies his cousin of these matters.

"When the colonel apprized him of the transfer of his property to Mactabb, and the intended emigration to Kentucky, he exclaimed, with uncontrollable emotion, 'My G—d!'; and burst into a passion of tears.

"His benefactor, who had never suspected him of so much feeling, endeavoured to comfort him, by suggesting a variety of topics of consolation. But it was all in vain; he continued to weep with a degree of convulsive agitation exceedingly painful. The long winter, which had frozen his feelings into ice, seemed to have broken up on a sudden, and the waters flowed forth scorning all restraint.

'Don't take on so, Ulysses,' said the colonel; 'I am not so poor but I can allow you something to live on when I am gone. Mactabb will receive you for a small allowance, and that I can spare without difficulty.'

'May the thunder and lightning strike Mactabb and all his race!' cried Littlejohn, suddenly checking his emotion, or rather turning it into another channel.

'Shame, Littlejohn, shame!—what has Mr. Mactabb done that you should set the thunder and lightning at him?'

'He's got Powhatan, d—n him!'

'Well, what of that? he came by it honestly.'

'I don't believe it. I don't believe it possible for one man to get the estate of another honestly. It stands to reason the Old Boy must help him, more or less.'

"The colonel could not forbear a smile at this theory of Mr. Littlejohn.

'The Old Boy sometimes helps people to get rid of an estate, I believe, as well as to get one. But I'll tell you what, Ulysses, I intend to give you Barebones. I can't bear to sell him.'

'Barebones, colonel!—I wouldn't have him if he carried a packsaddle of guineas; he's just fit to take a bag of corn to mill, and be hanged to him! Blame me if I believe in his pedigree.'

'You don't, Mr. Littlejohn? Let me tell you, sir—confound me, sir!—let me tell you, Mr. Littlejohn,'—and the colonel spoke between his shut teeth,—'that if your pedigree were as undoubted as that of Barebones, you might hold up your head a little higher than you do. Look here, sir,'—jerking out his pocket-book,—'look here, sir,'—taking out a piece of smokedried paper,—'look here, sir,'—unfolding it,—'dam, Kitty Fisher, sir; grandam, Slow and Easy, sir; great-grandam, Singed Cat, sir; great-great-grandam, Pettitoes, sir; great-great-great-grandam—'sblood! Mr. Littlejohn, I expect the next thing you do will be to call me the son of a tinker!'

"A moment after, the hand of Mr. Littlejohn was clasped in his own, for he remembered that Ulysses was a dependent, and himself his benefactor.

'Well, well, colonel, I'm sure I didn't mean to affront you; but that tobacco merchant has put me so out that I hardly know what I say. I beg your pardon for undervaluing poor Barebones.'

"This was the first time he had ever begged the colonel's pardon, and he did it now in compliment to his misfortunes."

Our author can never write many pages without his overpowering love of nature breaking forth, and these two volumes are not wanting in fine descriptions. The character and story of Bushfield, the backwoodsman, have something striking about them; and the election scene is full of life. The sketches of Western boatmen; of a village editor, and his wife, a village gossip; and of the itinerant preacher; though rough, are spirited. But the course of the story is painful, and, like most of the author's, it does not hang very closely together. It however ends happily.

I make but one more extract. The following oration of the old Frenchman of the old village—both passing away before the encroachments of the American people—is not only amusing, but suggestive.

"'Ah! monsieur,' said the landlord, an old remnant of the ancient régime: 'Ah! monsieur, the Yankee are one great people, but then she always so busy, busy, busy, morning, noon, and night. Diable! she don't give himselves time to say their prayers, I think. She come here among us, and she must ave new road: very well, the road is make at last. Eh bien! then she must ave a canal right long side of him, and everybody must give money for him. Very good, then we shall ave new streets, a new court-house, a new market, and a new church. So she come round for more money for that. Then she goes on, busy, busy, busy, never satisfied, more work, more money, and all for the dem publique good. Diable! I wonder what the publique ever do for me that I shall work for him as if he was the king himself? Well, monsieur, we ave got new road, new canal, new court-house, new market, and new church; and now I say to myself, ha, hah! I think she must ave satisfaccion at last. Phew! no such thing; she must ave town meeting to choose the police; then she must ave town meeting to choose the legislator; then she must ave town meeting to send the president and his bureau all to le diable, for something I don't know. Eh bien! all this done, I say ha hah! I shall dance and sing now a leetle. Phew! Morbleu, no such thing. Next time all this to do over again. The government machine out of order, she say, and must set it right again. So we go, year after year, making the grande improvement, and mending the government; and we Frenchmen, bongré, malgré, must do every thing de haute lutte, when we had much rather do nothing at all. Peste! that I shall be condemned to live in one dem country, always in want of improvement, under a government that always want mending. What you call? Ah! the dem self-government more trouble than she is worth, I think. For my part, monsieur, I like somebody shall take it off my hands, and let me dance a leetle some time."

## XV.

1832–1835. [ÆT. 54–57.]

LETTERS TO IRVING — CONTRACT WITH HARPER AND BROTHERS — LETTERS, TO BREVOORT AND IRVING — RANDOLPH OF ROANOKE.

AT the close of the year 1832 and beginning of the next we have several characteristic utterances of Mr. Paulding, in letters to Irving, then at Washington.

NEW YORK. Decr. 30, 1832.

A man by the name of Herring has applied to me for some particulars of your life and writings, to be used in a biography to accompany a likeness, for a publication called the National Portrait Gallery. Shall I respond to the villain?

And, in the succeeding one, (an answer to the former evidently having been received in the interim): —

January 7th, 1833.

You mistook me a little on the subject of the biography. I was applied to for facts, not to write the whole; but I have made interest to see the article before it is published, that I may if possible "restrain and aggravate" the fury of the writer, whose name I cannot learn.

A third closes with a threat. Whoever knew the two men will know also that this was indeed a dire menace.

March 7th, 1833.

When are you coming home? If you don't come soon we shall inflict another public dinner on you.

In 1833 and 1834 our author came before the public with no literary effort of any consequence. In November of the former year he entered into a contract with Harper and Brothers for the republication in uniform style of all his works then written; but circumstances prevented this from being ever fully carried out. The year 1834 renews the long-suspended correspondence with Brevoort, in a single letter addressed to him at Paris. Nothing exasperated Mr. Paulding so much as servility to foreign titles, and here he discharges himself, briefly, but very much to the point. The book he mentions I take to have been a translation into French of "Westward Ho!"

New York 26th March, 1834.

Dear Brevoort,

I thank you for the book, and especially for the pleasant letter which accompanied it. It is full of excellent matter, and realizes my ideas of how my excellent countrymen and countrywomen, with a few honorable exceptions like yourself, support the stern republican character abroad. There is not one in fifty that would not lick the dust at the foot of the Blood Royal.

He thus pleasantly refers to his friend's expected return.

Washington says you are coming home this spring. I am glad of it, because it will add one more of my old friends to the small number left, and because I think you ought to be here, to brighten the last few years of the good old couple at the good old home in the Bowery. They will grow young again.

I have mentioned that Mr. Paulding had, in his early experience at Washington, formed the acquaintance of John Randolph. They grew to like each other, and I find various allusions to their intercourse in our author's correspondence and memoranda. As early as February 28, 1816, he writes to Brevoort: —

I spent last evening with Jack Randolph, of whom I shall tell you something one of these days. We had much rare talk, and I could not help confessing, that, with all his weaknesses, he was one of the most delightful persons in the world. His conversation possesses a *piquancy*, as the French say, which I have met with nowhere else.

The promise in the above he makes good in the following letter, of March 26, 1816.

I have lately spent some choice evenings with Jack Randolph, who has treated me with singular attention since he found me out here. The other night Irving [William, no doubt] and I went over to Georgetown to beat up his quarters. We found him at least ten degrees below zero, a good deal indisposed, and I believe fancying himself much more so than he really was. At first it was rather so so — but at last we got him fairly up, with telling stories and talking about New York, where he was at college about twenty-seven years ago, and where he says he forgot all that he knew when he went there. He knows more of the *ancient* state of the city than any man I ever met with, and Irving and he fell tooth and nail at old recollections. . . .

In this way we went on, Randolph giving anecdote after anecdote, and story after story of some of the most distinguished men of this country. My memory is so bad that half of them have slipped away, and if they had not I could not do justice to the excellent dramatic manner in which they were given. . . . The time slipped away till almost twelve, and when we went away he thanked us for making him forget that he was sick when we came.

New York, October 19, 1831, he writes to Irving.

Our eccentric friend Randolph arrived here a few days ago,

apparently in the last stage of decay, but whether really so is more than I can tell, for he has seemed in this situation from the time I first knew him some thirty years ago.

Very late in life he made this memorandum: — "Gravity is not wisdom, nor merriment folly. I have known one man, at least, whose jests were often equal to the wisest precepts of philosophy, and that was JOHN RANDOLPH of Roanoke."

In the summer of 1835 "Letters from the South" were republished under the arrangement with Harper and Brothers, and with considerable alterations and additions. Among the latter was the character of John Randolph which I am about to quote. I have interpolated a few sentences from a newspaper sketch. It is well to remember that Randolph was born June 2, 1773, and died June 24, 1833. The characterization is referred to the year 1817.

### RANDOLPH OF ROANOKE.

Among the descendants of Pocahontas, the most remarkable are John Randolph and Bolling Robertson, each exhibiting in complexion and physiognomy indubitable traces of the common stock. The eyes of both are perfectly Indian — black, shining, and occasionally fierce. Indeed, I have never met with a man having a cross of the aboriginal, that did not show it like a blood-horse. The marks seem indelible, both in body and mind.

In my visit to Washington, four winters ago, it was my fortune to lodge in the same hotel with Mr. Randolph, and to be favored with his acquaintance, I might almost say his friendship, which, notwithstanding his alleged wayward disposition is, I am told, generally steadfast and sincere. He is certainly the most extraordinary personage I have known, and, on the whole, the greatest orator I have heard. There is wit in every thing he says, and eloquence at the very end of his long fingers. He is the last man in the world into whose hands I should wish to fall in a debate, for he cuts with a two-edged sword, and makes war like his Indian ancestors, sparing neither sex nor age. Yet his kindness is irresistible, and when he wishes to evince it, the tones of his voice and the expression of his eye go equally to the heart.

His style of oratory in Congress is emphatically his own. He is, indeed, original and unique in every thing. His language is simple, though polished; brief, though rich, and as direct as the arrow from the Indian bow. He often tides away, apparently, from his subject, but, however he may seem to drift without rudder or compass, never fails to return with a dash, illustrating it with flashes of living light. Though eccentric in the ordinary intercourse of life, there will be found more of what is called plain common-sense in his speeches than in those of any other member of Congress. His illustrations are almost always drawn from the most familiar sources, and no man is so happy in allusions to fables, proverbs, and incidents of the day. He never declaims, or sacrifices strength, clearness, and simplicity, to the more popular charms of redundant metaphor and full-rounded periods. He is abrupt, sententious, and laconic. Nothing, indeed, is more easy of comprehension than the expressed ideas of the great orator of Old Virginia. Though exceedingly irritable in debate, he is never loud or boisterous, but utters biting sarcasms in a manner the most provokingly cool, and a voice that suggests the music of the spheres. Such is the admirable clearness and perfection of his enunciation, that his lowest tones circulate like echoes through the hall of Congress. In short, in all the requisites of a great orator he has no superior; and, in the greatest of all, the power of attracting, charming, riveting the attention of an audience, no equal in this country.

Mr. Randolph has shared the fortune of most political leaders, in having his conduct misrepresented, his foibles — which, heaven knows, are sufficiently formidable — exaggerated, and his peculiarities caricatured, without remorse. The fault is, in a great measure, his own. He spares no adversary, and has no right to expect quarter from others. In this respect his fate may serve as a beacon, indicating the necessity of toleration in politics as well as religion. That he is capricious, and careless of wounding those for whom he has no particular regard, no one will deny. That he is impatient in argument, and intolerant of opposition, is equally certain; and the whole world knows that he is little solicitous to disguise his contempt or dislike.

But, whatever may be the defects of Mr. Randolph's temper, no one can question his lofty independence of mind, or his unsullied integrity as a public agent or a private gentleman. In the former character he has never abandoned his principles to suit any political crisis, and in the latter he may be emphatically called an honest man. His word and his bond are equally to be relied on — and as his country can never accuse him of sacrificing her interests to his own ambition, so no man can justly charge him with the breach of any private obligation. In both these respects he stands an illustrious example to a country in which political talents are much more common than political integrity, and where it is too much the custom to forget the actions of a man in admiration of his speeches.

Much of his peevishness may find its origin and excuse in his physical sufferings. Almost from boyhood he has not known the blessing of health, nor enjoyed even its anticipation. His constitution is irretrievably broken; and though he may live many years, they will, in all probability, be years of anxiety and suffering, imbittered not only by the absence of hope, but by the ridicule, instead of the sympathy, of the world, which is ever too apt to suppose that a man cannot be sick without dying. Men lingering under the slow consuming decay of a constitutional infirmity, and perishing, not by inches, but the hundredth parts of an inch, seem to me the most pitiable of the human race. The world, and even their nearest friends, come at last to believe their malady imaginary, their complaints without cause. They grow tired of hearing a man always proclaiming himself a victim to disease, yet at the same time appearing to take his share in the business, as well as the enjoyments, of society, and living on like the rest of his fellow-worms. "They jest at scars that never felt a wound," and the very circumstance that should excite additional commiseration, too often gives occasion to cold neglect or flippant ridicule.

In this painful and trying condition was Mr. Randolph when I saw him, and it is but fair to urge that some apology at least for his indifference to the feelings of others might be found in the harassing nature of his own. I know of no situation more aptly calculated to make a man a misanthrope; and those who are foremost and loudest in their condemnation, would do well to look into their own hearts, put themselves in his place, and then ask whether it does not naturally lead to, though it may not justify, occasional petulance, if not habitual ill-temper. I here speak of him as the world generally does. But so far as I saw him, and this was at all hours, he was full of benignity. His treatment of his servants, and especially of his own slaves, was that of the most indulgent master; and he always called his personal attendant "Johnny," which diminutive, to my mind, strongly indicated an habitual good-will toward them. It is thus we designate our familiar friends, and the children of our love. To me, from whose admiration or applause he could anticipate neither honor nor advantage, his behavior was uniformly kind, almost affectionate, and it will be long before I forget his melancholy, yet winning smile, the music of his voice, or the magic of his gentle manners.

We passed our evenings together for some weeks, or rather I may say the better part of our nights, for he loved to sit up late, because, as he was wont to say, the grave, not the bed, was *his* place of rest. On these occasions there was a charm in his conversation I never found in that of any other person. Old Virginia was the goddess of his idolatry, and of her he delighted to talk. He loved her so dearly, that he sometimes almost forgot he was also a citizen of the

United States. The glories and triumphs of Patrick Henry's eloquence, and the ancient hospitality of the patricians on James River, were among his favorite topics, of which he never tired, and with which he never tired me. In short, the impression on my mind, never to be eradicated, is, that his heart was naturally liberal, open, and gracious, and that his occasional ebullitions of splenetic impatience are the spontaneous, perhaps irrepressible, efforts of a debilitated frame, to relieve itself a moment from the impression of its own ceaseless worrying.

Mr. Randolph is, beyond comparison, the most striking person I have ever seen. He is made up of contradictions. Though his person is exceedingly tall, thin, and ill-proportioned, he is the most graceful man in the world when he pleases; and with an almost feminine voice, his whispers are heard across a room. When seated on the opposite side of the hall of Congress, he looks like a boy of fifteen; but when he rises to speak, he seems to stretch and expand his figure almost into sublimity, from the contrast between his height when sitting and standing. In the former, his shoulders are raised, his head sunk, his body collapsed; in the latter he is seen, his figure dilated, in the attitude of inspiration, his head raised, his long white finger pointing, and his dark Indian eye flashing at the object of his overwhelming sarcasm.

I regret to add, that this extraordinary man will, in all probability, survive but a few years. A premature decay seems gradually creeping, almost imperceptibly, over all his vital powers, and an irresistible, unseen influence, that baffles human skill and human means, appears to be dragging him like an inexorable creditor to the grave. At the age of forty-one or two, with wealth in possession, fame as his handmaid, and glory and power in bright perspective, he is a mere wreck of humanity; with light glossy hair parted over his forehead, and tied with a black ribbon behind; teeth white as ivory, eyes instinct with intellect, and a countenance seamed with innumerable wrinkles. At the distance of a hundred yards, he may be mistaken for an overgrown boy; approach him, and at every step his appearance changes, and he becomes gradually metamorphosed into a decrepit old man. You will then see a face such as you never have seen, never will see again; if he likes you, a smile such as you never beheld light up another visage; and when that passes away, a countenance wearing an expression of anxiety and suffering, that will make your heart ache if it never ached before.

Such is John Randolph, the descendant of Pocahontas, as he appeared to me. He may be self-willed, and erratic. His opponents sometimes insinuate that he is crazy, because he sees what they cannot see, and speaks in the spirit of inspiration of things to come. He looks into the clear mirror of futurity with an eye that never winks, and they think he is staring at some phantom of his own creation. He talks of things past their comprehension, and they pronounce him mad.

Would to Heaven there were more such madmen among our rulers and legislators, to make folly silent and wickedness ashamed; to assert and defend the principles of our revolution; to detect quack politicians, quack lawyers, and quack divines; and to afford to their countrymen examples of inflexible integrity both in public and private life.

# XVI.

1835–1836. [ÆT. 57–58.]

A LIFE OF WASHINGTON — A LEGEND OF THE BIRD'S NEST — THE TOMB OF WASHINGTON — THE CHARACTER OF WASHINGTON.

IN the winter of 1835–6 two small and unpretending volumes were published by Harper and Brothers, under the modest title of "A LIFE OF WASHINGTON. By James K. Paulding." They are at present kept in print in connexion with "The Family Library" of the original publishers. The Messrs. Duyckinck, in their "Cyclopædia of American Literature", thus characterize this work.

"It is an admirable production, and shows conclusively that the author is equally qualified for a different sphere of literature from that to which he has principally devoted himself. Though written with a steady glow of patriotism, and a full perception of the exalted character and services of the Father of his country, it is pure from all approaches to inflation, exaggeration, and bombast. The style is characterized by simplicity combined with vigor; the narrative is clear and sufficiently copious without redundancy, comprising all the important events of the life of the hero, interspersed with various characteristic anecdotes which give additional interest to the work, without degrading it to mere gossip, and is strongly imbued with the nationality of the author. Being addressed to the youthful reader, he frequently pauses in his narrative to inculcate the example of Washington's private and public virtues on his readers. The character of Washington, as summed up at the conclusion, is one of the most complete we have ever met with."

For this undertaking Mr. Paulding was, in one respect at least, eminently qualified. He was gifted with a thorough and sympathetic insight into the personality of Washington. Perhaps of all that have yet written his life he had the truest appreciation of *the man.* All his days, Washington was his model character.

In the Second Series of Salmagundi, in the number for January 19, 1820, he introduced a little narrative, which, if not strictly true, has a verisimilitude which almost dignifies it into the regions of authentic history. Certain details of this, as I learn from some remaining memoranda, were gathered at a very early period of his life. In the summer of 1861, at the solicitation of the late George P. Morris, I republished it in "The Home Journal", with other papers of my father's, prefacing it with some remarks, a portion of which I here reproduce.

"It may be worth while to state that this is not a mere fancy sketch. The scene is still to be recognized in the heart of the Highlands. The graves have not yet given up their tenants; the mouldering stones preserve their melancholy record; the old church partially maintains its ground, though about to be replaced by a new structure; and the house described is now 'The Bird's Nest,' so styled by Mr. John Brown, at one time its owner, and as great an oddity as ever lived, who will be remembered by old play-goers in

Boston in the character of Tony Lumpkin. Altered and added to, it is at present the residence of Upjohn, the architect. The road to this has been changed within a few years, but the ravine is as it was, and one of the old cherry-trees, a very patriarch of its race, yearly puts forth healthy leaves, among which other birds yet sing their unchanged notes. The water-course in front of the house now carries only a tiny rill, but the brook below still leaps its way to the lake-like river still sentinelled by the stately mountain heights.

"Colonel Beverly Robinson, in the right of Susannah, his wife, was the landlord under whom the tenancy was held. The old couple bore a name yet familiar to Highland ears as one of the most respectable in the county of Putnam.

"But we are not, at the present writing, sure that the author's recollections, or the old lady's perhaps confused reminiscences, have not betrayed him into an error in the statement that the house was used, (at all events for any length of time), as the quarters of General Putnam. As regards the concluding incident, there is no one living to give us any information, but we are satisfied that it rests upon some tradition picked up in the author's early experiences in Westchester county, and, through a pardonable freedom, interwoven with the present sketch."

Here follows the paper. I call it

### A LEGEND OF THE BIRD'S NEST.

"Who does not love to list the old wife's tale
Of former days, told in her rambling way,
And full of repetitions — yet most rare,
And worthy of the ear of list'ning youth,
Gathered about the rousing winter's fire?"

I love to talk with old people who remember the

revolutionary war, and hear them tell those stories of domestic heroism, of solitary and patient suffering, they have treasured in their memories, and which escape the notice of the historian. It is from these rural chronicles that we often gather trivial incidents that let us into the true characters of illustrious men, who, when in public, act before the great audience of nations, but who, in the solitary farm-house, or rural village, among people too lowly to be any restraint upon their actions or deportment, appear in their night-gown and slippers. The little drama, thus simply exhibited in the unstudied narrative of talking age, to me is far more interesting than pompous details of fallen empires or dethroned kings, whose weakness or ambition, whose follies or crimes, drew down upon them the ruin they deserved.

Besides exhibiting more of the real picture of human life than a hundred swelling biographies of dead or living heroes, these traditionary narratives combine the simplicity of truth with the interest of romance and the beauty of poetry, which are indebted to this source for a great portion of their most charming incidents. There is also another advantage in this legendary lore which history seldom possesses. History is for the most part hearsay; tradition, like the witness in a court of justice, relates what it has seen, and the impressions communicated to the listener are those of the actor or the spectator himself.

In one of the romantic and sequestered scenes that abound along the banks of the Hudson, resided, a few years ago, an old woman, who, though above four-score, had retained all her faculties, and especially the faculty of speech. The house in which she lived had been the quarters of General Putnam, during that gloomy winter in which our army lay in the Highlands, and had often been honored with the presence of WASHINGTON. It was a large farm-house, that, having never been contaminated with paint, retained a truly Quaker-like simplicity; and was so little an object of respect to the tenants of the farm-yard, that the chickens made no ceremony in coming in and picking up the crumbs that fell from the good man's table. It was of considerable length, one story high, and its whole appearance accorded with the homely, careless simplicity which still characterizes the establishment of an honest, independent, American farmer.

Before the door ran a mountain-brook, which, in its rapid course toward the river, had ploughed a deep ravine, whose sides were covered with grass, and skirted by a row of English cherry-trees almost a century old. Here hundreds of chirping birds came to steal cherries, and sing their merry madrigals undisturbed; for the old lady had more than she wanted, and so had her neighbors, so that there was enough for birds and all. Below the house the brook became a torrent, and forced its way among immense masses of rocks shadowed with dark hemlocks and solemn pines, with now and then a wild flower trembling on the brink of the steep, and by a succession of cascades at length tumbled into the river, forming a little cove of alders, and all the tribes of shrubbery that love the fresh water-side.

The whole landscape was shut in by lofty mountains, woody and waving, at whose foot rolled the majestic stream, which was seen here and there, like a cluster of little lakes reposing in the cool shadows of the hills. Within about a half mile of the house was a singular-looking church, which, though neither picturesque nor magnificent nor antique, gave a cast of greater dignity to the scene, by connecting the glorious works of the Creator with the grateful homage of his humble creatures. I remember going there one Sunday morning, some years ago, and being struck with the rustic simplicity not only of the church but also of the preacher, the service, and indeed the whole congregation. But what most excited my attention was the good dame who is the heroine of this story. She sat in a pew, close by an open window which looked into a corner of the burial-ground, where, under more than a dozen gravestones, reposed the remains of all that portion of the family which she had survived. Here lay her parents, her children, and grandchildren; here she could receive a sad, impressive, lesson of the inevitable fate of all that breathe; and here she doubtless reconciled herself to her own, by the cheering hope that she was going to meet more dear friends than she would leave behind her when she died.

Being accustomed to visit an old and hospitable friend whose mansion is not far from the place I have been describing, I formed an acquaintance with the worthy dame by often stopping in my rambles, to rest myself, and listen to her stories about WASHINGTON and Putnam, and other revolutionary heroes of less note. For fear my frequent visits may excite a little scandal among some of my gossiping readers, I may as well take this oportunity to mention, that she had a husband at the time of which I am speaking, who was older than herself. He died a few years ago;

and all that I remember of him is, that he was a little old man, with a head as white as the winter snow on the tops of his native mountains, and that at the age of eighty he used to turn out of a frosty morning to cut up a load of wood by way of exercise.

My chief pleasure in the society of this aged dame consisted in hearing her talk of the great names that frequented her home "in the war-time." I would give much if I carried in my memory some, even remote, recollection of how WASHINGTON walked, and looked, and smiled, and danced — for he was accustomed, during his arduous struggle for the freedom of his country, to relax from his weight of overwhelming cares by often going down a sprightly country dance. I am acquainted with a lady who was frequently his partner, and whom I look upon with peculiar veneration on that account, since, to have been in habits of social intimacy with that man, is, in my mind, sufficient to give dignity to his surviving cotemporaries. Nay, I freely confess, I have sometimes found it in my heart to envy even the worn-out, ragged, and crippled soldier of the revolution, on witnessing the honest pride with which he boasted of having fought for the liberties of his country by the side of GEORGE WASHINGTON. Having once in my life had an opportunity of visiting Mount Vernon, since the death of him whose presence has consecrated every spot around and given to the very trees and blades of grass a nameless value, I paid particular respect to the old German gardener, who bragged of having raised cauliflowers for the General; and got out of the carriage at the park gate on purpose to shake hands with the gray-headed negro who opens it, because he told me he remembered Master George when he was a little boy.

Such being the nature of my feelings on this subject, I used to listen with silent interest to the rambling traditions of this sibyl of the Highlands. Her family, I ought to have mentioned, had been, for more than half a century, the tenants of a gentleman who joined the royal standard at the commencement of the troubles, and forfeited his estate in consequence. Though warmly attached to the cause of freedom, it was natural for the good dame to lament, as she often did, the worthy landlord, who had always been sociable at the house, and treated her and hers with those little attentions which cost nothing to those above yet are so gratifying to those beneath. She would occasionally sneer at the upstart pride of those who had succeeded him, and I remember her once pathetically alluding to the period when the parson never began the service till the lord of the manor made his appearance. In short, she still cherished in her heart, unknown to herself, a latent spark of toryism; and while she missed no opportunity of telling a story to the credit of WASHINGTON, could never be brought to use any other prayer-book than one given her by the old landlord, which contained all the prayers for King George and the royal family.

But for all this, WASHINGTON was her hero. She had a picture of him hung up just below her best looking-glass, and whenever she looked that way, it reminded her of something the General said or did, or some event of those doleful times when the foot of an enemy pressed almost every threshold in the land. She would look at the picture with the affection of a mother, and exclaim:—"Ah! he was a good man. I remember he used to come over sometimes, nay, very often, to talk over matters with General Putnam, who had his quarters here. If ever man loved his country, it was General WASHINGTON. I could tell, but I am old, and lose my memory every day—I could tell of his perplexities, his watchings, cares, and sufferings of mind and body, which I believe he never let any one see but myself; and I shall never forget his kindness when I lost my youngest son. My boy was quite a hero among the young men of the hills, and night after night used to go out with parties of militia, beating up the plundering *Yagers* that came from below and carried away every thing they could find, to the ruin of many of our poor people, who stayed between the lines because they were old, and knew not where else to go.

"One night—it was the twentieth of January—I can recollect *that*—in the dead of night, my son and his little troop were surprised in turn by a party from below, while warming themselves in a house, which the enemy surrounded in black silence and then set on fire. In attempting to escape they were all butchered by the *Yagers*, who hacked them down, though they begged for quarter. The next day, while I was out at a neighbor's house, my son's body was brought home by some people who knew him; and when I returned, there I saw it, with the blood frozen in the gashes with which he was covered.

"I don't remember what became of me till I found myself sitting in our old arm-chair, and the General standing just by, with his hat in one hand and the other resting on the back of the chair. 'Mother,' said he, when he saw I was come to myself—'Mother'—and the word made me so proud I almost forgot what had happened—'Mother—you have given a son to your country—a brave man to his God. Go now to your room, I will see every thing done.' I went, for no one could say nay to him when he soothed or commanded, and they buried my boy like a soldier. The troops fired, while the General himself stood over the grave, and the pride of a mother almost overcame her affection. Time, hardships, and more sorrows that succeeded each other for years afterward, drove away the bitterness of this bereavement; although when the floor was washed, or the sun shone bright upon it, we could see the stain of blood where the body had lain. I can talk of these things now, for when I think of the death of my son, I remember also that he died in the service of his country, and his country's father followed him to his grave."

In the republication of "Letters from the South" in the summer of 1835, he has expressed the feelings aroused by a visit to the original burial-vault at Mount Vernon.

THE TOMB OF WASHINGTON.

You have had so many descriptions of this illustrious spot, that I shall confine myself to a detail of my impressions on contemplating the simple tomb where repose the remains of a man who has left behind him a fame more enviable than that of any mere mortal that ever breathed the breath of life. If it were mine, I would not exchange it for all the vainglories of all the conquerors and destroyers of mankind, from Sesostris down to Napoleon.

The tomb is situated on the summit of the high bank of the Potomac, and commands a view of the fine expansion of the river below. It partakes of the sobriety of Washington's character. A pathway, walled on either side, leads you to a plain door of wood imbedded in brick-work, over which, in the rear, rises a hillock covered with trees. This is all. At first my impressions were those of disappointment, at the absence of art and decoration. But a better feeling came over me, and soon I felt the inspiration of this touching simplicity stealing into my inmost soul. I forgot every thing before me, and remembered only the man. There was no majestic work, impudently obtruding itself, to draw off my attention toward the triumph of art and set me to criticising the taste and genius of the artist; there was nothing, in short, to impair the single idea of Washington. His life and actions passed swiftly in review before me, as I sat with my eyes riveted on the door that inclosed his sacred dust; and that pure, unmixed, complete character, "without fear and without reproach," gradually embodied itself in my fancy. The silence and repose of the scene was profound, except that now and then the little birds, that had made their nests in the clump of trees which overshadowed the tomb, chirped over my head. It was a calm, sultry, autumnal morning; the leaves were unruffled by a single breath of air, and the wide expanse of the river below was all one glassy mirror, burnished by the rays of as bright a sun as ever shone in the heavens.

Could the proudest creations of art add interest or dignity to such a scene? I felt they could not; that it was out of the power of man to embellish what nature had made so perfect, or to ennoble the moral excellence of him whose glory I was contemplating. He stands by himself, occupying a position which few will ever approach; his glory is without spot or stain; his whole life one uninterrupted virtue. In the midst of the most harassing vicissitudes, with the destinies of this New World on his shoulders — in the depths of almost hopeless adversity, when the fate of his country hung, day after day, year after year, suspended by a single hair — he was a hero. When, having won for his country the prize for which he had so long contended, it was in his power to appropriate it to his own purposes, he was a patriot. And when placed, by the united voice of the civilized world, on the pinnacle of human glory, he was a sage. His head neither turned, nor did his heart become corrupt. He sailed along, like the eagle, easily and gracefully, in the highest heaven — majestic, without effort or affectation; and while the eyes of mankind were upon him, never for a moment forgot he was but a man.

Such a being, thought I, wants no monument. While his name is in the mouths of devoted millions; while his virtues are embodied in every page of the history of his country; and while his glory accompanies the rising sun through his daily course from east to west — to what purpose pile masses of marble upon his bones? He who had no parallel in his life, should have none after death. Others have become illustrious by their tombs; let it be his distinction to owe no part of his glory to marble, architects, or statuaries. The truly great may be safely left to history, poetry, and tradition. Let him, then, enjoy the privilege of sleeping undisturbed in the midst of his kindred ashes. There let him rest in peace, embalmed in imperishable glory, till the trumpet shall sound, and the dead of thousands of years arise to judgment.

But, as for monuments, there is a better evidence of our veneration for him. It lies in preserving the liberties he bequeathed us, and, as far as possible, sailing in the bright wake he has left behind him.

Finally, in this "Life," published late in 1835 or early in 1836, and written, as the Preface declares, for the youth of the country, Mr. Paulding gives his matured views. We have Washington in the time of darkness and doubt:—

"The picture presented to my imagination is that of a lofty and expanded mind, struggling with difficulties, not for an hour or a day, but through a series of years, each one increasing the weight of his anxieties, and investing him with still more insuperable difficulties. He was indeed a man of many cares, perplexities, disappointments, and sufferings; and nothing could have supported him in these endless trials of his patience and his fortitude, his body and his mind, but that consciousness of duty which is founded on the rock of ages, animated and inspired by a patriotism which nothing could shake or undermine. With him the animating principle was neither the love of glory nor the ambition of power. His station for a long while offered him no hope of the one, no present possession, and scarcely any anticipation, of the other. Many is the time, no doubt, that, instead of glory, he looked forward to exile, or an ignominious death; and instead of the wreath of victory, anticipated a crown of thorns. The conquerors of kingdoms and the desolators of the world fade into utter insignificance when brought face to face with the man of our pride, our affections, and our reverence; and far greater, as well as far more an object of admiration and love does he appear, to my mind, in the midst of disaster and defeat, than did Cæsar when making his triumphal entry into the capital of the world, laden with the spoils and followed by the captives of a hundred nations of barbarians."

And here is the hour of Washington's triumph.

"At the dead of the night, a watchman in the streets of Philadelphia was heard to cry out, 'Past twelve o'clock, and a pleasant morning — Cornwallis is taken.' All but the dead resting in their last sleep awoke at this glorious annunciation. The city became alive at midnight; the candles were lighted, and figures might be seen flitting past the windows, or pushing them up, to hear the sound repeated, lest it should have been nothing but a dream. The citizens ran through the streets to inquire into the truth; they shook hands, they embraced each other, and they wept for very gladness. None slept again that night, and the dawn of the morning, which brought new confirmation of the happy tidings, shone on one of the most exulting cities that ever basked in the sunshine of joy.

"The news ran like fire on the prairies along every road, and through every by-place of the land. It seemed to fly on the wings of the wind, or to be borne by some invisible messenger. No one could tell from whence it came, but it came invested with a charm that rendered confirmation unnecessary. Everybody believed it, for all, even in the darkest days of the Revolution, had cherished a hope, which carried with it almost the force of inspiration, that Washington would, beyond all doubt, one day give liberty to his country. That hour was now come, and the souls of the people expanded with unutterable joy. For years they had stared misery in the face, and suffered in its iron grasp. They had reaped many harvests of bitterness, and they now expected to reap those of peace and plenty. They had passed through the dark valley of the shadow of death, and were now about to emerge into the regions of light. There was but one single and united voice throughout the whole land, and that shouted the name of Washington, Deliverer of his Country."

I close with the last pages of the work.

"In analyzing the character of Washington, there is nothing that strikes me as more admirable than its symmetry. In this respect it is consummate. His qualities were so nicely balanced, so rarely associated, of such harmonious affinities, that no one seemed to interfere with another, or predominate over the whole. The natural ardor of his disposition was steadily restrained by a power of self-command which it dared not disobey. His caution never degenerated into timidity, nor his courage into imprudence or temerity. His memory was accompanied by a sound, unerring judgment, which turned its acquisitions to the best advantage; his industry and economy of time did not render him dull or unsocial; his dignity never was vitiated by pride or harshness, and his unconquerable firmness was free from obstinacy or self-willed arrogance. He was gigantic, but at the same time he was well-proportioned and beautiful. It was this symmetry of parts that diminished the apparent magnitude of the whole; as in those fine specimens of Grecian architecture, where the size of the temple seems lessened by its perfection. There are plenty of men who become distinguished by the predominance of one single faculty, or the exercise of a solitary virtue; but few, very few, present to our contemplation such a combination of virtues unalloyed by a single vice; such a succession of actions, both public and private, in which even his enemies can find nothing to blame.

Assuredly he stands almost alone in the world. He occupies a region where there are, unhappily for mankind, but few inhabitants. The Grecian biographer could easily find parallels for Alexander and Cæsar, but were he living now, he would meet with great difficulty in selecting one for Washington. There seems to be a height of moral excellence, which, though possible to attain to, few ever approach. As in ascending the lofty peaks of the Andes, we at length arrive at a line where vegetation ceases, and the principle of life seems extinct; so in the gradations of human character, there is an elevation which is never attained by mortal man. A few have approached it, and none nearer than Washington.

He is eminently conspicuous as one of the great benefactors of the human race, for he not only gave liberty to millions, but his name now stands, and will for ever stand, a noble example to high and low. He is a great work of the almighty Artist, which none can study without receiving purer ideas and more lofty conceptions of the grace and beauty of the human character. He is one that all may copy at different distances, and whom none can contemplate without receiving lasting and salutary impressions of the sterling value, the inexpressible beauty, of piety, integrity, courage, and patriotism, associated with a clear, vigorous, and well-poised intellect.

Pure, and widely disseminated as is the fame of this great and good man, it is yet in its infancy. It is every day taking deeper root in the hearts of his countrymen and the estimation of strangers, and spreading its branches wider and wider to the air and the skies. He is already become the saint of liberty, which has gathered new honours by being associated with his name; and when men aspire to free nations, they must take him for their model. It is, then, not without ample reason that the suffrages of mankind have combined to place Washington at the head of his race. If we estimate him by the examples recorded in history, he stands without a parallel in the virtues he exhibited, and the vast, unprecedented consequences resulting from their exercise. The whole world was the theatre of his actions, and all mankind are destined to partake sooner or later in their results. He is a hero of a new species: he had no model; will he have any imitators? Time, which bears the thousands and thousands of common cut-throats to the ocean of oblivion, only adds new lustre to his fame, new force to his example, and new strength to the reverential affection of all good men. What a glorious fame is his, to be acquired without guilt, and enjoyed without envy; to be cherished by millions living, hundreds of millions yet unborn! Let the children of my country prove themselves worthy of his virtues, his labours, and his sacrifices, by reverencing his name, and imitating his piety, integrity, industry, fortitude, patience, forbearance, and patriotism. So shall they become fitted to enjoy the blessings of freedom and the bounties of heaven."

# XVII.

1836–1838. [ÆT. 58–60.]

SLAVERY IN THE UNITED STATES — OF NEWSPAPERS — THE BOOK OF ST. NICHOLAS — THE WOOING OF — THE DEATH OF — LETTERS TO KEMBLE.

IN 1836 Mr. Paulding published, with the imprint of Harper and Brothers, a small volume entitled SLAVERY IN THE UNITED STATES. The *animus* of the book may be considered as given in a single sentence of the Introduction. "It will be perceived, in the course of the following discussion, that the writer does not consider slavery, as it exists in the United States, an evil of such surpassing enormity as to demand the sacrifice of the harmony and consequent union of the states, followed by civil contention and servile war, to its removal."

This work it were idle now to dwell upon. Events have superseded opinions; and we have all cause to be thankful that a terrible question has, partially at least, disposed of itself.

I find in a letter to Irving, in this year, an explanation of our author's habit of writing for the newspapers, which is worthy of every man's consideration.

Since however it appears inevitable that the newspapers are to give the tone to public opinion, it would seem desirable that they should be influenced if possible by those who will give them a proper direction. If men of good principles keep aloof from all participation in newspapers, they will naturally fall into the hands of interested, factious, and unprincipled demagogues, and become sheer instruments of mischief. In no other country has the daily press such a wide influence, and I don't know what will become of us if that influence is directed by men without talent or principles.

At the close of the year 1836, or some time in 1837, appeared THE BOOK OF SAINT NICHOLAS, "translated from the original Dutch of Dominie Nicholas Aegidius Oudenarde." The title page bears the date 1836. The copyright was taken out on the 25th of February, 1837. The "Dedication" "To the Societies of Saint Nicholas in The New Netherlands, commonly called New York", is dated "Nieuw-Amsterdam, July, 1827"—no doubt a misprint. It is not improbable that the volume was prepared for the holidays of 1836, delayed, held back, and issued for those of 1837. It is the impression of the Messrs. Harper, the publishers, that it was chiefly made up of stories previously printed in a fugitive shape.

As its title implies, this book deals, for the most part, with legends of the patron Saint of New York. Premising that he is represented as having been apprenticed to a baker, I quote from the first paper this account of his wooing:—

"Little Nicholas, our hero, was a merry, sweet-tempered caitiff, which was, doubtless, somewhat owing to his living almost altogether upon sweet things. He was marvellously devoted to cakes, and ate up numberless gingerbread alphabets before he knew a single letter.

"Passing over the intermediate years, of which, indeed, I know no more than the man in the moon, I come to the period when, being twenty-four, and the term of his apprenticeship almost out, he fell desperately in love with the daughter of his worthy master, who was a burgomaster of forty years standing. In those unprecocious times, the boys did not grow to be men and the girls women, so soon as they do now. It would have been considered highly indecent for the former to think of falling in love before they were out of their time, or the latter to set up for young women before they knew how to be any thing else. But as soon as the worthy Nicholas arrived at the age of twenty-four, being, as I said, within a year of the expiration of his time, he thought to himself that Katrinchee, or Catharine as the English call it, was a clever, notable little soul, and eminently calculated to make him a good wife. This was the main point in the times of which I am speaking, when people actually married without first running mad either for love or money.

"Katrinchee was the toast of all the young bakers of Amsterdam, and honest Nicholas had as many rivals as there were loaves of bread in that renowned city. But he was as gallant a little Dutchman as ever smoked his way through the world pipe foremost, and did not despair of getting the better of his rivals, especially as he was a great favourite with the burgomaster, as, indeed, his conduct merited. Instead of going the vulgar way to work, and sighing and whining out romance in her ear, he cunningly, being doubtless inspired by Cupid himself, proceeded to insinuate his passion, and make it known by degrees to the pretty Katrinchee, who was as plump as a partridge, and had eyes of the colour of a clear sky.

"First did he bake a cake in the shape of a heart

pierced half through by a toasting fork, and presented it to her, smoking hot; the which she received with a blush and did eat, to his great encouragement. A month after, for he did not wish to alarm her delicacy, he did bake another cake in the shape of *two* hearts entwined prettily with a true lover's knot. This too she received with a blush, and did eat with marvellous content. After the expiration of a like period, he did contrive another cake in the shape of a letter, on which he had ingeniously engraven the following couplet:—

'Wer diesen glauben wöhlt hat die vernanft verschworen,
Dem denken abgesaght sein eigentham verlohren.'

If the reader comprehendeth not the meaning of this, I do hereby earnestly advise him to set about studying the Dutch language forthwith, that he may properly appreciate its hidden beauties.

"Little Katrinchee read this poesy with a sigh, and rewarded the good Nicholas with a look which, as he afterward affirmed, would have heated an oven.

"Thus did the sly youth gradually advance himself in the good graces of the damsel, until at length he ventured a downright declaration, in the shape of a cake made in the exact likeness of a little Dutch Cupid. The acceptance of this was conclusive, and was followed by permission to address the matter to the decision of the worthy burgomaster, whose name I regret hath not come down to the present time.

"The good man consulted his pipe, and after six months' hard smoking, came to the conclusion that the thing was feasible. Nicholas was a well-behaved, industrious lad, and the burgomaster justly decided that the possession of virtuous and industrious habits without houses and lands, was better than houses and lands without them. So he gave his consent, like an honest and ever-to-be-respected magistrate.

"The news of the intended marriage spoiled all the loaves baked in the city that day. The young bakers were so put out that they forgot to put yeast in their bread, and it was all heavy. But the hearts of the worthy Nicholas and his bride were as light as a feather notwithstanding, and when they were married it was truly said there was not a handsomer couple in all Amsterdam.

"They lived together happily many years, and nothing was wanting to their felicity but a family of chubby boys and girls. But it was ordained that he never should be blessed with any offspring, seeing that he was predestined to be the patron and benefactor of the children of others, not of his own. In good time, and in the fullness of years, the burgomaster died, leaving his fortune and his business to Nicholas, who had ever been a kind husband to his daughter, and a dutiful son to himself. Rich and liberal, it was one of the chief pleasures of the good Nicholas to distribute his cakes, of which he baked the best in all Amsterdam, to the children of the neighourhood, who came every morning, and sometimes in the evening; and Nicholas felt his heart warm within his bosom when he saw how they ate and laughed, and were as happy as, ay, and happier than, so many little kings. The children all loved him, as did their fathers and mothers, so that in process of time he was made a burgomaster, like his father-in-law before him."

There is a simple pathos in the description of the Saint's death, and its effect on his fellow-citizens.

"The illustrious visitor staid all night; and the next morning, as he was about to depart, the aged Nicholas said to him,

'Farewell — I shall never see thee again. Thou art going a long journey, thou sayest, but I am about venturing on one yet longer.'

'Well, be it so,' said the other. 'But those who remain behind will bless thy name and thy memory. The little children will love thee, and so long as thy countrymen cherish their ancient customs thou wilt not be forgotten.'

"They parted, and the prediction of the good Nicholas was fulfilled. He fell asleep in the arms of Death, who called him so softly, and received him so gently in his embrace, that though his family knew he slept they little thought it was forever.

"When this news went abroad into the city, you might see the worthy burgomasters and citizens knocking the ashes out of their pipes, and putting them quietly by in their button-holes; and the good housewives ever and anon lifting their clean white aprons to their eyes, that they might see to thread their needles, or find the stitches as they sat knitting their stockings. The shops and schools were all shut, the day he was buried; and it was remarked that the men neglected their usual amusements, and the children had no heart to play."

There are several of the little stories in this collection that are sprightly and spirited. But I am obliged to pass them by.

In 1837 we come upon a correspondence between James K. Paulding and his friend and brother-in-law, Gouverneur Kemble, then a member of the House of

Representatives. The first preserved, dated New York, 14th Sept, 1837, ends in this characteristic style: —

Gertrude and the boys are with Mrs. Philipse, [widow of "the chieftain", and now residing at Tarrytown Westchester County, on the Tappaan Zee], whose situation the more I see the more I admire. The other moonlight night, I walked the piazza with a segar, and as I looked out on the glorious bay glittering in the moonbeams, its shores fretted with dark woody points projecting into the waters, impressions such as I had thought buried forever under the rubbish of years awoke in my heart, and I felt young again. I am going up this afternoon. We are invited to a *Tableau Vivant* I think they call it, this evening at Mr. C.'s, where I shall figure in a satin embroidered jacket that I flatter myself will put Master Wash's nose out of joint. The fellow has a seraglio of dowagers about him, whose flattery would turn the head of any man not hardened into indifference by the frequent repetition of the dose.

Adieu. Write often and believe me

Yours always

J. K. PAULDING.

He writes again, New York, 2d February, 1838: —

My dear Gouv,

I sympathize with you in the anticipated necessity of making a speech. It is a thing of habit exclusively, and the great obstacle to success is too great a flow of ideas, without a sufficiency of words to express them. Now a man can do without ideas in Congress, but a want of words is the deuse and all.

Here is an allusion to literary matters in his usual tone of philosophy, under date of New York, 3d March, 1838.

You must excuse my bad writing. An accident many years ago to the little finger of my right hand is becoming more and more perceptible, and the finger becomes inactive after writing a few lines. I regret this exceedingly, as it destroys all the pleasure of writing. Perhaps it is all for the best, and may be the means — under Providence, as the pious ones say — of saving me from the common fate of authors, namely, that of trifling away in old age all the earnings of youth.

# XVIII.

1838–1840. [ÆT. 60–62.]

SECRETARY OF THE NAVY — LETTERS, TO KEMBLE, IRVING, AND BREVOORT — A GIFT FROM FAIRY LAND — LETTER FROM GREENOUGH, THE SCULPTOR — THE MAINE BOUNDARY — JOHN FORSYTH, OF GEORGIA — STEAM — HEMP — TRAVEL — POLITICS — PHILOSOPHY.

IN May of the year 1838 Mr. Paulding was offered the position of Secretary of the Navy in the Cabinet of Mr. Van Buren; which, after some hesitation, he accepted. There are a number of references to this in his letters to Gouverneur Kemble. For example: —

NEW YORK. 11th May, 1838.

I doubt my capacity for the situation; but I have found in every new station I have occupied, the difficulties vanish before me, and a man knows not what he can do till he tries.

NEW YORK. 16th May, 1838.

I received your letter inclosing that from the President, which could not but be gratifying to my feelings. I yesterday accepted the offer, and await the result with Christian resignation.

NEW YORK. 17th May, 1838.

In thinking, as I do almost all day long, on the step I have taken, I am extremely doubtful whether I have not done a foolish thing. But of the results of acts done with honest and honorable motives no man should be afraid, and so I have made up my mind to meet all the consequences to be anticipated by one who has more than fulfilled the wishes of his enemies, by writing twenty books instead of one.

Mr. Paulding's commission bears date June 25th,

1838, and I presume he entered at once on his duties. Previous to this, viz., on the 15th June, 1838, he wrote to Kemble from New York, blowing out, as I suppose, against Osceola, the Seminole chief.

How is Poinsett [Secretary of War] getting along? I hope he is quite recovered, and that he will be soon rid of the Indian heroes. I say heroes, for it seems only necessary for a bloody Indian to break his faith; plunder and burn a district or two; massacre a few hundred soldiers; and scalp a good number of women and children; to gain immortal honour. He will be glorified in Congress; canonized by philanthropists; autographed, and lithographed, and biographied, by authors, artists, and periodicals; the petticoated petitioners to Congress will weep, not over the fate of the poor white victims, but that of the treacherous and bloody murderer, who will receive his apotheosis in the universal sympathy of all the humble echoes and hypocritical followers of that prince of hypocrites old Johnny Bull. There, I feel a little cooler after this explosion.

Mr. Paulding of course soon found that he had not removed into a bed of roses. He writes to Irving from Washington, 30th July, 1838, specifying sundry annoyances, and goes on thus: —

My young midshipmen and lieutenants too, are extremely bilious at this season of the year, and when I order them in service answer me by a request for permission to accompany mamma to the White Sulphur Springs for their health. I am as you know a pretty obstinate fellow, and have already begun to let them know that these things will no longer be permitted. . . . And I am in hopes by degrees to realize some of the expectations which the nation so liberally anticipates from me, God knows why. . . . On the whole however I don't regret the step I have taken, and though my labors are heavy, it surprises me to find the mornings pass away so swiftly. I cannot sufficiently regret that the death of Dusky Davy Longworth prevents me from testifying my grateful recollection of his excellent hot cakes the which he dispensed so liberally in his little backroom, by making him a chaplain in the Navy. But he has slipped through my fingers, and I must endeavor to quiet my conscience by doing something for that most amiable rascal, his son Tom.

The letter concludes with an allusion to Irving's improvements near Tarrytown.

Farewell my dear Washington. May your trees grow like unto Jack's beanstalk, and the blessing due to him who causes two blades of grass to grow where only one grew before, light on your head.

Decr. 24th, 1838, he offers various inducements to his friend to pay him a visit at the seat of government, and ends:—

So pray bestir yourself and come, if it be only to see a gentleman of leisure metamorphosed into a pack-horse.

At the close of the year 1838 Mr. Paulding published anonymously, in one volume, through D. Appleton & Co, a charming book of Fairy Tales, illustrated on steel by J. G. Chapman, and entitled A GIFT FROM FAIRY LAND.

The arrangement of the letter press and the plates for printing was peculiar, and the absence of the artist from this country renders it well-nigh impossible to re-issue it. To do so without the engravings would be a pity, so admirably have the illustrations rendered the spirit of the stories.

The book was not so successful as one would have expected. It found however at least one appreciative reader, in the sculptor Greenough, then at Florence, at work on his statue of Washington. Mr. Paulding was in correspondence with him about these years upon this very subject of the statue, and, then and thereafter, attended to his interests in that respect at Washington, in a spirit worthy of the artist and the country. Writing to our author from Florence, Decr. 14th, 1839, Greenough incidentally remarks:—

"I recognized your pen at once in the gift from fairyland, which was truly a treat to us all—my wife was delighted with the novelty you have given to that form of invention. This is what we want—not a starveling and puritanical abstinence from works of fancy and taste, but an *adaptation* of these to our institutions, and a harmonizing of them with our morals or what we mean to be such."

Sound and judicious doctrine, this; worth pondering, one may say.

To his early friend Brevoort, Mr. Paulding writes, January 20th, 1839:—

I was comforted with your approbation of my course here. I believe I have done some good already, and if Congress and the newspapers don't prevent me, may do some more. In the meantime, I endeavor to do right, and calmly meet the consequences.

And elsewhere in this letter:—

You won't believe it, but I am the greatest slave in Washington, except my master the President.

And of certain grand dinners given by himself; and especially one:—

It was voted a great thing, but a few more such victories and Pyrrhus is undone. The fight lasted four hours.

May 16, 1839, he writes again to the same.

On the whole however, I don't regret coming here. If I outlive my term of service, and come out with credit, it will be a good stopping place for an old man, and I will sit down quietly for the short remainder of my life. If my friends would encourage me on, it would serve to strengthen my resolution, and support my spirits. I must necessarily make many enemies, and these can always find plenty of party newspapers in which to vent their spleen. Approbation is not half so active as abuse, and enemies are always more industrious than friends. Still I am content. There is a diabolical satisfaction in the exercise of power, and the head of the Navy is the most absolute of all despots.

Remember me affectionately to Mrs. Brevoort, and especially to the old ante-diluvians of the Bowery, and believe me my dear Brevoort, Yours always,

J. K. PAULDING.

Of course, during his continuance in the office of Secretary of the Navy, Mr. Paulding was overburdened with serious work, and had no time for literature. But his correspondence with Irving and Kemble during these three years is quite full, with some amusing comments on matters in Washington. As these things however do not fall within the scope of my design, I compress the important concerns of his Secretaryship into as brief compass as I conveniently can.

Mr. Paulding's first, and continued, effort during his official term, was for the restoration in the Navy of a proper subordination, which circumstances had sadly impaired. To Kemble he writes, April 10, 1839:—

As to myself, my great object is to restore the discipline of the Navy.

March 25th, 1839, to the same.

The President stands by me manfully, and please God, if I

live, and Congress does not counteract me, I will make both high and low young and old know who is their master, before I have done with them.

October 20th, 1840, to the same.

If I go out of office next Spring, it will be with the reputation of a tyrant, but should I remain four years longer, the benefit of my course will be seen and felt. I am prepared for either, and I may truly say indifferent to both, for the labours of four more years, such as I have lately passed, will hardly be repaid by their fruits.

The honor of his country was dear to Mr. Paulding's heart, and though earnestly desirous of peace during the Maine Boundary difficulties of the year 1839, it annoyed him excessively to note the delay of Congress to provide the means for taking due precaution in the business. He writes Brevoort, May 16th of this year.

Let war come when it will, suddenly, or by gradual approaches which any wise man can see, I predict it will find us unprepared, not from any fault of ours, but of Congress.

Mr. Forsyth was then Secretary of State, and Mr. Fox the British minister—both able men. The diplomatic contest was of course carried on by them; while, as regards General Scott, who was sent to the frontier, my father often bore testimony to the judicious management of his part of the affair. Mr. Fox, (Mr. Paulding used often afterward to say), from his habits of life, kept us always on the defensive. He turned night into day, and had a paper ready at daylight every morning. I myself, returning from Georgetown College at dusk, have more than once seen him just emerging from his house for his morning stroll.

Mr. Paulding was fond of sketching the characters of those with whom he came much in contact, and, in a commonplace book of much later date than this period, I find the following outline of

JOHN FORSYTH, OF GEORGIA.

This gentleman and myself were in long habits of intimacy, and for some years associated in public life. He had genius, and talents of the highest order, and was probably the readiest debater that ever sat in either house of Congress. His voice was extremely musical, and he had a readiness and fluency of speech accompanied by graceful action that rendered him one of the most pleasing speakers of his age. His mind was quick of comprehension; so quick that I believe he depended on it entirely: and seldom, if ever, did he study any subject thoroughly. He was naturally indolent, fond of society, especially that of women, and had no inconsiderable taste in the fine arts. When in Congress, it was a long time before he gave himself the trouble to make a set speech, and it was principally owing to the influence of a friend of mine, who belonged to the same mess and was aware of his capacity, that he finally overcame his *vis inertiæ*. When he did so he delighted everybody. When Secretary of State, I had sufficient opportunities to scan him more closely. He was not one of the mischievous *busybodies* who think they must always be doing something, and oftentimes get into mischief by meddling with every thing. He would be amusing himself while the little pettifogging politicians were fidgetting and whispering about nothing; but on all great occasions when the honor or interests of the country were concerned, he acted with a spirit, decision, and energy, becoming a great statesman and patriot. He always maintained his right of precedence over Senators, Judges of the Supreme Court, and foreign Ministers, and never permitted them to go before him at dinner or any formal occasion. In all other respects he was one of the most courteous of men, and his manners were eminently easy, graceful, and conciliating. I preserved an uninterrupted friendship with him to the day of his death, and there are few men whose memory is accompanied by more agreeable recollections.

Mr. Paulding was not given to novelties. When Secretary of the Navy Board, the bursting of a patent carbine nearly put an end to him. Perhaps from this circumstance he imbibed a prejudice against all experimental weapons for the rest of his days. He rather shook his head at 68 lb. Paixhan guns, as being too cumbersome for easy handling on board ship. Nor was he inclined to go headlong into a steam marine, though he was not unwilling to "humor" the thing a little.

The "Fulton", indeed, had been built before his time. But she was rather a floating battery for harbor defence, than a sea-going steamer. She was an immense and powerful mass, her momentum when once in motion so great that it was no easy matter to stop her. It was now proposed to build something to vie with the English and French war-steamers. His letters to Gouverneur Kemble often allude to this. He writes, June 16th, 1839.

If I had time, I would endeavour to place the subject before the public on *both* sides, with a view of allaying the steam fever now raging among us. But such fevers, like all others, must pass through their various stages, and the people of the United States must have some mania to excite them, whether it be a merino, a *morus multicaulis*, a canal, a railroad, or a steam mania. . . . We must yield the palm to the majority in this as in other things; for, whatever may be his opinions, the man who opposes the world is a fool for his pains. I am willing therefore to go with the wind, though I don't mean to carry full sail, and keep the steam enthusiasts quiet by warily administering to the humour of the times; but I will never consent to let our old ships perish, and transform our Navy into a fleet of sea monsters.

June 8th, 1839, to the same.

My dear Gouv, I am *steamed* to death.

April 10th, 1839, to the same.

I am afraid too of consulting too many wise men, lest I should fare as Panurge did when he took counsel as to the propriety of taking to himself a wife, and followed the advice of a fool at last. According to custom we have had Boards to sit and cogitate, and disagree, and compromise, so that in the end nobody will be responsible for a failure if one should take place. If they don't settle the matter soon, I shall dissolve them into empty air, and take the whole matter on my own shoulders.

This, in effect, he finally had to do; and the result was the production of two noble vessels, The Missouri and The Mississippi. Both underwent the doom of fire, The Missouri at anchor on a peaceful morning in the friendly harbor of Gibraltar, and her mate in the dead of night while attempting to pass the batteries of Vicksburg, with the din of war about her, and the fierce waters of the river whose name she bore clamoring for what the other element might spare.

Other subjects of consequence to the Navy engaged

his attention, such as the obtaining of better iron for anchors; and, notably, the production of an American Hemp equal to the best imported. This he looked upon as a national interest. He was not the first Secretary by any means to whom this matter had occurred; but his long experience as navy agent had no doubt impressed on his mind the vital importance of being independent of any foreign supply. Experiments had been made—all failures; resulting from an apparently insuperable prejudice against the processes of *water-rotting* hemp, as injurious to health. Was then this essential article of naval equipment to be forever subject to the chances of war? Mr. Paulding pondered it. Clearly there could not but be a remedy. Where? How to be got at?

To him thus casting about for means came, on other, though kindred, business, a certain David Myerle—being one of those men raised up by Providence to accomplish enterprises that foil all meaner spirits. Truly, a man of mark—one of those apt to be stigmatized by superficially-acute men as enthusiasts; but who, when combining with this great gift a practical ability courage and energy, and taking hold of an idea not in words but in reality as a "mission", effect the wonders of time. Mr. Paulding had the sagacity to appreciate this character, and, as it has since turned out, unfortunately for all his worldly prospects, induced him to undertake the enterprise, and enter into a contract of supply.

This David Myerle, in the face of innumerable obstacles, succeeded in establishing the production of water-rotted hemp as a branch of domestic industry, the success being entirely due to his own force and perseverance. As a reward for having added incalculably to the resources of his country, he lived to become almost if not quite blind, over papers, in the sickening position of a claimant before Congress — lived until he came to be cruelly known, among those that withheld from him his justice, by the terribly-grotesque designation of "the water-rotted hemp man."

He had substantially fulfilled his contract, and delivered his hemp, which through some underhand influence was, to his ruin, rejected. This was after Mr. Paulding had left the Department. Sixteen years a petitioner for his rights, seventeen favorable reports were made upon his claim; repeatedly it passed the Senate or the House, but not concurrently; and at last, (sixty five thousand dollars having been the amount admittedly due him in the beginning), a report was made recommending the payment to him of forty four thousand and four hundred dollars, which was cut down to thirty thousand, and so settled. Scarcely the salary of a clerk for those years — much less than half the simple interest on the debt — insufficient, in all probability, to pay his expenses in securing it. Then he died.

Doubtless among many his memory is still loaded with the imputation of having been an impostor, a madman, or a cheat. Nevertheless he was the first, practically and in such a way as to make an impression on the producing classes, to furnish the best quality of hemp, native grown. I learn by inquiry at Washington, that at this moment "American water-rotted hemp *would* be used in the Navy, if it could be procured;" but that "it is impossible to obtain it." Whether the discouragement met with by the first successful experimentor, or the general break-up of agricultural routine in the hemp-producing states, is the cause of this condition of things, I am unable to state. I only know that he who first made American water-rotted hemp, made it, as it were with his heart's blood.

Mr. Paulding's disinclination to fudge and flummery was deeply seated. An illustration of this occurred in the summer of 1840, on the occasion of a trip to the White Sulphur Springs, undertaken for the sake of his wife's health. It happened that another party were going forward at the same time, at the head of which was a man of imposing presence. Of course the stage agents were on the look out for the Secretary, and at a little town on the way one morning, pitched upon this gentleman as the great official. In his honor therefore six horses were put to his stage instead of four. Meantime, as things were being made ready for starting, Mr. Paulding could not be found; but when "the secretary" was fairly off, he emerged from the kitchen chimney-corner, placidly puffing his cigar. Apologies were tendered for the mistake, but he cut them short by remarking to the agent that four horses could break his neck as well as six.

He was ere long to be relieved from the weight of public dignities. The great Log Cabin revolution was coming on, and the mutterings of the storm grew louder and louder. But Mr. Paulding was always a philosopher, even to the extent of admitting himself sometimes in error. Thus he writes Kemble from Washington, 4th Novr., 1839:—"I know that we are all apt to lay the blame on others, but so far as my experience goes, I have always been obliged to confess, that the stone lay at my own door, else I should not have stumbled."

Accordingly he viewed the chances of the approaching election very coolly. He writes, at various dates, to Irving and Kemble.

TO IRVING.

WASHINGTON, 3d March, 1840.

I hear you have bought Mrs. Philipse's place, which I have sometimes squinted towards as the spot where I would like to doze out the remainder of my days, should I outlive my honors.

TO IRVING.

WASHINGTON, 2d June, 1840.

The rumors of resignations in the Cabinet, are, so far as I know, totally without foundation, and, as to being turned out next March, we defy the d——l and all his works, Log Cabins, Hard Cider and all. I should not much mind it myself, for I assure you a man works hard for a livelihood here, and is expected to spend all his money in giving entertainments, which as everybody is invited to nobody thanks him for. The Patroon is well and hearty.

TO IRVING.

WASHINGTON, 17th Septr., 1840.

We are not much frightened here as yet, and have great confidence in the final result of the elections. It will not quite break my heart if things go the other way, for, to a gentleman of leisure like myself, it comes rather hard to work like a horse and be abused like a pickpocket for my pains. If things go on in this way, no gentleman will consent to govern such a pack of scandalous rogues, and blackguards only will condescend to become great men. To leave the administration now, however, would be cowardly, and notwithstanding the newspaper authority, I have at no time contemplated such a course.

Farewell — may your garden flourish, and ease and quiet be your portion forever.

Mr. Kemble's term in Congress was to expire on the next fourth of March, and he was not up for re-election.

TO KEMBLE.

WASHINGTON, 20th Oct., 1840.

Judging from my own experience in political life, I should suppose you do not regret the prospect of a little quiet, after such a stormy season. Public stations are becoming little better than pillories, in which a man is set up to be pelted with old shoes and rotten eggs, and the head of a party is either a demigod or a demon.

Finally, after the election:—

TO IRVING.

WASHINGTON, 11th Novr., 1840.

The question being now settled, I am perfectly resigned to my fate, and cannot resist the inclination to rejoice at the prospect of getting rid of a laborious, vexatious, and thankless office, in which my duty has been almost always in direct opposition to my feelings, and I have been obliged to sacrifice private to public considerations. . . . . . . . . . .

I have not yet decided where I shall pitch my tent. My inclinations point to Tarrytown, but you have anticipated me in the possession of Mrs. Philipse's house. I feel a sort of yearning, after having completed the circle of life, to return and end where I began. I shall not be able to call myself rich, but when I remember that I set out from that memorable village with seven dollars in my pocket, I ought not to complain. I believe I have finished my public life, and the experience I have had in high office gives me no very keen appetite for a renewal.

In whatever situation I may be, or wherever I cast anchor, be assured my dear Washington, that I shall ever retain that sincere and steady regard I have constantly cherished for my oldest friend.

# XIX.

1841–1843. [ÆT. 63–65.]

RETIREMENT FROM PUBLIC LIFE — RETURN TO NEW YORK — DEATH OF HIS WIFE — LETTER FROM MARTIN VAN BUREN — TOUR THROUGH THE SOUTH AND WEST — LETTERS — ANDREW JACKSON — THE MISSISSIPPI — THE PRAIRIE — IN PRAISE OF THE SPINNING WHEEL.

ON the fourth of March, 1841, Mr. Paulding ended his public career. He had served the United States for three and forty years. Before the close of his term of office the health of his wife had so far failed that her condition was almost hopeless. She was removed to the house of her brother, William Kemble, in Beach street New York, and Mr. Paulding rented one a few doors off. Before this was prepared for occupation she died, on the 25th of May, 1841. In this extremity he turned once more to his "oldest friend", whom, in a few sad words partly addressed in another hand, he summoned to join him in following her to her grave.

During this year his health was not good, and he was probably too much depressed in spirit to work in his old fields. Early in the next spring it was suggested by ex-president Van Buren that he should join him in a projected tour to the South and West.

In the year 1839 Mr. Van Buren had purchased the estate of Lindenwald, in his native county, near Kinderhook, and thither he retired on his defeat in the election. Thence he wrote to Paulding: —

"My dear Sir,

I am extremely happy to hear that you go with us. We propose to leave here on a week from Monday, and to stay in N. York but a single day. I shall accept no dinners, and will make all your speeches for you that can't be avoided. So be ready. In great haste

Very truly yours

M. VAN BUREN.

K. H. Feby. 3d, '42."

The above promise is no doubt in answer to a stipulation on Mr. Paulding's part as a condition precedent to his acceptance of the invitation. Mr. Van Buren used afterward to tell with much glee how skilfully his companion on this excursion evaded the delegations, deputations, progresses, parades, receptions, processions, addresses, serenades, and other annoyances, which are the part and lot of noted politicians, and which should be considered in mitigation of their sins. In particular, he would relate, how, on one occasion, while crossing one of the great prairies of Illinois in a carriage on a dry and dusty day, Mr. Paulding was unusually talkative, and charmed with the scenery. Suddenly he became reserved, silent, and apparently out of sorts. He had been previously threatened with fever and ague, and Mr. Van Buren naturally inquired:—"Why, Paulding, is there any thing the matter with you?"

The indignant ex-secretary grimly jerked his thumb away off to the left, where, low down on the horizon, a small puff, as it were of smoke or dust, was dimly to be descried:—"Another d——d Committee!" And so it proved. He was caught where there was no escape.

Mr. Paulding adverts to this matter, during this tour, in several letters. In one he observes: "Mr. Van Buren was kidnapped by a Committee at Detroit"; and in another objects to "this supervision of Committees." He however, in the latter, goes on to say: "But it would be churlish to complain of what proceeds from the kindest feelings, and most liberal hospitality."

I cannot follow our author through the journey. I suppose his general experience is pretty fairly indicated in the following extracts from a letter to a niece, Miss Margarette T. Kemble, written at "The Hermitage", May 2d, 1842.

> There was a great turn out at those places, but I kept out of the way as much as possible, for you know there can be but one Punch to a Puppet-show. . . . On landing [at Nashville] we were received into the bosom of a crowd of some thousands whom I wished in the Red Sea, for I have a great dislike to being pushed about here and there, and having my toes trod on by fellows with hob nails in their shoes. I met one of them at Columbia [Tennessee] the other day, in the crowd in the yard of the Court House, who planted his foot on one of my corns with such emphasis that the print of the hob nails remains on my boot to this day. "Sir," said I, "I wish you would take your foot off mine." "Sir," said he, "I would with great pleasure, but I can find no other place to put it in." This appeared to me a special good reason, so I proposed we should take turns, five minutes at a time, and we got on very amicably during the rest of the ceremony, during which I shook hands with about five thousand people, some of whom squeezed my fingers together so tight that it took two days for them to separate, and for that time I was web-fingered. . . .
>
> If I were only travelling on my own hook, I should cer-

tainly think myself a great man, but as it is, my pride every now and then sustains a mighty fall, by seeing the rustical and barbarous Corydons staring at Mr. Van Buren with open mouths, and taking no notice of me. However I am consoled by the kindness of the "better sort", the aristocracy, and especially the venerable Blue Stockings, who have stultified me into limestone with talking of Boz, The Lady's Book, and Brother Jonathan.

Whatever may be the ultimate verdict of History as to the influence the life and character of Andrew Jackson produced upon his country, one thing is certain. There was a magnetism about the man which involved every one who fell within the circle of his personal acquaintance. Mr. Paulding, who had met him in Washington at the close of the war of 1812; who, at his request wrote to him occasionally; and who at the period to which we have now arrived spent three weeks at his house; — did not escape this witchery.

In 1837 he had written to Kemble from New York: "He was *sui generis.* The power of man is the power over his fellow men. It is this alone that enables him to do wonders. Mr. Calhoun has happily dashed off this in the single phrase, that he 'had the power of imprinting his own feelings on the community.'"

And from a memorandum in a common-place book and an article published in The Democratic Review — both subsequent to the general's death, which occurred on the 8th of June, 1845, — I piece together this character.

ANDREW JACKSON.

He was indeed an extraordinary man; the only man I ever saw that excited my admiration to the pitch of wonder. To him knowledge seemed entirely unnecessary. He saw intuitively into every thing, and reached a conclusion by a short cut while others were beating the bush for the game. His reasoning was impulse, and his impulse inspiration. His genius and his courage were his guides. One pointed out the path; the other prompted him in the pursuit. He never sought an object that he did not succeed in attaining; and never fought a battle that he did not win. His political opponents ascribed his success to good fortune; but Fortune, though she often does us a single good turn, soon becomes tired of tagging at the heels of imbecility and folly. To win always is the best proof of skill in the player.

He began his public career in Tennessee, at a time when — as an old lady, who came up with the first party to Nashville, once told me — "there was neither law nor gospel" there. In such a state of things personal qualities give the law, and courage assumes its proper rank as the first of virtues, because it is the great conservator of all the rest. Here he soon gained that ascendency over the wild spirits he had to cope with, which he ever after maintained in his intercourse with his fellow men. Many anecdotes are told illustrative of his quick decision, his indomitable courage, and his inflexible determination. There was nothing on earth he despised so much as cowardice, and his highest eulogium on his favorite, General Coffee, was, "Sir, he was as brave a man as ever stepped."

General Jackson was not only an honorable, but an upright, man, and equally scorned a mean, as a dishonest, act. Whatever he might have been in his youth, he was a pious man in his old age; and though, as Corporal Trim says, "our armies swore terribly in Flanders", the general had conquered the habit entirely before his death.

At the time I visited him at the Hermitage he was in a condition of extreme physical debility, but his intellect was as clear and bright as ever. He was the shadow of a man in body, but the substance in mind. Tall, fleshless, straight as an arrow, and with a profusion of snow-white hair, his appearance was sublime; and his manner more kind, graceful, and benevolent, than that of any man who has ever fallen under my observation. It was not the politeness of conventional habits, but the courtesy of the heart; and his deportment toward his family, his guests, and his slaves, was that of a patriarch of old, presiding over his flocks, his herds, and his dependents. At this period he might almost be said to live without food, for he ate less than an infant. His long table was crowded, nearly every day, by visitors who came from far and near to see him; but, though he sat down with them, and shared in the gay freedom of the hospitable board, he never tasted any thing but a little rice and milk.

Never I believe did the mind of any man so completely predominate over his body. During the last two years of his life its energies kept him alive when his natural powers were exhausted, and probably no man ever died with less pain or less fear. Peace to his spirit! I equally admired and loved him, not only for his high heroic character, but for his private virtues.

Notwithstanding all annoyances, Mr. Paulding came home delighted with his tour, and more than ever impressed with the idea of his country's magnificent extent and destiny. Among the results of this excursion were two sketches of the great features of the Western Country, written in 1842 or 1843.

THE MISSISSIPPI.

"The Father of Rivers", as it was called by the Indians, whose names of places persons and things are so apt and expressive, is assuredly one of the wonders of nature. To the eye it presents itself as the greatest body of fresh water collected and conveyed in one channel, to be found on the face of the globe. Those who take into consideration the number and magnitude of its tributaries; the depth of its channel; and the velocity of its current forever setting in one direction; must be convinced that none of the great rivers of the earth can compete with it in the vast tribute of waters it bears to the ocean. To the imagination it appeals with still greater effect, as the reservoir of a region whose bosom is yet a mystery; as the great artery into which flow all the rivers, that, like the veins of the human body, permeate that vast undefined world justly styled "The Great West", winding its majestic course a distance of three thousand miles, and forming the connecting link between the rough winter of the North and the abode of perpetual spring and summer.

I arrived in New Orleans at dawn of day, by way of Lake Pontchartrain, about the middle of April, and my first visit was to the Mississippi, then in full flood. The first thing that attracted my attention was that the water in the gutters flowed rapidly from the river, instead of towards it; the next, that I found myself walking up hill in approaching its bank. But the sight of the river drove these oddities from my mind at once. The current was sweeping along, its surface just on a level with its margin, and seemed to be one vast collection of boiling eddies, conflicting which should go foremost. The opposite shore was one dead level, bounded by the distant forest and the horizon, and the river reminded me of a full bumper which a single drop would overflow. These low levee banks contribute to increase the apparent magnitude of the stream, by offering no interruption to the range of the eye as it wanders over the wide expanse of turbid waters, the impression of whose depth is enhanced by the impossibility of anywhere seeing the bottom, thus leaving them for the imagination to fathom. Altogether, though the river was not so wide as others I had seen, the conviction of superior importance was immediate and supreme. The truth is, my imagination was dwelling on its almost interminable course; its numberless tributaries; and its unique characteristic of entire independence on the Ocean, whose tribute it rejects, and whose inroads it laughs to scorn.

The formation of new points of land, and islands, is constantly going on in this river, which is perpetually robbing Peter to pay Paul. If it cuts off a point of land in one place, it is pretty certain to form another somewhere below, with the spoils filched from above. The islands are established much in the same way. A great tree grounds at some projecting point, or some shallow, of the river, and intercepts fragments of drift wood, vast quantities of which come floating down during the high stage of the waters. Here the sand and sediment gather rapidly, until a bank appears above the surface. Sometimes these accumulations are caused by eddies in the current, and it is quite surprising in how short a time they become clothed with trees. The Cotton tree everywhere abounds, and at the proper season the whole atmosphere is filled with its gossamer, which sails about in the wind, and is occasionally very painful to the eye. This contains the principle of vegetation, and, settling down on these new formations, almost immediately produces a little forest of cotton wood, of such regularity and beauty as can scarcely be described. Every year brings new accessions to the land, and a new growth of cotton trees, which thus exhibit a regular gradation, from the tiny plant just springing up at the edge of the water, to the high tree on the elevated part which was first formed. Nothing can be more beautiful than these terraces of verdure, each annual growth of which, though higher than that of the succeeding year, is as uniform as a cropped garden hedge, each one presenting a different shade. The last growth, just rising apparently out of the water, is of an exquisitely soft and delicate green, but the tints of the successive terraces gradually deepen, until the eye at last rests on the dark hues of the primeval forest. The effect of these new formations, especially of the islands, is exceedingly agreeable, and indeed, striking. The gradations of the annual growth of trees convey the impression that they are planted on a conical mound, and give to the eye all the effect of a considerable elevation, although the surface of the earth on which they stand is perhaps nowhere more than a few feet above the level of the river. At a little distance, they may be mistaken for hills two or three hundred feet high.

In the course of the whole voyage I never saw twenty miles of the river at the same time. It is continually resolving itself into what the boatmen call "points and bends", to wit, on one hand a vast magnificent curve of many miles, opening a sea of waters, on the other a point of forest jutting out and apparently shutting up the river. You seem continually sailing on a lake, and the opening and closing of these vistas is inexpressibly grand and beautiful.

People generally complain of the monotony of the Mississippi, but I never became tired of the grand uniformity of the scene, which only serves to impress itself more deeply and permanently on the memory and imagination.

The Mississippi at night, and especially on moonlight nights, appears in all its glory, and, during my voyage of eight days, we were favored with them, without the interruption of a single storm, and scarcely a single cloud. An almost unchanging calm prevailed, and under the magic of the moonbeams all the unamiable features of the river disappeared. The vast expanse of waters, sometimes two or three miles wide, was one untroubled glassy mirror, edged by a frame of dark forest, rising like a perpendicular wall of marble from the water, and following its graceful curves in all directions. The boiling eddies that everywhere disfigure its surface and agitate its bosom, vanish in the lustre which envelops them, and the opaque deformity of the current can no longer be distinguished. The skies of this region, until you approach the climate of the North, are of deeper blue, and purer transparency, and I sometimes fancied I could see far beyond the stars, whose radiance, however, is not so keen as in our frosty winter nights. Nothing is heard but the puffing of the steam and the champing of the wheels, to which voyagers soon become so accustomed that they cease to excite attention; and the forest-lined shores exhibit no sign of life or animation, except it may be a far-distant gleam from a fire, kindled as a signal to stop and take up a passenger. Occasionally a steamboat passes down the stream, or a broadhorn, sliding along as quietly as death itself, adding stillness to the scene. The quiet is profound, yet not dreary; for every thing around and above, is sublime or beautiful. It is Nature, in all her grandeur, reposing in the lap of Night.

Here is a companion picture:—

THE PRAIRIE.

The Prairie is not all grass, being everywhere interspersed with flowers of every hue and odor, from the wild rose to the wild sun-flower. These are not mixed together, but grow, each species by itself, in beds of several hundreds or thousands of acres. In one place the blue, in another the red, and in a third the yellow, predominates. They jealously guard the purity of their respective castes, and seldom mingle with each other. To the eye, however, as it ranges over the extended plain, the prevailing, and indeed general, tint, is a soft yet brilliant light olive green, which distinguishes it in a striking manner from the deep color of the lines of forest which grow almost exclusively on the banks of the rivers, whose course they invariably indicate. The soil is a black mould, of varying depth, and inexhaustible fertility; but wants both wood and water.

The Prairies are a sort of *lusus naturæ*, and those who attempt their description undertake a difficult task, because there is nothing in Nature with which to compare them; and to give a just idea of their features and complexion requires analogies not to be found in the imagery of the mind. You may talk of vast meadows, but no one can form an idea of a prairie by comparing it with the largest meadow he has ever seen. The Prairie has a character, a physiognomy, and an atmosphere, of its own. Just around you it is all reality; at a distance it is all doubt, delusion, mystification. Distances are magnified, or diminished; what seems close by, is often a great way off; and what shows dimly afar, is almost within reach of the hand. What, in passing over, seems a perfect plain, exhibits in perspective a succession of light waving hills rising one above another pencilled in the skies. It is always level under your feet, and yet you see a perpetual succession of little eminences, behind, before, and all around. At one time you behold a solitary house looming up on a rise, which, when you approach it, is a flat expanse, apparently without beginning or end; at another, a distant wood, whose long straight line of deep foliage darkens the sky in which it seems to stand self-supported: — at all events, beneath is vacancy.

Occasionally you see something sailing across this ocean of land, distinguishable almost as far off as a ship at sea. This is a wagon, freighted with the goods and chattels of a pilgrim journeying to the land of promise, and manned by a troop of lusty children. At first you can see nothing but the peaked ends of the wagon-top, covered with linen or canvas, shaped like gaff-topsails, and one cannot resist the impression always conjured up by the strange resemblance which an open prairie-scene bears to an ocean on which now and then a vessel heaves in sight. Hence these wagons are aptly called "Prairie Schooners."

When the atmosphere is hazy, as it generally is on these vast plains, the scenery seems dancing before the dizzy eye, and all sorts of incongruities present themselves. Cattle appear grazing in the air; hills and islands of trees floating on the water; and every object, whose opacity or magnitude renders it visible at a distance, seems translated from its appropriate element. It is beyond the power of language — I might almost say, imagination — to exaggerate the strange and beautiful combination of what is with what is not, sporting together on these boundless plains. The eye becomes wearied at length with being thus perpetually at fault, and the mind almost revolts at the deception of the senses.

About this period also we have the following: —

### IN PRAISE OF THE SPINNING-WHEEL.

Some forty years ago, I resided in a retired village, built on a narrow level, between a range of high rugged mountains and a wide but rather shallow river, which afforded navigation neither to steamboat nor canoe, though occasionally an adventurous boy would launch himself in its swift current on a plank, and succeed in crossing, after floating down the stream a mile or two. This, however, was considered a great feat, and the successful navigator another Columbus. A large brook, tributary to the river, flowed through the village, after leaving a deep and narrow gorge in the mountain. Wild for the most part, it presented on its margin here and there a bit of greensward which contrasted agreeably with the surrounding desolation. Subject to great rises during heavy rains and at the melting of the snow in the spring, it would overflow these little meadows, sometimes to a depth of several feet, thus rendering a residence in the valley dangerous, and obliging the inhabitants to place their rustic dwellings up among the rocks on the side of the mountain.

The situation of one of these was peculiar. The building, which was constructed of logs in the most primitive style, was placed on a flat projecting rock, perhaps an hundred feet above the stream; and underneath, a path wound along its border. When a lad, I used frequently to indulge in the philosophic amusement of angling, and have often seen the good woman of this hold walking back and forth on the rock high in the air, and turning her big spinning-wheel, whose musical and soothing hummings might be heard, keeping time as it were to the murmurs of the brook, and forming a most agreeable concert amid the solitude of the hills.

This was many years before Domestic Industry was banished from the fire-side, and when every housewife did her own spinning, assisted by her rosy-cheeked girls, instead of carrying her wool and flax to the factory and returning home to idleness and ennui.

An aged and an old-fashioned man, I hope to be pardoned if I take this occasion to indulge in grievous lamentations over the banishment of the spinning-wheel from among our country people. It furnished the most graceful as well as wholesome employment of all the circle of domestic labors. It afforded a gentle exercise; it filled up those hours of idleness which inevitably occur in the most industrious families, with an occupation which was rather an amusement than a toil; and it was a tidy, almost lady-like, art, administering alike to the comfort of the body and the peace of the mind. But, alas! the spinning-wheel has given place to the spinning-jennies, and our blooming rustic maids are transferred to the slavery of the manufactory; or, having little or nothing to do at home, resort to the mischievous alternative, of either gadding abroad, or killing time in the perusal of cock-and-bull stories at a shilling a-piece, which, for the most part, only addle their brains, excite their passions, and pervert their imaginations into a thousand fantastic distortions.

The foregoing must not be considered as mere declamation, but as the serious reverie of an old man, "looking through a glass, darkened", over the long vista of departed years.

# XX.

1844–1848. [ÆT. 66–70.]

PHILOSOPHY OF LIFE — REMOVAL TO HYDE PARK — THE OLD CONTINENTAL; OR, THE PRICE OF LIBERTY — EXTRACTS FROM — LETTERS FROM MARTIN VAN BUREN — AMERICAN COMEDIES — LETTER TO KEMBLE — THE HUDSON RIVER RAIL-ROAD.

IN a letter to one of his sons, in 1844, Mr. Paulding gives his philosophy of life: —

Whatever may be your inclinations as to your future life, I shall not interfere with them, assured as I am, that, to be content anywhere, and in any situation, is the great secret of happiness, and that one of the great means of attaining it is to follow one's own tastes, provided they are innocent and do not interfere with those of others.

A life in the country, if accompanied by those tastes and resources which render even rainy days pleasant, and either fill up our leisure time or render us insensible to its pressure, is, in my opinion, on the whole most conducive to virtue as well as happiness. But no well-educated gentleman should ever flatter himself that the rural life is made for him, unless he possesses a natural taste for rural employments and the beauties of nature, as well as intellectual resources, to keep him from the necessity of resorting to low and vicious indulgences, merely to pass the time.

In the summer of 1845 Mr. Paulding purchased a residence at Hyde Park, in the county of his birth, and thither he removed in October of the same year.

The house was situated at one of the most beautiful points of the Hudson, and the neighborhood afforded ample scope for that enjoyment of nature which was his passion. Here he again employed part of his time in literary avocations, and, in 1846, published through Paine and Burgess, New York, a novel in two volumes prepared some years before. He called it THE OLD CONTINENTAL; OR, THE PRICE OF LIBERTY.

The latter title is the more appropriate, as indicating the aim of the work, which is definitely stated in the author's prefatory address

"TO THE READER.

THOUGH some of the personages, and a portion of the incidents, of the following tale, are either historical or traditionary, it makes no pretensions to the dignity of a historical romance. The design was, to convey to the mind of the reader some idea of the spirit, the sufferings, and the sacrifices of a class of people who are seldom, if ever, individualized in history, yet who always bear the brunt of war and invasion. The hero of the piece once actually existed, and exhibited in his youth many of the qualities here ascribed to him. Some of the adventures detailed were well remembered by the old people of the neighborhood, few, if any, of whom are now living. Others took place in different parts of the country, at various times; and the whole may suffice to give at least a faint picture of the price paid by our fathers and mothers for the freedom we enjoy."

I give a few extracts bearing on this leading idea. The hero of the story, as the war goes on, cannot stand remaining at home, and, with the consent of his grandparents, (his mother being dead and his father already with the army), sets out to join the revolutionary forces. He makes for, and reaches, the nearest post.

Our adventurer first sought his father, and the meeting was affectionately solemn. But after the parent had welcomed his son, he began a long lecture on the impropriety of leaving home, where his presence was required for the protection of the old people, and the cultivation of the farm.

"Besides," added the captain, "you would have seen me soon, without coming here. I was about asking leave for a few days, as early as next week—however, John, I should not find fault with you for taking all this trouble to see me. So give me your hand, you are heartily welcome."

"But, sir," replied John, "I did not come to see you: that is, I did not come on purpose."

"No? what then brought you here?"

"I came to fight for my country, sir!"

"You? why, you're but a boy, a chicken—what will you do amongst our old cocks?"

"Crow, and fight like the rest, father."

"Pooh, John! go home and take care of the farm, and the old people. I'm sure you've run away without permission."

"No, on my word, sir, they consented."

"What! mother too?"

"Yes sir. She opposed it at first, but at last said to me, 'well go, John, fight for your country, and take care of your father.'"

"Did she, the dear old soul?" exclaimed the captain, drawing his hand across his brow; "but why should I doubt it, when I have seen so many of our women with the hearts of men in their bosoms? John, you can hardly remember your mother, you were so young when you lost her. Though brought up tenderly in a quiet city, I verily believe she never knew what it was to fear for herself. I have seen her twice in situations that made old soldiers turn pale, without a change in her countenance. If you ever turn coward, John, you will disgrace both your parents. But you are too young for a soldier of freedom. Can you live without eating; sleep without covering; fight without shirt to your back, or shoe to your foot; without pay, and without the hope of victory? If you cannot, you'd better go home. Look at *me*, John."

John ran his eye over the poor soldier of freedom, and though he had been absent little more than a year, was struck with the change in his face and person. He had grown very thin; his brow was seamed with deep furrows; his hair, which was only a little grizzly when he left home, was now almost white, and a deep scar on his cheek gave token of his having been within arm's reach of an enemy. Cap he had none, but its place was supplied by a coarse wool hat, of a grim, weather-beaten hue, ornamented with a little faded plume, now of a most questionable colour. His epaulet was of the tint of rusty copper; his garments not only worn threadbare, but rent in more than one place; he wore a common leather stock, and his clumsy cowhide boots, the soles of which were gradually departing from the upper leathers, were innocent of oil or blacking. His sword was cased in a scabbard of cartridge paper made by his own hands, and his entire appearance presented no bad emblem of the fortunes of his country.

"Well, John, what do you think of me?"

John made no answer. His heart was too full for words, but he thought to himself, "Such is ever the price of liberty!"

"But don't be discouraged, boy. Though I seem rather the worse for wear, I have plenty of money. Look here —" and the captain drew from his pocket a handful of paper money, with a smile that partook of bitter irony. "See how rich I am, if I could only persuade people to take these rags for money. I offered Mangham, the pedlar — you know him, I believe, a wary rascal — a hundred dollars for a pair of stockings, a luxury I have not enjoyed for some time: but the fellow answered, 'No, captain, if I want to be charitable, I give things away; but when I trade, I expect something of equal value for my goods.' He offered to give me a pair for old acquaintance sake, but I could not bring myself to that. So you see me barefoot, with a pocketful of money."

"If I were in your situation, sir, I would resign and go home. Let *me* take your place, while you get a little rest and clothe yourself. I can't bear to see you look like a beggar."

"No, my son," replied the captain, with a firm determination, unalloyed by a single spark of enthusiasm, "no, John; when I first put on this old rusty sword, I swore never to lay it down till my country was free, or all hope of freedom was at an end. I mean, if God spares my life, to keep my oath, let what else may happen. If my country cannot give me shoes,

I will fight barefoot; if she cannot afford me a hat, I will fight bareheaded; and if she can't pay me for my services in money, I will live in the hope of being repaid hereafter by her gratitude. I know she gives us the best she has to give — that she shares in our sufferings — and may God forsake me, when I desert her!"

Such were the men who bore the country on their shoulders, through peril, doubt, and despair: such the unknown heroes, who live only in the blessings they bestowed on posterity. And here lies the mystery which has puzzled the world, namely, the achievement of independence in the face of apparently insuperable obstacles presenting themselves at every step and every moment, which cannot be explained but by the virtuous firmness, the unwavering patriotism, not more of the high than of the low; not more of those whose names will forever remain objects of national gratitude, than of those whose names were never remembered. The soul that animated and inspired the revolution, spoke from the lips of this nameless soldier.

Taken prisoner subsequently, and having escaped, he reaches the old homestead to find more of the price of liberty paid.

Just as the rising sun glanced his golden beams athwart the dewy fields, he found himself looking from higher ground into the smiling vale where nestled his long lost home. He saw the moss-covered roof of the old stone house, standing in all its loneliness; but no smoke rose from out the chimney-top, as was wont at that hour, and the absence of this token of life and animation smote like the cold hand of death on his heart. As he gazed around on the fields, he saw neither cattle nor sheep, and the conviction rushed on his mind that he had come too late. He approached the door of the once peaceful mansion with fearful anticipations, and found it standing wide open. He looked in, and saw a sight that thrilled his very soul with mingled anguish and desire of revenge. The good old housewife was sitting, with the head of the old man resting in her lap, while his body lay extended on the floor, which was covered with blood. A plaintive moaning announced that he still lived, but the wife was silent as the grave. Her pale, wrinkled face, was turned toward heaven, as if appealing to its justice, or in humble resignation to its decrees; her few gray hairs were without the accustomed covering, and she neither complained nor wept. As John stood contemplating this scene of woe, incapable of moving, and almost lifeless, she drew a long, deep sigh, and at length murmured, as to herself, these melancholy words—

"My son is dead, my husband is dead, and John will never come home again. Why, O Father of mercy!, why can't I die too?"

In an instant John was on his knees by the side of his grandfather.

"Mother!", cried he—for he remembered no other—"mother, see! I *am* come home, never to leave you alone again, so help me heaven!"

She looked at him wistfully, as if scarcely recognising the speaker, or comprehending his speech, and seeing the bloody gash in his head, murmured as to herself—

"More murder — more murder — all but me can die!"

John took her cold, withered hand, and wept over it. There is a magic power in tears of heartfelt sympathy, that communicates with the hearts of others, and awakens even despair to recollection. She looked in his face a while, and by degrees recognized her grandson.

"Oh! John! John! why did you leave us here all alone? See what has come to us," and she pointed to the bleeding head in her lap.

Here is the successful appeal of a Quaker's wife to her husband, in behalf of her boys who are eager to fight for their country's liberty.

"Friend Ruth," said he, "abide thee a little. Thee has been putting wicked notions into the heads of these foolish boys, and spiriting them on to mischief; even now they depart to join in the unlawful business of defending their country. Thee art but half a Quaker, Ruth. What evil spirit possessed thee?"

"No evil spirit, friend," replied Ruth, with a mild and simple fervour. "No evil spirit, friend Nathan; but almost every day, for more than a year past, I have seen the smoke of our neighbours' buildings rising over yonder hill, and I knew who it was that set them on fire. I have heard story after story of farms laid waste, cattle driven away, old men and women abused, even unto death, and young maidens insulted and outraged by the lawless soldiers from beyond the seas. And when I saw and heard all this, I said to myself, in the bitterness of my heart, am I the mother of women, that my sons should be idle at home, while their country is bleeding? Nathan, thou art a Friend, but thou art still a man. Thou hast sons with stout hearts and willing minds; wouldst thou see thy country — that generous country which opened its bosom to thy fathers, in times when no other refuge was left them on the face of the earth, ravaged and subdued by the descendants of our ancient persecutors — trodden under foot, crushed to the earth in cruel bondage, by those who, at the same time, if they should triumph, will persecute our faith as they did in past days, and make us again exiles or martyrs? Couldst thou see this, oh Nathan! and not lend a hand in such woful times of need? — couldst thou, friend Nathan?"

As usual, we have many quaint bits of description or moralizing. I close with an extract involving both. Here are the lovers, about to part.

They rambled under the stately elms and plane trees, that overshadowed the clear murmuring stream, and now began to exhibit the many coloured tints of autumn. The maples and sumach, already displayed their scarlet foliage, most beautiful in decay; the hardy brood of autumnal flowers were on the wane, and the blue-birds, the meadow-larks, and the robins, were collecting in flocks, preparing for the sunny regions of the south. There was a sober, calm serenity, almost bordering on melancholy, in the aspect of the earth and skies; a soothing gentleness in the murmurs of the stream, and the soft whisperings of the dying leaves, which ever and anon, smitten by the frost, fell in spiral eddies to the ground or dropt into the brook, apt emblems of some dear and well remembered companion, on his way to the home of all the living, the region of eternal suffering or eternal rest.

Every object around them was calculated to awaken and foster the purest and tenderest emotions of the heart, and the impression that their parting now might be to meet no more, imparted a deep solemnity to the feelings by which they were inspired. Love, engrossing, overpowering love, filled all their hearts—prompting a thousand innocent endearments, such as, at a time like this, may be claimed without assurance, and granted without indelicacy. The silent solitudes of nature are not the promoters of the guilty passions; it is where the human race herd together in crowds, amid luxurious seductions appealing to the senses and the imagination through every avenue of the heart, that the passions become epidemical, spreading like contagion from one to another, until the entire mass becomes diseased and corrupted. There is no incitement to sensuality in the charms of nature; no seduction in her music; no mischief in her smiles; no luxurious fascination in the rich bounties she pours out with such a lavish hand; and they who would secure to themselves the cheapest, the purest, and the most enduring source of innocent enjoyment, should cherish in their inmost heart a feeling of admiration for that stupendous and beautiful fabric, which, more than any other work of his hand, displays the wisdom, the goodness, and the omnipotence of the great Architect of the universe.

About these years a correspondence was going on

between Mr. Paulding, and Mr. Van Buren who had settled at Lindenwald near his native village, in which they used occasionally to rally each other about their farming operations. It is pleasant, as exhibiting the cheerful subsidence into private station of two men who had played parts in great dramas. The burden of much of Mr. Van Buren's side, half in a serious half in a jocose vein, is — muck. A couple of specimens must suffice. Here is one of the braggadocio letters. Mr. Van Buren had a large farm, Mr. Paulding but forty acres.

M. VAN BUREN TO J. K. PAULDING.

"LINDENWALD. Sunday. April 25, 1846.

My dear Sir,

Your potatoes will go by the Eagle of the ensuing week. You must be sure and not plant before *the full of the moon* which will be about the 13th of May. You must cut the potatoes into two pieces each and put only two pieces in a hill — positively no more. This will plant four acres, and if your *small farm* will not allow you that much, give the seed to your neighbors rather than encumber the ground with them. If you want reasons, a very unreasonable requirement, know that the Carters have treble the number of eyes that all other kinds have."

[Mr. Van Buren here diverges into a humorous defence of his housekeeping arrangements, and then recurs to the farm; speaks of his plantings — one thousand Pear and two thousand Apple trees in the ground, and eight thousand Apples on the way; states that he shall plant seventeen acres in potatoes, and has sowed "*ninety bushels* of oats. Think of that and weep."]

. . . . . . .

"P. S. You have behaved badly in not coming up. The sun and moon would stand still if I were to leave my farm at this moment."

The above allusion to "the full of the moon" reminds me that Mr. Van Buren used to tell of an old Dutchman, a neighbor, who tried to dissuade him from laying a stone wall when she was on the wane. And now we get upon the great and all-engrossing topic.

M. VAN BUREN TO J. K. PAULDING.

"LINDENWALD Feby 13th, 1847.

My dear Sir,

More curiosities from the muck bed. Since yesterday the learned Cooney [his factotum] has found, six feet under the muck a considerable quantity of charcoal like the enclosed. How came it there? He seems to think it affords tolerable proof that the world has once been destroyed by fire. . . . .

We find also frequently what we are sure is marl, but, as you once said, it will not effervesce, and be hanged to it. I think however that I have a specimen which has some lime and I mean to test it by mixing it with the muck. I can't think that Nature would have put the two materials so beautifully together without some good object.

That you may not bewilder yourself too much with these interesting matters, I send also for your amusement a letter from my queer friend —— in relation to another friend of ours who has taken his departure, which please return.

Very truly yours
M. VAN BUREN."

In 1847, Carey & Hart, Philadelphia, published in one volume four "AMERICAN COMEDIES"—so styled. Mr. Paulding was responsible for but one of these productions—his present editor for the rest. It had been wiser in both to have kept them all out of print.

In the spring of the same year his brother Nathaniel broke up his business as a wine-merchant in the city of New York, and went to reside with him. My uncle was immediately seized with a furor for working in the garden, and to this Mr. Paulding alludes, Sept. 12th, 1847, in a letter to Irving, whose brother Ebenezer had a similar passion.

"P. S. Remember me to my old friend Capt. Greatheart, and tell him Uncle Nat can beat him all hollow in his exploits in the garden."

Mr. Paulding had all his life been an interested observer of, and profuse writer on, public affairs. In the latter years of his life the corruption of parties and decay of patriotic spirit often excited his animadversions. He writes to Kemble:—

HYDE PARK. Duchess Cy.
February 18th, 1848.

. . . I remember I used to tell you, the administration, in trying to break down Mr. ——, would break down themselves, and I think it will prove true. It seems from your report they are beating the bushes for a candidate, and don't care much whether they put up a 'possum, a woodchuck, or a muskrat, provided he can win the race. This is a poor state of things, and if the People have no more honesty than their rulers, we have nothing left but to trust to Providence, which I have no doubt will take care of us, since it seems quite clear that we are instruments in his hands for great purposes. We have got on the right track; we believe in destiny, and that makes destiny.

. . . . . . . .

But anybody will do for a President now-a-days. The office is fast sinking into contempt and insignificance, and I think it will not be long before the incumbent will be a mere cipher. Congress is every day paring away the Executive authority; and they will probably soon add to the just prerogative of declaring war, that of making peace on their own terms. We want a sturdy military man as President, who would not shrink from a contest with the noisy machine at the Capitol, and who dared to assert his just prerogatives, like Old Hickory. In my opinion we are in great danger of being tyrannized over by legislation, and that the country will soon be governed by "resolutions" instead of laws. But I have of late arrived at a conclusion which conduces greatly to my repose. I am convinced that so long as we have room for expansion, and the People can sow their wild oats all over the continent, we can't be ruined, either by President or Congress. . . . . . .

But the Americans are very devils at scribbling, and about equally divided between the *Cacoethes Scribendi* and the *Cacoethes Loquendi.* I should like to see a President that could neither write nor talk.

The above extracts are, in the letter, intermingled with remarks upon various Presidential candidates and other political notabilities, which are diverting enough, but which I suppress. He now branches off to a subject that had annoyed him extremely, and his treatment of which exhibits very favorably the honesty of his character.

I am of opinion — though it goes against my own particular feelings — that both the interests of the public and those of the Company require the Rail Road to be carried along the edge of the river. I have read Jervis's Report, and though I don't think much of his taste in the picturesque, I think him perfectly right in his general conclusions, and shall submit, like a true patriot, to be annoyed for the good of the Public, though no compensation I can expect to receive will prevent me from wishing it had pleased Providence to render the other route the most advantageous.

This was pretty fair for a man whose chosen and special abhorrence was a Rail-road.

# XXI.

1849. [ÆT. 71.]

THE PURITAN AND HIS DAUGHTER — DEDICATION OF — MORSELS OF WISDOM — EULOGIUM ON THE DIVINE TOBACCO PIPE — THE WILD MAN IN THE WILD WOODS — BLOOD-PUDDING LITERATURE — CAPTAIN ABIEL SKEERING — EXCOMMUNICATION OF THE DEMON OF WATER POWER — AN OLD AUTHOR'S PARTING ADVICE TO HIS READERS.

FOR the copy of a letter containing the first hint of our author's next publication I am indebted to Colonel J. Grant Wilson. The letter was addressed to his father, Mr. William Wilson, a friend of Mr. Paulding resident at Poughkeepsie, and one of the rather uncommon cases of a dealer in literary wares who had at the same time a taste and a talent for literature.

TO W. WILSON.

HYDE PARK, DUCHESS COUNTY.
Dec. 17th, 1848.

Dear Sir: Having nothing to do in the farming way this winter, I have undertaken to *splice* the "Puritan's Daughter", as they do steamboats, by cutting them in two, and putting a piece in the middle. With dovetailing here a little, loitering by the way, and stopping now and then to have a talk like Cooper, I shall be able to stretch it to the proper dimensions, I hope, without doing it much damage. Indeed, I think, on the whole, it will rather be improved. It will cost me, however, more labor than writing it in the first instance. It will make two volumes, such as "The Old Continental", perhaps a little larger.

When you go to New York, and get among the trade, I

wish you would see what kind of arrangement (for cash) you can make with those Philistines. I could have it ready in about a month, and should not be easily induced to take less for it than the old price agreed on by —— ——. Had they not declined all further negotiation on the subject, in so careless a style, I should have held myself bound to offer the work on the old footing, but as it is, I don't think I owe them the compliment.

Pray let me have a few lines from you reporting progress, when you make any, as I don't expect to visit Poughkeepsie till spring. I am dear sir,

Yours very truly

J. K. PAULDING.

P. S.—Screw as much out of those rogues as you can, as I contemplate some great agricultural experiments next spring.

The book above referred to came out in 1849, under the auspices of Baker & Scribner, being a novel in two volumes, entitled THE PURITAN AND HIS DAUGHTER. The moral of this is, that a very conscientious man may make those to whose happiness it is his duty to minister, very unhappy—on principle.

The "DEDICATION" is highly characteristic.

TO THE MOST HIGH AND MIGHTY SOVEREIGN OF SOVEREIGNS, KING PEOPLE.

MAY IT PLEASE YOUR MAJESTY—

IT was the custom, previous to the commencement of Your Majesty's auspicious reign, for every judicious author to dedicate his work to some munificent potentate, who, by virtue of the Divine Right of granting pensions, held, as it were, the purse-strings of inspiration; or to some neighboring prince, or noble, whose rank in the State, or whose reputation for taste, might serve, if not as a guarantee to the merits of the work, at least, in some measure, to overawe the vinegarized critics from falling foul of it with tomahawk and scalping-knife.

I, however, may it please Your Majesty, choose rather to go to the fountain-head — the source and grand reservoir of dignity and power — and scorn to skulk behind the outworks, when I flatter myself I may have the good fortune to effect a lodgment in the very citadel itself, under the immediate protection of your most sacred Majesty, to whom only, of all potentates, can be justly applied the great maxims: "The king can do no wrong" — "The king never dies."

You alone reign by Divine Right: you alone inherit the privilege, and exercise the power, of judging the past, directing the present, and presiding over the future. You alone are the great arbiter of living and posthumous fame; for being yourself immortal, it is yours to confer immortality on others. Your empire is self-governed and self-sustained. You require neither fleets, armies, nor armed police, to enforce your decisions, for your fiat is fate. You can set up kings and knock them down like nine-pins; you can make and unmake laws at pleasure; you can make little men great, and great men little: your will, when you choose to exert it, is despotic throughout the nations of the earth, for Your Majesty is the only sovereign that ever existed who could justly boast of universal empire.

Not only is your power without limit, but your judgment infallible in the selection of favorites, and the bestowal of honors. If you call a pigmy a giant, a giant he becomes; and if you dub a man a fool, the wisdom of Solomon cannot save him from the Hospital of Incurables. The reputation of heroes, statesmen, sages, and philosophers, is entirely at your mercy; you keep the keys of the Temple of Fame, and none can enter without your royal permission. In short, when Your Majesty issues a decree it must be carried into effect, for with you there is nothing impossible, and all must obey him who is himself all.

It is for these, and other special reasons, which I forbear to enumerate lest I should tire Your Majesty's royal patience, that I have, as it were, turned my back on the rest of the world, and selected Your Majesty as mine own especial Mæcenas, knowing full well you are of all patrons the most munificent and discriminating. May it please Your Majesty then to issue your Royal Bull, directing that no critic shall presume to mangle this my work with a stone hatchet, or dissect it with a butcher's cleaver, unless he can give a good reason for it; that it shall be puffed and trumpeted to the uttermost confines of your universal empire, insomuch that it shall go through as many editions as the Pilgrim's Progress, or Robinson Crusoe; that all members of Congress, past, present, and future, shall be furnished with a copy at the expense of Your Majesty, and what is more, be obliged to read it — unless their education has been neglected; that whoever ushers it into the world shall make a judicious distribution of copies; and above all, that Your Majesty will order and direct some munificent bibliopole to publish it, at the expense of the author.

Relying thus on the powerful aid of Your Majesty, I considered it my interest, as well as my duty, to consult Your Majesty's royal palate in the conception and development of this my humble offering; and having been assured by an eminent publisher that Your Majesty relishes nothing but works of fiction and picture-books, I hereby offer at the footstool of your royal clemency a work, which, though containing a great many truths, has, I flatter myself, so dextrously disguised them that Your Majesty will not be a whit the wiser. If I appear, or affect to appear, as an adviser or instructor to Your Majesty, it is not that I have the presumption to suppose that Your Majesty requires either advice or instruction, but because it is next to impossible for an author to dissemble the conviction that he is wiser than his readers.

Having, for a long time past, been sedulously occupied in studying Your Majesty's royal tastes, I am not ignorant of your preference for high-seasoned dishes of foreign cookery, most especially blood-puddings, plentifully spiced and sauced with adultery, seduction, poisoning, stabbing, suicide, and all other sublime excesses of genius. I am aware also that Your Majesty, being yourself able to perform impossibilities, believes nothing impossible. Possessing this clew to Your Majesty's royal approbation, I solemnly assure you I have gone as far as I could to secure it, with a safe conscience. I have laid about me pretty handsomely, and sprinkled a good number of my pages with blood enough, I hope, to make a pudding. If I have any apology to make to Your Majesty, it is for permitting some of my people to die a natural death, a thing so unnatural that it has been banished from all works of fiction aiming at the least semblance to truth.

I am aware, may it please Your Majesty, that it is one of the established canons of critical and other criminal courts, that killing is no murder; and that a writer of fiction is not amenable to any tribunal, civil, ecclesiastical, or critical, for any capital crime, except murdering his own story. But, may it please Your Majesty, I am troubled with weak nerves, and my great-grandfather was a Quaker. I am, therefore, naturally averse to bloodshed, and have more than once nearly fallen into convulsions over the pages of Monsieur Alexandre Dumas, whom I consider a perfect guillotine among authors. In short, may it please Your Majesty, I abjure poisoning, or smothering with charcoal, and confess myself deplorably behind the spirit of this luminous age, which is as much in advance of all others as the forewheel of a wagon is ahead of the hind ones.

Your Majesty will, I trust, pardon the most devoted of your servants, for thus intruding on your valuable time. But it is a notoriously well-established fact that authors are a self-sufficient race, who think themselves qualified to direct Your Majesty's opinions. I therefore make no apology for so universal a failing, and shall limit myself on this head, to beseeching Your Majesty's forgiveness for introducing to your royal patronage so many honest, discreet women, not one of whom hath the least pretensions to figure at Doctors' Commons, the criminal court, or in modern romance.

As this is a time when empires are overturned, and potentates exiled, by romances and newspapers, I deem it incumbent on me to conclude this my humble Dedication, by assuring Your Majesty that I have not the most remote intention of meddling with those dangerous edge-tools, politics and polemics, any farther than seemed necessary to render probable the conduct of the actors, and the incidents of my story. I solemnly declare that I have no idea of interfering with Your Majesty's regal prerogative; that I have no design against Your Majesty's royal person; that I am neither High-Church nor Low-Church, Socialist, Red Republican, Anti-Renter, Agrarian, or Philanthropist, but a peaceable disciple of the doctrine of passive obedience and non-resistance in all cases where Your Majesty's prerogative is concerned.

One word more, may it please Your Patient Majesty. Not considering myself as writing a historical fiction, or bound by the strict rules of matter of fact, I have indulged in one or two trifling anachronisms, which I refrain from pointing out, in order that Your Majesty may have the pleasure of detecting them yourself.

I am,
May it please your Majesty,
Your most gracious Majesty's
Most Faithful,
Most Humble,
Most Obedient,
Most Devoted Servant,

THE AUTHOR.

Here we have what may be called the lesson of the book, and what he styles —

SOME MORSELS OF WISDOM

CRAMMED DOWN THE READER'S THROAT IN SPITE OF HIS WRY FACES.

All men, says our wise old friend, and, as is affirmed

by scandalous persons, all women, have a way of their own, and like to have their own way. Now there is an infinite variety of nothings in domestic life, which, though in themselves of no importance, constitute the most fruitful source of trifling disagreements and contradictions that too often in the end produce coolness, if not alienation. We have somewhere heard of a couple of the fondest, best tempered people in the world, who unfortunately, one day, in the middle of a long, gloomy, drizzly week in November, during which the sun suffered a total eclipse, fell into an argument on the question, whether people have ten fingers, or only eight fingers and two thumbs. They parted without settling the controversy, and the next day it was renewed with additional vivacity. The habit grew upon them, and each party waxed more warm as well as obstinate. They began to complain bitterly of the peevishness of each other, and finally agreed to a separation on the ground of incompatibility of temper. Were it possible to penetrate the deep mysteries of wedlock, it would probably be found that in a vast many, perhaps a majority of, cases, matrimonial dissentions arise from a difference of opinion on matters of not the least moment and to which the parties are totally indifferent.

Harold was a man of principle. He did everything on principle, and often applied his principles to things that involved no principle whatever. Susan, too, was governed by principle; she was obstinately good, though to do her justice, it was only passive obstinacy, that of non-resistance. No earthly motive could tempt her to do wrong, or act against her settled conviction. It would have been better for both, had they confined their adherence to principle to those acts which involve the obligations of duty to ourselves and others; but they went much farther, and when there was neither right nor wrong in the case, strictly adhered to principle. Yet with all this, Susan possessed a temper of the sweetest complacency, and never on any occasion contended with her husband. When, as sometimes happened, Harold found fault with her, she would only ply her needle with greater rapidity, and exclaim — "My dear, I don't hear — I don't hear."

That perseverance, our old friend continues, nay, obstinacy in doing right, is a noble characteristic in man or woman cannot be denied; and yet it requires to be kept within certain bounds, or it may chance to degenerate into obstinacy in doing wrong. Nothing is more common than to mistake prejudice for principle, or the suggestions of passion for the dictates of reason. The desire of having our own way, the mere indulgence of the will, is often the substitute for a conviction of right, and in many, very many, cases, what is called acting on principle is only an excuse for a determination to do as we please. Even conscience is not an infallible guide, else we had not so often seen whole nations forgetting the obligations of humanity charity and justice, and exterminating each other for a mere difference of opinion. It is however the best we have; and though partaking in the common weakness of our nature, should be handled with gloves, lest from a sleeping lamb it become a raging tiger.

There are a vast many occasions, particularly in the daily intercourse of domestic life, in which it is not worth while to be obstinate, and where opposition is oftener the result of wilfulness than reason. It is in yielding to others in such small affairs that what is called good nature consists. This is the honey that sweetens the cup of human life; the great cement of our social relations, which consist as much in mutual forbearance, as in mutual good offices. A married pair should equally keep clear of the two extremes, of absolute independence, and grovelling submission. Most especially should they avoid all argument, which is only another name for contention. The wise old gentleman from whom we have again quoted, is clearly of this opinion, and earnestly recommends the example of a friend of his, who, whenever his wife expresses dissent to any opinion or proposition, invariably replies, "well, my dear, then there is an end to the argument," — takes up his hat, and quietly goes about his business.

The same old gentleman begs to caution our readers against a fundamental error of a certain married couple with whom he was on terms of intimacy, whose domestic harmony was grievously undermined by a habit of contending, not which should have his, or her, way, but which should concede it to the other. This produced very serious conflicts, which generally ended in the husband exclaiming, "Zounds, madam, do you think to always have your own way? I desire you to understand that I too have a will of my own." The old gentleman, however, observes, that this is rather an uncommon case, and constitutes an exception. He further remarks, that argument between the rival domestic powers is most of all dangerous where both parties agree; and affirms he has seen two people exceedingly discomposed, at finding, after a long and warm discussion, that there was in fact no difference of opinion.

Mr. Paulding at this period had been a temperate and methodical smoker for about half a century, as I suppose, and in this work he gives us, as he terms it, an

EULOGIUM ON THE DIVINE TOBACCO PIPE.

" MOTH," said Master Hugh Tyringham to his trusty squire, who was philosophically solacing himself with the truly republican relaxation of the fragrant pipe. We call it republican — not to say democratic — because it is emphatically the poor man's luxury, innocent, cheap, and refreshing; one that he can enjoy at home in summer on his porch, in winter by his fireside, without seeking abroad for vagrant pleasures; one that, while it produces a gentle, harmless excitement, leads to no excesses like the mischievous inspiration of wine, and whiles away the time in the intervals of exhausting labor. Well have the wise red men of the woods selected the pipe as the seal of reconciliation, the token that the bloody hatchet has been buried, for it is the very emblem of peace and repose. Would any man wish to calm his troubled spirit, ruffled by the rude elbowings of the busy world, or wasting away with disappointed hopes or never-ending toil; would the philosopher wish to explore the depths of some unfathomable doubt or metaphysical mystery; would the poet aspire to reach the highest heaven of inspiration, or the lover seek to indulge himself in weaving a web of fancied bliss; —

let him light his pipe, and, like the fabled wand of the magician, it will conjure up before him such a host of happy ideas, that he will no longer seek the fruition of dull reality.

Were we to attempt to exhibit a picture of content — the only real happiness this earth affords — one that would attract the envy of mankind, we would set before them yonder gray-headed Dutch farmer, not fat, but round and portly, with his brown, ruddy face, calm as the noble river that flows along his verdant meadows. He is seated under his porch, one of the last remaining types of the little cocked hat erewhile worn by the great Frederick of Prussia and other celebrated warriors. He has finished his haying and harvest, his barns are full, and generous plenty laughs him in the face. It is a delightful summer evening, and it is not yet time to go to rest. No wind but the sweet southwestern zephyr, which the Indians say comes from the abode of the Great Spirit, ruffles the leaves or the waters; no noise but that of the rural concert of tinkling bells and lowing herds, nothing to awaken the wickedness of man, or afford his great enemy a bait to lead him astray.

He has lighted his pipe, and the eddies of smoke ascend in spiral volumes, gradually fading away in boundless space. Beside him sits a wholesome dame plying her knitting needles, and now and then it is clear, from the old man taking the pipe from his mouth, that they are exchanging a few words. On the lower step of the porch, and at a respectful distance, sits honest Coony O'Brien, of the Emerald Isle, a hired man, who, saving that he sometimes makes a respectable blunder, is as honest and well spoken a person as one would wish to meet with. He has saved from his wages enough to pay his brother's passage to the land where labor meets its due reward, and rollicking abundance is born of liberty. Coony, too, is modestly smoking the stump of a pipe, black as ebony, and counting the days till the coming of his brother. Notwithstanding all the loyal and orthodox writers of England say of Irish ignorance, barbarity, and that sort of thing, they certainly have strong natural feelings and affections, and if they are impatient of the process of starvation, we must expect the apple to sputter a little while roasting. The honest fellow looks so comfortable that we could almost find it in our heart to wish we were Coony O'Brien.

A plague on those musty moralists who would feed the world with crab apples; who rail against the majesty of tobacco, and seek to deprive the poor and lowly of their cheap, as well as harmless, solace in the few short hours of cessation from labor. And most especially a plague on those pestilent rulers who leave the expensive luxuries of the rich unburdened, only to lay the load on the poor man's enjoyments. Smoke away, honest, portly Dutchman, and smoke away, Coony; if this is the worst thing you do, would we were in your old shoes.

And now a picture of another tone. It should be borne in mind that the scene is supposed to be in the South-Easterly portion of Virginia.

### THE WILD MAN IN THE WILD WOODS.

In the depths of the vast primeval forest, where echo had never replied to the axe of the woodman, the great instrument of civilization, — on the margin of a nameless lake, whose dark waters, though pure as the skies, reflected no object of the earth — was assembled a band of red men, a race made for the shade, as the white man is for the sunshine. The lake, several miles in circumference, lay in the centre of swamps whose limits were almost undefinable, and its approaches were at that period only known to the savages who roamed its borders. It was a gloomy, wild, fantastic scene, silent as death, and melancholy as the grave, yet decked with a profusion of flowers and flowering vines of gorgeous tints and various odor, that "wasted their sweetness on the desert air." There every production of nature around the margin of the lake seemed to spring out of the water; for the land, if so it might be called, was nothing but floating earth, that quivered like a jelly under the light foot of the Indian. Vast cypress trees, with slender limbless trunks, and tufted heads towering to the skies and rocking with the slightest breeze, rose from the water apparently self-supported on its surface; and with the exception of a level spot on the southern shore which loomed some ten or twelve feet above the surface of the lake, the entire margin was one dead level morass of decayed vegetables saturated with moisture. A numb and moody silence reigned far and near; no woodland minstrel caroled his joyous notes in these pathless wilds, whose unapproachable recesses were never cheered by the rays of the sun even in winter, for the trees were all evergreens and knew no change of seasons. At intervals during the day, a lonely woodpecker, the hermit of the forest, might be heard tapping some rough-barked tree; and sometimes the monarch eagle was seen in solitary majesty resting on a dry limb, silent and motionless, as if he were the guardian genius of this gloomy empire.

The hour was near midnight, and a large fire, around which a crowd of dusky figures were moving back and forth, tinged the melancholy cypress trees with a silvery lustre, and threw a long line of light athwart the dark water. It was an Indian council of the surrounding tribes, whose deputies had met together at this secret hour, in this secret haunt, to devise the plan of a general attack on the intruding white man, and practice those preliminary rites which were always the precursors of war to the knife. It is the characteristic of the savages of North America, that they have always some old injury to remember, or some new one to avenge. Though without historians to record their wrongs, they never forget them; and a legacy of revenge is handed down from generation to generation. Time never heals these wounds, however slight; and when these motives are wanting, a dream interpreted to suit the purpose, a whim of some old woman, a fraud of some mountebank, or a real or pretended desire to appease the spirits of the dead, is sufficient to rouse the ever restless savage to war and rapine.

The following comes almost as pat in this year, 1867, as it did eighteen twelvemonths ago, during the "Yellow Cover" era. It formed the introductory chapter to the second volume, and is there headed by the words — "A preface which ought to have preceded the first volume of this work."

## BLOOD-PUDDING LITERATURE.

It hath been a mooted point with that class of philosophical inquirers which so usefully occupies itself with discussions that can never be brought to a conclusion, whether the age gives the tone to literature, or literature to the age. It is a knotty question, and, not being of the least consequence to any practical purpose, it will be passed over with the single remark, that it is quite useless for an author to write in good taste if the public won't read, and equally idle for the public to cherish a keen relish for polite literature if there are no authors to administer food to its appetite.

It is certain, however, that owing either to the excessive refinement and intelligence of the age, or it may be, to causes directly the contrary, the present taste of the venerable public is exceedingly carnivorous. If any conclusion can be drawn from those classical productions which are so industriously hawked about by the genuine representatives of the illustrious "Dicky Doubt," who, by an allowable figure of speech, may be called the handmaids of the Muses, there must be an exceedingly voracious appetite in the reading community for all sorts of breaches of morality and breaches of the peace, not omitting smothering, poisoning, and suicide. Authors do not mind committing murder in cold blood, or perpetrating any other atrocious crime, any more than they do borrowing an idea from some old, forgotten writer; and the most timid, delicate, nervous lady in the land, who would shriek at the apparition of a caterpillar, or run away from a butterfly, is now so accustomed to battles, robberies, poisonings, and assassinations, that it would not be altogether surprising if we some day hear of one of the elite, after going the rounds of polite literature, and committing a few murders in the way of poisoning, together with some other fashionable *et cœtera* — (not proper to mention by name, though the thing itself is highly aristocratic) — making a most brilliant exit by blowing up a whole square of houses and perishing in their ruins.

There was a time — it was in the dark ages, previous to the apotheosis of phrenology and animal magnetism — there was a time when the records of crime, and those exhibitions of human depravity which disgrace the name of man and make angels weep, were confined to the romance of the police, and the last dying speeches of convicted and converted murderers. A taste for these was considered as characteristic only of the vulgar and depraved, and they seldom ascended to the parlor or the drawing-room, except by stealth. At present, however, it appears that the most fashionable species of romance is a sort of Newgate calendar, in which the crimes and depravity of the lowest and worst species of real human beings, are cast into the shade by the creation of imaginary monsters.

The reader, however, is not to conclude from these preliminary remarks that we meditate the presumption of finding fault with the prevailing taste for blood-puddings and concentrated soup of depravity. On the contrary, with the amateurs of thorough-going barbarity and wickedness, we are perfectly willing to defer to the taste of the venerable public for that species of meritorious romance, which, if any thing can achieve it, will assuredly, in the shortest possible time

—with the aid of the "diggings" of California—bring about that Golden Age, when the saint and the assassin shall lie down in peace together; when the sword shall be turned into a bowie knife or a revolving pistol; firemen meet at midnight conflagrations without broken heads and bloody noses; and last and greatest miracle of all, the bright star of Bethlehem cease to be the torch of discord.

We are full of hope that the time is not far distant, when the human heart shall have become so mellowed and humanized by being accustomed to these pictured horrors, these atrocious crimes, and this total degradation of the human species exhibited in polite literature, that certain portions of select readers will have lost all perception of the distinction between virtue and vice, and the good and bad will mingle together in perfect harmony. Thus the world might at length be brought to a perfect good understanding, and no more blood be shed, except in romances.

Doubtless the experiment is worth the trial, and we propose in this our second volume to flourish the besom of destruction somewhat liberally. Hitherto, we have only killed two or three honest people, in fair fight, and, as yet, not one of our actors is qualified for a hero of romance. But we shall do better in future, by introducing, in due time, a gentleman so utterly divested of any attribute that might redeem him from abhorrence, that he cannot fail to conciliate the favor of the judicious reader. It shall go hard with us, too, if we don't commit a most exemplary murder soon. If it comes not in our way, we will seek it. If we can't kill by retail, which is much the most emphatic and striking, we will go at it by wholesale, and demolish entire communities without regard to age, sex, color or condition. Should all our resources fail, we will murder our story, and smother ourselves with charcoal to escape public justice.

The course of the story carries the principal characters to New England, and the Down-East captain who transports them from Virginia is thus taken off.

CAPTAIN ABIEL SKEERING.

The vessel which carried Harold and his fortunes was in all respects so unlike a Liverpool or Havre packet of the present day, when far greater pains are taken to make people comfortable abroad than at home, that to compare would only be to contrast them with each other. She was sorely laden with a miscellaneous cargo of such inconceivable articles, that though the insertion would save us at least a dozen pages of wear and tear of thought or invention, we are compelled to give it up in despair. It was a veritable cargo of notions, and the bill of lading almost as capacious as Captain Skeering's flying jib. The cabin, the lockers, and the rat holes, were all stowed choke-full; and Harold, on insinuating himself into his berth, found his pillow stuffed with tobacco stems, which every body knows are an excellent commodity for snuff-making. Now Captain Skeering well knew, that though the good people of Naumkeag abhorred smoking, yet did many of them quiet their consciences by snuff-taking.

Touching Captain Abiel Skeering, he was one of those strange, unaccountable, nondescripts, that never were, and never will be, found anywhere but in his own country. He cultivated a little farm, cobbled shoes in winter, and at intervals caught codfish, either along shore, or on the coasts of Newfoundland and Labrador. Between whiles he traded to the Manhadoes, Virginia, and the West Indies, up Connecticut River, and the Lord knows where. There was not a hole or corner in which he did not poke his bowsprit to smell out a bargain; and, what is very remarkable, he never went anywhere without finding one. He once made a capital speculation by being cast away on Cape Cod, not by defrauding the underwriters, but by exchanging rusty nails for wampum. In short, he was one of those wise men who never fail to convert a misfortune into a benefit. He was unquestionably an expert seaman, for he went where no one else ever thought of going; and though he never saw, heard, nor dreamed of a nautical almanac, managed to find his way all the world over, by dint of a combination of skill, luck, and sagacity. He was undoubtedly amphibious, and, for aught we know, his mother might have been a mermaid, for his marine instincts seemed equal to those of our Indians in the woods.

Though, to use his own expression, "he had followed the sea ever since he was knee high to a grasshopper," he never met with but one disaster, out of which, as before stated, he made a capital speculation. Captain Skeering was, withal, an easy, quiet, good-tempered man, and reasonably honest; though, when it came to a bargain, it must be confessed he shaved rather close. Like all wise men, he preferred asking questions to answering them. He, moreover, smacked enormously of the Puritan, and he and

Harold got on exceedingly well together, notwithstanding the latter was sometimes a little put out, by the captain putting in at rivers, creeks, bays, and inlets, to see if there was any thing stirring in the way of a bargain, though to all appearance there was scarcely room to stick a pin in his vessel. He knew what people at ever so great a distance wanted, quite as well as, if not better than, they did themselves; and if he could only be set going, you might pump out of him more practical knowledge than would set up an academy of science.

As our author, in his first successful appearance before the world, had, in the "Autumnal Reflections" of Salmagundi, given evidence of a profound and sympathetic communion with Nature, so, in this his latest published work of any consequence, he fails not to give token of his unabated loyalty to her. Hear how he attacks her direst enemy.

EXCOMMUNICATION OF THE DEMON OF WATER POWER.

At length they reached the banks of one of the fairest rivers of the New World, fed by a hundred winding streams, that, like the veins of the human body, convey the life-giving fluid from one extremity of the frame to the other. Coasting upward along its level alluvial banks where no tangled forests impeded their course, they at length arrived at the foot of a beautiful cascade, as yet unspoiled by the hand of that busy meddler, man; who, in this age of progress, wickedly sacrifices all the beauties of nature, and banishes all the naiads and the nymphs from their wonted haunts, to make way for that monstrous pagan demon, yclept the water power. There is some satisfaction in knowing that at least one half of these sacrilegious caitiffs, who thus outrage the divinity of nature, are punished for their impiety even in this world. Sometimes retribution comes in the shape of a freshet, that sweeps away all his "improvements," as the rascal calls them, into chaos and night. The insulted river-god rises in his wrath, and in an hour avenges the atrocities of years. Sometimes the task devolves on another element, and the flames perform the work of destruction; and at others political economy punishes this conspiracy against the rights of nature, by letting loose her mysterious jargon of supply and demand, maximum and minimum, specific and ad-valorem duties; and last of all, the avenging spirit is let slip on them in the form of a new tariff without protecting duties. Thus are the ringleaders of this crusade, the votaries of the demon of water power, punished in their generation, besides being compelled by the prickings of a guilty conscience to join a temperance society and perish on water.

Listen, again. This is, as it were, the farewell of an old author to that circle of readers with whom he had for so many years fared cheerfully along the journey of life. It may be held to be his parting advice to whatever readers he may hereafter have. It is his innocent theory of enjoyment, summed up in a few words.

The sun had just slipped behind the distant hills that rose in waving outlines above the level borders of the river, and left a flood of glory behind him in the evening sky. A range of airy and fantastic clouds drowsing quietly in the lap of Heaven skirted the horizon, never moving, but perpetually varying in shape and color, and exhibiting, in their changes, all the colors of the rainbow. The river slept in a dead calm. Not a single tiny wave broke on the white pebbled shore, and not an object moved on its surface but a little skiff, paddled by two negroes, who kept time to the homely, yet pathetic old ditty, which has for its burden "Long time ago." In the silence and distance its simple pathos was exquisitely touching; and the plagiarist mock-bird, after stilling his song and listening a while, vainly attempted to catch its plaintive melody. It was one of those scenes which, though they awaken no joyous feelings, are dear to the senses, the imagination, and the memory. When not overwhelmed with sorrow, or smarting under the lash of remorse, they seldom fail to inspire a pleasing and luxurious melancholy, divested of all painful recollections of the past, all gloomy anticipations of the future. We confess our delight in lingering about such scenes as this we have just sketched, and that we would fain inspire our readers with a taste which can at all times be so easily gratified. It is a cheap, as well as blameless, luxury; it costs no sacrifice, and is followed by no regrets; it is one of those pleasures for which we pay nothing, in the past, the present, or the future; and, in a world where every good we enjoy seems to be so dearly purchased, it is a great privilege to banquet at the feast without paying the reckoning. It is, moreover, a pleasure at all times and everywhere within reach; and, while it appeals to the senses, is, at the same time, a step in Jacob's ladder leading from earth to Heaven, since there is an inseparable link between the great Architect of the Universe and his glorious works.

# XXII.

1849. [ÆT. 71.]

EXTRACTS FROM AN UNPUBLISHED POLITICAL WORK — THE AMERICAN PEOPLE.

"THE Puritan and his Daughter" is the most carefully written of Mr. Paulding's productions. It is also, as I have said, his last published effort of any pretence. But it by no means follows that henceforth he laid aside his pen. On the contrary, so long as his strength lasted, he was as industrious as ever; but his labors for the most part took the direction of politics, and he wrote for reviews and newspapers. The tendency of our National sentiment and policy, both as to home and foreign affairs, gave him much uneasiness. Always jealous of the influence of England, he feared her approaches in Central America; and the heart-burnings which resulted in the late civil war were daily looming up into more angry significance. His views on these subjects he put forward through every channel available to him.

He had occupied himself at intervals for years with a political work which was never published. He called it "The mother and daughter; or, The United States and The United Kingdom. By Suum Cuique." A few sentences will give an idea of the comparison the author draws between his two competitors.

Liberty often sleeps, but never dies.

The sentiment of loyalty, I might almost say the love of country, is becoming too weak to resist the youthful attractions of the New World. Not the fabled songs of the Syrens along the sunny shores of Italy were half so alluring as the voice of Liberty, with the cornucopia in her hand, chanting a welcome to her capacious bosom.

America is the poor man's inheritance.

Old and decayed governments are made up of abuses, and one might as well attempt to wash the dirt out of a mud wall, as to renovate them. There will be nothing left of the structure.

English writers sneer at these American auguries. Be it so; yet what is destiny but a belief in destiny? One begets the other.

From this work, (incorporating a few hints from other sketches), I take the following character of and warning to

THE AMERICAN PEOPLE.

The People of the United States have been considered by foreign writers as a congregation of shreds and patches, without any peculiar or distinctive character. But this is a great mistake; since, taking into consideration their numbers and the extent of the territories they occupy, they clearly appear to be the most homogeneous nation in the world. With a few trifling exceptions, they all speak one language and one dialect; though of a great variety of sects, all are

Christians; and, though descended immediately from a variety of nations, share the common rights of one great family. Whatever disparities may prevail among them at first, they in a little while become cemented together by the strongest of all bonds, that of Liberty and Equality. Although in the United States, as everywhere else, unequal distributions of wealth necessarily occur, from unequal opportunities, exertions, capacity, or fortune, yet such distinctions are not, and cannot be, permanent. The exclusive right of the first-born is not recognized, and the possessions of the wealthy man dwindle into a competency for each of his children. Generally speaking, the grandsons are obliged to begin the world anew. Thus the moneyed Aristocracy of one generation becomes the laboring Democracy of the next; and thus those bitter hereditary feuds between the few and the many, which elsewhere become more inflexible and malignant by being handed down from father to son, can find no root. The aristocrat looks forward to his posterity's becoming democrats, and the poor democrat anticipates for his children, if he does not gain it himself, a place among the rich.

The history of the first race of white men which occupied the Atlantic states is not yet, and I hope never will be, forgotten. It should be one of the earliest lessons of our children, for it furnishes admirable examples of piety, courage, unconquerable patience, and never-dying hope. When Poetry shall once again devote herself to heroic themes, and glorious endeavor restore to the noblest of the arts its most noble attributes, the early history of this country, its heroes, and its martyrs, will assuredly take its appropriate place among those themes which more than any of the works of man partake of immortality.

The inhabitants of this region came of excellent stocks originally, and have been greatly improved by being transplanted to a sphere of action which, from the first, called into requisition all the highest qualities of manhood, and gave full exercise to their courage, their fortitude, their patience, and their inventive powers. They occupied, for generations, the frontier post in the progress of Christianity and civilization. They were the forlorn hope of human Liberty, and bore the brunt, not only of every obstacle which Nature herself could place in the way of men, but of the never-sleeping never-dying hostility of an enemy, as has been truly said, "the most subtle, the most bloody, and the most formidable of any on the face of the earth." In this obscure position, among wintry storms and in the midst of interminable forests, these few, laborious, nameless, heroes, wrought out a work which, in future times, when the destiny of this New World is accomplished, will be the miracle of distant ages. Never let their posterity forget what a sublime responsibility rests upon them to carry out this great work and consummate this glorious beginning.

The descendants of these courageous, much-enduring, men, have not altogether degenerated. They have, indeed, approximated once more to European habits and refinements, but much of their primitive individuality remains. They are still, as a people, distinguished for activity of body and mind, versatile capacity, and a spirit of enterprise, coupled with a certain mental hardihood prompting them to deeds and undertakings which those who have been fettered to the great treadmill of the Old World have neither the genius to conceive nor the courage to attempt. Accordingly they have achieved results which scarcely have a parallel in History.

The people of the Atlantic states, especially the Eastern and Middle, are probably, in proportion to their numbers, the most commercial in the world; and, certainly, the most expert and daring seamen in existence are there to be found. The men of New England have a singular aptitude for nautical life; are equally hardy, adventurous, and skilful; and being, for the most part, brought up in habits of sobriety, retain their vigor and activity to a much later period of life than almost any other class of sailors. Success, when it does not lead to a foolish confidence which neglects the means by which it was attained, is one of the elements of strength, and the seamen of the United States are not only animated by the recollection of repeated triumphs, but are likewise conscious of having obtained a reputation which is one of the best guarantees for their future conduct.

The inhabitants of what is aptly styled "The Great West" constitute a species of men of a most racy and peculiar character. The greater portion of them are natives of the older states or of Europe, and retain some of the habits and modes of thinking characteristic of the places of their birth, in a sufficient degree to distinguish them from each other. But being thrown together in one great and entirely new sphere of action, they have assimilated through the force of circumstances — by the absolute necessity of adopting the same modes of life, and of coping in the first instance with similar hardships, privations, and dangers. Thus they have in some measure acquired a new being. Both their minds and their bodies have undergone a change. The one partakes of that expansion which is presumed to result only from study and contemplation, but which is much more frequently due to the exercise of the faculties on a great scale and in situations perpetually stimulating self-dependence under the most trying circumstances; the other becomes more hardy, vigorous, and alert, by wrestling with more formidable difficulties and fatigues.

Those petty obstacles which deter others from great undertakings are to such men only stimulants to action. Thus they have acquired what is their characteristic — an independence of mind, a self-reliance, which to a great extent discards the authority of names, precedents, and established opinions.

This race inhabits the richest region of the earth, the valley of the Mississippi, a vast empire capable of supporting in abundance a hundred millions of people. They are increasing beyond example, and will continue to increase; for there is nothing there of such value as man, and men, like money, will go where they are most wanted and of most worth.

Should I personify this people, I would say — The Backwoodsman is a soldier from necessity. Mind and body have been disciplined in a practical warfare. He belongs to this continent, and to no other. He is an original. He thinks "big"; he talks "big"; and when it is necessary to toe the mark, he acts "big." He is the Genius of the New World.

It is upon this continent that the superfluous millions of Europe, where "the land grows weary of her inhabitants," are seeking and finding an asylum; and here, that, in the sublime words of George Canning, "THE NEW WORLD WILL REDRESS THE WRONGS OF THE OLD." It affords the means of happiness and prosperity to all those who pine in hopeless poverty and irremediable insignificance, for want of a proper opening for the development of those physical and intellectual qualities which are the common gift of a common benefactor. Hither comes man, to resume his ancient dignity, as lord of the creation; and to enjoy the free use of that reason which has made him master of the world. He comes to relieve himself and his posterity from the burden of ages, from that weight which in his native land presses him to the dust, so that, in the language of the old Puritan, "though the most precious of all animals, he is more vile and base than the earth he treads upon." He comes, not to a strange land, but to a home; not as an alien, to remain for life debarred from all voice and influence in the choice of his rulers, or the making of those laws to which both life and property are subjected, but to share with the descendants of common parents, after a brief probation, all the rights of a free citizen of a free Commonwealth. Surely Providence will prosper such a land, and keep it long sacred as a refuge to mankind. Not all the pigmy politicians of the earth can arrest the progress of what has been grandly called "A DELUGE OF MEN DRIVEN ONWARD BY THE HAND OF GOD."

With the exception of foreign immigrants — who, however, from being placed in similar situations very soon accommodate themselves to the same emergencies — the people of the United States have grown up in a new world presenting an almost unbounded sphere for the exercise of all their energies, physical, intellectual, and moral. From their very first step on this continent they have breasted in their progress a series of labors, dangers, privations, and sufferings, such as perhaps no other civilized race ever encountered with equal fortitude and equal success. Their whole history is one continued struggle with the obstructions of Nature, and the opposition of her sons. They have had to subdue both man and the earth; the wild beast, and the wild Indian; the floods, the forests, and the very elements themselves. This has been their uniform course for more than two hundred years; and, consequently, a great majority of them are now precisely in that intermediate state between the extreme refinement which approaches effeminacy and the ruggedness which admits of no softening influences — a state the most favorable to the complete development of man.

Equally uncorrupted by luxurious indulgence and undebased by abject poverty; equally exempt from the burden of hopeless toil and the temptations of perpetual idleness; equally free from the shackles of despotism and the license of anarchy; equally master of body and mind; accustomed from their youth, and from generation to generation, to a breadth of action and contemplation almost without limit or circumscription; — the faculties of the American People operate on a scale of which the masses of other countries, crimped and cribbed as they are in one little circle of unvaried, unrewarded, labor, can form no conception whatever. The Americans feel that they have subdued a world with the rifle, the axe, and the plough;

and the recollection of the past is to them the mirror of the future. The laborer in the field, the mechanic at his trade, and the shopkeeper behind his counter, has his imagination wandering into distant regions of the land which hold out a prospect of speedier independence; and the Mississippi boatman as he floats lazily down the stream, as like as not is anticipating the period when he will become commander of a steamboat, member of Congress, or founder of a State.

The United States contain, in proportion to their population, a greater amount of physical strength and activity than is to be found in any other nation. In the new states almost all the men are young, at least in full vigor of body and mind; and there is not to be found among them that old world class, debilitated in all their faculties by a long continuance of excessive and monotonous labor, and miserably sustained by an inadequate supply of wholesome food. Throughout the country the inhabitants have exhibited those attributes indispensable to the pioneer. Though averse to war, they are emphatically a martial race. There is not a more dangerous people under the sun to take by the beard; and although they often get a broken head in the outset, they almost always give a broken back in the end. In a word, the Americans are a young nation, and only such achieve miracles; they are a free nation, and Liberty creates her own career.

That such a people, so circumstanced, are destined to play a conspicuous part in the great drama of the future seems very probable, if not certain. They are the cradled Hercules of the present time. Like the fabled demi-god, they too have their choice to make between a splendid and a happy destiny; between a government which shall become great and powerful by sacrificing the liberties and prosperity of the people, and one that shall devote all its wisdom and its energies to the sustaining of those interests.

I see that this is to become perhaps the greatest empire the world ever saw, and hope it may also be the happiest. But that this may be so, those manners, habits, and principles, on which the permanent prosperity of every nation reposes, must be preserved. The American People have incurred a weighty responsibility to the human race, for whose sake as well as their own they should cherish, as the apple of their eye, those virtues which enabled their forefathers to triumph over every impediment of Nature, and their more immediate progenitors to leave behind them a legacy richer than any diadem that ever descended from an imperial brow. Should they, as there is too much reason to fear, through that strong desire for personal independence and personal distinction which is one of our noblest characteristics, degenerate into sordid worshippers of gold; should they, from whatever motives, adopt the essential policy and principles of European governments, while preserving merely the outward forms and phrases of Democracy; should they fall asleep under the shadow of the tree of Liberty, while it is distilling poisons: then will it be reduced to a certainty that men cannot govern themselves, and that, like the wild beasts of the forest, they must be chained, to prevent them from devouring each other.

If the people of the United States cannot sustain a free government, or if they suffer themselves to be enslaved either by force or fraud, then may the human race read their doom; for never was there, and never can there be, a people placed under circumstances more favorable to its preservation. The moment they cease to be free they will merit the scorn and contempt of the world.

Let it be said again:—It is only by cherishing those principles and preserving those wholesome and manly habits and virtues by which their freedom was acquired, that they can hope to retain it; for never yet was there a nation that did not sink into abject slavery when it had lost those noble traits. When the love of pelf becomes the ruling passion, and the golden calf the only divinity; when money is made the standard by which men are estimated, and held as the sole agent in the attainment of that happiness which is the common pursuit of all mankind: then will this majestic fabric of Freedom, like every other that has yet reared its lonely front in the great desert of the world, crumble to pieces, and from its ruins will arise a hideous monster with Liberty in his mouth and Despotism in his heart.

Let it be said again, and yet again:—If Liberty cannot dwell here, she belongs not to the earth, and must be sought for in the skies. The experiment of this New World will be decisive of the problem whether man in his fallen state is fitted to be other than a slave.

# XXIII.

1850–1852. [Æt. 72–74.]

LETTERS, TO T. CADWALLADER, G. KEMBLE, MISS E. P., W. I. PAULDING — THE LITERARY WORLD — ALMORAN THE WISE — THE OLD MAN'S BLESSINGS.

Some of our author's newspaper articles at this period are surprisingly full of a spirit and vivacity as of youth. But I pass them by, and draw more freely than heretofore on his correspondence, which is equally characteristic, and will more appropriately illustrate the remaining years of his life. Almost to the very last there occur touches of that whimsical philosophy which was natural to him. I shall present these letters and fragments of letters in chronological order, but make no pretence of narrative to connect them. They are the separate grains of sand whose passage in the hour-glass is the wasting away of time.

TO GENERAL THOMAS CADWALLADER.

Hyde Park, Duchess County. March 6th, 1850.

. . . . . I am of opinion that a man never becomes old so long as he don't think himself so; and that he should keep the secret from himself as long as possible. So long as he can busy himself about something — no matter what, so it be not absolutely wicked — he may still enjoy life, especially if he can relish his dinner, tipple his whisky punch, and turn up the ace of trumps now and then.

TO GOUVERNEUR KEMBLE.

HYDE PARK. Novr. 22d, 1850.

My dear Gouv,

. . . Though I have lately discovered that I am five years younger than I thought myself, I am daily becoming more averse to locomotion, and seldom leave my premises, except to visit Hyde Park or Poughkeepsie, on business. But you must not suppose from this that I am growing misanthropic, or even indifferent to my friends whom I love the better the older I grow. As to the world at large, I acknowledge my respect does not keep pace with my age, any more than I can keep pace with the progress of the age, which I begin to think is advancing like a crab, backward, in every thing but rail-roads, steam-packets, and machinery — meaning no disrespect to your vocation.

. . . . . . . . . . .

But when a man differs from all the rest of the world, the best thing he can do is to hold his tongue, and console himself with the conviction that he is wiser than all the blockheads put together. I am in somewhat of this happy state at present, and, as the vulgar say, "Look down on all creation."

TO GOUVERNEUR KEMBLE.

HYDE PARK. Duchess County. February 23d, 1851.

To-day it is Spring, and I am become a new man, as happy as a fly the first time he suns himself at the window.

The following is to a young lady of about fourteen. The "free-soilers" referred to were the Irish laborers on the Hudson River railroad then being built, who sometimes helped themselves to the products of other people's ground.

## TO MISS E. P.

HYDE PARK. Duchess County.
February 24th, 1851.

My dear Emily,

I received your letter, and as it was the only billet from a young lady I have been favored with for at least half a century, I assure you I felt very proud on the occasion. As the ice has broken up here, and the Spring is approaching, I hope you will pay us a visit by and by when the strawberries are ripe, and the Free-soilers have done blowing rocks. Lizzy and Kemble, and all the children, are going down to spend a month at Cold Spring, and Brother Nat and I mean to have a jovial time of it in their absence, as we shall be free from the despotism of Petticoat government, and not be obliged to shave ourselves every day.

. . . . . . . . . . . . . . . .

Good bye — remember me to all, and may you grow up an honor to the family.

Your friend and admirer,
J. K. PAULDING.

## TO W. I. PAULDING.

HYDE PARK. Duchess County. May 20th, 1851.

. . . . . There is so little news stirring in this quarter, and so little variety in our daily occupations, that it is difficult to eke out a decent epistle without resorting to abstractions. Like the Vicar of Wakefield, "all our adventures are at the fire side, and all our migrations from the blue bed to the brown." Yet our lives — at least mine — are not tedious, for you will learn one of these days that habit supplies the place of variety, and that the man who goes through a regular routine of the same humdrum occupations and enjoyments is quite as happy as he who seeks pleasure in perpetual change. The former is the peculiar solace of age, the latter the peculiar characteristic of youth; and it is thus that the two extremes of life are pretty much on a par in the pursuit of happiness. One woos the staid old woman, Repose, the other the brisk young damsel, Excitement. But I am getting figurative again, and had better return to matters of fact.

And first as to the weather, which, like the President or the Corporation, is a fair subject for abuse to every freeborn Republican citizen. We have had much rain, considerable fog, plenty of North-Easters, and very little sunshine, for some weeks past. Yet the Spring has crept out gradually, and at this moment every thing around looks beautiful, in spite of wind and weather. It is now precisely the season when the grass is most gaily green, and the foliage most soft and fleecy. If the sun would only shine out a little more I should be quite happy, in spite of taxes and Corporation improvements, two great blessings that result from the people enjoying the inestimable privilege of choosing the greatest rascals among them for Aldermen and Members of Assembly.

## TO GENERAL THOMAS CADWALLADER.

HYDE PARK, Duchess County. Septr. 20th, 1851.

. . . . In the first place I differ with you *in toto* as to the pleasantness of Rhode Island, which I utterly denounce, as a region of fogs, vapors, porgies, tautogs, and quohogs; where they grind all their corn with windmills, and call Apple sauce Apple butter. I once spent some five or six weeks at Newport. Though midsummer, I found it so cold, that when the sun shone — which was once a week or so — I used to get on the sunny side of the house to smoke my segar; and when it did not, I was glad to make friends with the cook, and sit in the chimney corner while she was baking johnny-cakes. The very thought of Rhode Island makes my teeth chatter, and at this moment I feel very chilly. As to the sea breeze, in my opinion it is ten times worse than

Aurus or Boreas, or any of the rascally winds Ulysses shut up in his bags. I don't wonder you were all glad to return to your warm comfortable home. The great use of going to these watering places is to learn by actual comparison the comforts of home.

In 1851 and the two years following, Mr. Paulding contributed to "The Literary World" a few brief articles, which he entitled "Odds and Ends, by an obsolete writer." He was fond of embodying an important moral in a short story, often choosing for it an oriental dress. One of the most striking of these occurs in a paper styled "Happiness" furnished to this periodical. A favorite idea with him, he had illustrated it before; but had, probably, at the moment, forgotten the fact. I reproduce it here in a shape derived from several versions.

### ALMORAN THE WISE.

The dervis Almoran, called by way of distinction "The Wise," had obtained a great reputation, by studying the Koran, devoting himself to the welfare and happiness of all true Mussulmen, and persecuting the Jews, the Christian dogs, and the followers of Hali, without mercy.

Almoran the Wise was accustomed to spend much of his time seated cross-legged in a shady grove by the side of a bubbling fountain on the shore of the Bosphorus, smoking his long pipe, and buried in contemplation. His thoughts would often revert to the nature and condition of man, so full of inequalities and contradictions, and apparently so irreconcilable with infinite justice, wisdom, or mercy. "Mashallah!," would he say to himself:—"Why is it that a small portion of mankind are rolling in wealth, and enjoying honors dignities luxury and power, while the great mass of their fellows may be said to be preserved from starvation only by perpetual toil? Why is it, O Allah!, that a few enjoy every thing without labor, and the many nothing without it? Why are the mind and the body of the slave subjected to the will of the master, while the master can do as he lists and go where he pleases? And why is it that while one is surfeited with all the delicacies that pamper the palate, thousands and tens of thousands are perishing for lack of food? Surely, surely the blessings of Providence are unequally distributed. Methinks, if I were to create a world, I would order things differently; and secure to my fellow creatures, with the exception of the Jews, the followers of Hali, and the Christian dogs, a more impartial diffusion of happiness."

As Almoran, the wisest of all the disciples of the Prophet and the oracle of the Chief-mufti of Stamboul, sat thus one day, trying to find out the true road to happiness in order that he might benefit his fellow creatures by communicating the discovery, his speculations were interrupted by a man richly clothed, who, approaching, sat down and sighed heavily, crying out at the same time, "O Allah, I beseech thee to relieve me of life, or the burdens with which it is laden!"

Almoran, who was a sort of amateur of misery, because it afforded him the pleasure of administering consolation, drew near to the man of sorrow, and kindly inquired the cause of his griefs:—"Art thou in want of food, of friends, of health, or any of those comforts of life that are necessary to human happiness; or dost thou lack the advice of experience, or the consolations of sympathy? Speak, for it is the business of my life to bestow them on my fellow creatures."

"Alas!" said the stranger, "I require none of these. I have all and more than I need of every thing. I have all the means of happiness but one, and the want of that renders every other blessing of no value."

"And what is that?" asked the dervis.

"I adore the beautiful Zulema; but she loves another, and all my riches and honors are as nothing. I am the most miserable of men; my life is a burden, and death would be to me the greatest of blessings."

Before Almoran could reply, there approached a poor creature, clothed in rags, and leaning on his staff, bowed to the earth with a load of misery. He sat down moaning, as if in great pain, and, casting his eyes upward, exclaimed, "Allah! be my star; for I have none other!"

The dervis went to him, and kindly said, "What aileth thee, poor man? Perhaps it may be in my power to relieve thy distresses. What wantest thou?"

"Every thing", replied the beggar; "health, food, kindred, friends, a home — every thing. I am an outcast and a wanderer, destitute of every comfort of life. I am the most miserable of mankind; for, in addition to my own sufferings, I see others around me revelling in those luxuries for lack of a small portion of which I am perishing."

At this moment a third man lounged along with

sluggish steps and languid look, and, casting himself down by the side of the fountain, stretched out his limbs at free length, and yawning desperately, cried out, "Allah! what shall I do? what will become of me? I am tired of life, which is nothing but a nursery of wants, that when supplied produce only weariness or disgust."

Almoran asked him also: "What is the cause of thy distress? what wantest thou?"

"I want a want," answered the other. "I am cursed with the misery of fruition. I have wasted my life in acquiring riches that brought me nothing but disappointment, and honors that no longer gratify my pride or repay me for the labor of sustaining them; I have been cheated into the pursuit of pleasures that turned to pain in the enjoyment; and my only want is that I have nothing to desire. I have every thing I wish, and yet I relish nothing."

Almoran paused a few moments, utterly at a loss to find a remedy for this strange complaint; then said to himself:—"Allah preserve me!, I see it is all the same whether men want one thing, every thing, or nothing. It is impossible to make such beings happy, and may I eat dirt if I trouble myself any more in so vain a pursuit."

Then, taking up his staff, he went on his way, a wiser man.

The following verses, the ripe expression, so to speak, of that mellowed cheerfulness which characterized our author's declining years, appeared in The Literary World, November 6th, 1852.

## THE OLD MAN'S BLESSINGS.

**"Honor thy father and thy mother, that thy days may be long in the land whicl the Lord thy God giveth thee."**

You think, because I'm fourscore years,
And halt a little in my gait,
My life is one of cares and fears,
And that no blessings on me wait;

You think I sigh for days long past,
When Hope his lamp bright beaming bore,
When all was light from first to last,
And not a shadow loomed before;

That, 'stead of this young phantom dear,
Lighting my path as on I stray,
The spectres foul of guilt and fear
Are my companions on the way;

That nothing now to me is left,
But patience to endure the load
Of added years, each one bereft
Of blessings which the last bestowed.

But trust me, friend, it is not so;
Age has of joys its hidden store,
As rich as youth can e'er bestow,
Which memory reckons o'er and o'er.

Remember that the withered leaf,
Just ere it falls to rise no more,
Discloses, for a period brief,
A brighter tint than e'er it wore.

Remember, too, in the command,
Those who their parents honor here,
Shall live long in the promised land,
And revel in its bounteous cheer.

Old age must then a blessing be,
  Since 'tis the boon which God doth give
To those whose filial piety
  Merits the chosen bliss, to live.

What though my head is white as snow,
  My forehead ploughed in many a furrow,
My body bent like Indian bow,
  And I a stick am fain to borrow!

What though my sight begins to fade!
  I still can find my way along—
What though my hearing is decayed!
  I still can hear the woodland song.

And though young Fancy's feasts are o'er,
  I am not yet condemned to fast;
Drawing from Memory's ample store
  As rich a treat as Hope's repast.

As o'er my shoulder back I peer,
  I see no spectre's ghastly grin,
No scowling imps of guilt or fear,
  Born of, and now avenging, Sin.

Some marks there are, I must confess,
  Long time chalked up behind the door—
Some old offenses, more or less,
  I wish were rubbed from out the score.

But He who gave His blood for all,
  I hope has shed one drop for me,
When He atoned for Adam's fall,
  On the high cross of Calvary.

This world is still a cheerful scene,
  The sunshine still is clear and bright;
The waving woods and meadows green
  Still give my heart a mild delight.

'Tis like the summer twilight eve;
  Though not so bright as morning's ray,
Yet soft and sweet, and hard to leave
  As the more gorgeous tints of day.

What though grim death, with iron hand,
  Hath severed many a kindly tie,
And many of my kindred band
  In yonder church-yard mouldering lie;

Old friends — a few — still hover near,
  Nursing, like me, the feeble flame,
Who, though they all new faces wear,
  Are still in heart and soul the same.

And best of all, a little band
  Of noisy imps climb up my knees,
And ramble with me, hand in hand,
  Along the brook, among the trees.

The old trunk, though its limbs decay,
  Puts forth new shoots from year to year,
And 'neath its shadows, rich and gay
  The grass upsprings, the flowers appear.

Then why should I of age complain?
  If 'tis a punishment to prove,
God would not promise it to man
  As a reward of filial love.

Content to live, content to die,
  I care not when king death appears;
But, if 'tis God's good pleasure, I
  Don't fear to live an hundred years.

# XXIV.

1852–1855. [ÆT. 74–77.]

LETTERS, TO J. S. SIMS, MISS E. P., W. I. PAULDING — THE FLIGHT OF TIME — THE STORY OF AN AUTOGRAPH — RELATIONS BETWEEN IRVING AND PAULDING.

In the year 1852 Mr. Paulding fell into a correspondence with the Honorable Joseph S. Sims, of South Carolina, a gentleman with whom he appears to have shared an unanimity of feeling which through the medium of letters, (for they never met), ripened into a sincere and lasting friendship.

This correspondence originated in an application on the part of Mr. Sims for some particulars of Mr. Paulding's life. Accordingly, the letter of April 10th 1852 is a brief autobiographical sketch. From this I have already quoted some passages bearing on his earlier days. What now follows describes himself, his surroundings, and his opinions, at the age of nearly seventy four.

"Perhaps you may wish to know something of my habits, manners, disposition, and tastes. From having lived so much alone in early life, when my thoughts rose and died without utterance, I am what may be called a silent, contemplative, man, and I speak more with the pen than the tongue. In fact I find great difficulty in arranging my thoughts for a speech; and it is only when I take pen in hand that they fall into the ranks, like a company of militia when the captain flourishes his sword and gives the word to dress to the right. Though threescore and fifteen, I have not lost the rural feeling, but enjoy the beauties of Nature with all the zest of youth, as I ramble about my farm, or sit on my piazza which commands one of the finest prospects in the world. I build castles too, sometimes, though they are somewhat frail, and, like the houses in New York, are apt to tumble down before they are finished. I never was avaricious, and have outlived my ambition. Having in my progress through life passed from the lowest to one of the highest stations, through various intermediate stages, and learned from experience that what men cannot find at home they will never acquire abroad, I am tolerably content as I am, and sigh for no change. If the fabled Fountain of Youth flowed at my feet, I doubt whether I should be tempted to drink."

. . . . . . . . . .

"My family consists of my bachelor brother — the retired merchant — my eldest son, his wife, and an increasing brood of children. I work a little out of doors, when the season and weather is pleasant, and, during the long winters here, read Fairy Tales of which I am very fond, write occasionally, and amuse myself with the children. By way of interlude, I sometimes laugh at the 'Old Fogies', their doughty rivals the 'Young Americans', the Milleniumites, the Transcendentalists, and the Universal Philanthropists. I don't believe in 'Progress', or that one age is much wiser than another; because, in my opinion, every age forgets as much as it learns: nor that every change is an improvement. But still I am on very good terms with myself, and the world, which has always treated me better than I deserved; though I don't think it as wise as it thinks itself, and am of opinion that if it could exchange a little of its superfluous knowledge for an equal proportion of honesty, it would gain by the bargain. I doubt the practicability of reforming mankind by 'excitements', and the supposed facility of making them better than God made them. In a word, I am in possession of competence, and as much health as I have a right to expect; have a reasonable good appetite, and sleep sound — a sign of a quiet conscience — or none at all."

Having, according to request, given a careless list of his works, he concludes: —

"All these, having lost the charm of novelty, are now nearly out of print, and it is somewhat doubtful whether any of them will reach Posterity."

TO J. S. SIMS.

HYDE PARK. Duchess County. July 10th, 1852.

I have arrived at an age in which the loss of dear friends and relatives seem to be the only calamities worth lamenting, and one of my most earnest hopes is, that I may not live to mourn over the bier of any of the few yet remaining.

[A prayer not granted. Almost eight years of life were still before him.]

I thank you . . . for your kind wishes for a peaceful close to my long career. When it comes, I hope I may die without pain, and without fear, for these are the only poisoned arrows in the quiver of death.

TO J. S. SIMS.

HYDE PARK. Duchess County. May 29th, 1853.

Old as I am, I still revel in green fields and green woods, and had rather listen to the Boblincons than to Sontag or Alboni.

TO J. S. SIMS.

HYDE PARK. Duchess County. Novr. 10, 1853.

You can scarcely imagine what an antipathy I have to cold. I hate cold puddings, cold beds, and especially cold water and cold weather ; and I could sometimes find in my heart to wish myself a bear that I might retire from the world the first hard frost, and not make my appearance again till Spring. But it has pleased Providence to make me a man, and like a true Turk, I submit to destiny.

. . . . . . . . . .

The Puritan and his Daughter is my favorite work, whether because it was the last of my offspring, or for some other cause.

TO J. S. SIMS.

HYDE PARK. Duchess County. July 14, 1854.

Mr. Irving and I have got to be a couple of Old Fogies. I am seventy six and he seventy three, and as we live some hundred miles apart, we seldom see each other nowadays. The chances are that we never meet again. He is, as you opine, a man of most pure and excellent heart — but — remember it is a profound secret — he is as testy and quick on the trigger as your most obedient humble servant: who sometimes stumbles over a straw, and kills a mosquito without the least compunction.

The last meeting that occurred between the two veteran authors was, I think, some years before this, in September, 1850. Mr. Irving's age is mis-stated, he having been at this time but seventy one.

TO MISS E. P.

HYDE PARK. Novr. 23d, 1854.

My dear Emily,

. . . Brother Nat and I, hearing it is becoming the fashion, talk seriously of letting our beards grow, as shaving every morning takes up time, and ours is precious. As I have a great ambition to appear to advantage in your presence next summer, I should like to have your opinion on the subject.

TO J. S. SIMS.

HYDE PARK. Duchess County. Oct. 13, 1855.

. . . . Death has been busy about me of late. Within the last year I have lost a brother and a sister, both between the ages of eighty and ninety, when life becomes little more than a theme for memory, and there is little room for anticipation except beyond the grave. They left behind the most precious of all legacies, a good name, and died without fear and without reproach. Of eight brothers and sisters but myself and one brother remain, and I am the youngest but one of them all. . . .

We two are the last of the brood, and I believe I may say with truth there are few old men living who are sliding down the hill of life more smoothly, and at the same time looking forward to the end of their journey more calmly than we two old patriarchs. Old age creeps on us almost imperceptibly, and I find that as the degrees of longitude grow shorter as we approach the poles, so every passing year slips away more imperceptibly, and leaves fewer traces behind. Every day is so much like the others that there is nothing to mark the course of time.

A strain of idea somewhat similar to the above he put into verse about this time, or perhaps a little earlier.

THE FLIGHT OF TIME.

Time flies with youth, writes many a sage,
But old men know time flies with age.
Still swifter roll the passing years,
As near our journey's end appears;
The closer we approach our homes,
The down-hill course more fleet becomes.

Just as the weary, worn-out, nag,
Whose strength is gone, whose spirits flag,
Pricks up his ears, and mends his pace,
At sight of his night's resting place.

TO W. I. PAULDING.

HYDE PARK. Duchess County. Decr. 11th. 1855.

Though not exactly infirm, I begin to feel the effects of age, and repose has become necessary to my health, and most especially to my comfort. Habit is to age what variety is to youth, and it is a great blessing that when we become incapable of pursuing one we can enjoy the other.

At the close of the year 1855 occur the last letters that passed between Mr. Paulding and Mr. Irving. They are due to an application for the latter's signature, made in behalf of a friend by the young lady correspondent whose initials have already appeared in these pages. The circumstance will bear pursuing into its details, as illustrating the kindly and cheerful spirit with which two old men regarded each other, friends of early days, and the great world, of which to be sure neither of them had cause to complain. Mr. Pierre M. Irving has given his uncle's letter in Vol. IV. of his "Life." I reproduce it here, as necessary to the connexion of what perhaps might be styled

THE STORY OF AN AUTOGRAPH.

Enter Prologue, (per post):—

TO MISS E. P.

HYDE PARK. Duchess County. Decr. 16th, 1855.

My dear Emily,

Though I have in my time received many letters from Mr. Irving, my papers are in such a state of confusion that I don't know where to look for them. I have however written to him to send me his autograph for one of the most beautiful young ladies in this or any other world, and have no doubt he will put on his specs and write his name in the best possible style. When received I will lose no time in sending it to you.

I am looking out for Spring, but it will be long in coming, and have such a decided antipathy to Winter, that I sometimes almost wish I could, like Sir Bruin, creep into a hollow tree and make one nap of it. But on the whole the time slips away so rapidly, that I lose a day, and sometimes two, almost every week. . . . I wish you all a Merry Christmas, and send you two kisses, one for Christmas the other for New Year. I should like to deliver them in person, for they always remind me of the balmy breath of spring and the dews of morning on the opening rose.

Your affectionate old friend,

J. K. Paulding.

The action begins in earnest.

TO WASHINGTON IRVING.

Hyde Park. Duchess County. Decr. 16th, 1855.

My dear Irving,

One of the most beautiful young ladies in this or any other world has written to me, to know if I can find an autograph of yours among my letters. I dare say I have more than one in my possession; but my papers are in such confusion that I don't know where to look for it. I therefore request you will be kind enough to send me your name written in your best manner that I may forward it to this paragon of a young lady.

I hope you are sliding smoothly down the hill, and like myself reasonably exempt from those infirmities of age which so often render old men a burden to themselves and all around them. Brother Nat and I, now the last of the brotherhood, are jogging on together in good humour with each other and with the world, ever since we both became confirmed optimists. It is a species of philosophy that saves men a world of trouble. I am, my dear Washington,

Very truly yours,

J. K. Paulding.

The plot thickens.

TO J. K. PAULDING.

"Sunnyside, Dec. 24, 1855.

My dear Paulding,

I enclose an autograph for the 'paragon of a young lady', whose beauty you extol beyond the stars. It is a good sign that your heart is yet so inflammable.

I am glad to receive such good accounts as you give of yourself and your brother, 'jogging on together in good humor with each other and with the world.' Happy is he who can grow smooth as an old shilling as he wears out; he has endured the rubs of life to some purpose.

You hope I am 'sliding smoothly down the hill'. I thank you for the hope. I am better off than most old bachelors are, or deserve to be. I have a happy home; the happier for being always well stocked with womenkind, without whom an old bachelor is a forlorn, dreary animal. My brother, the 'General', is wearing out the serene evening of life with me; almost entirely deaf, but in good health and good spirits, more and more immersed in the study of newspapers (with which I keep him copiously supplied), and, through them, better acquainted with what is going on in the world than I am, who mingle with it occasionally, and have ears as well as eyes open. His daughters take care of us both, and keep the little world of home in perfect order.

I have had many vivid enjoyments in the course of my life, yet no portion of it has been more equably and serenely happy than that which I have passed in my little nest in the country. I am just near enough to town to dip into it occasionally for a day or two, give my mind an airing, keep my notions a little up to the fashion of the times, and then return to my quiet little home with redoubled relish.

I have now my house full for the Christmas holidays, which I trust you also keep up in the good old style. Wishing a merry Christmas and a happy New Year to you and yours, I remain, my dear Paulding,

Yours ever, very truly,
WASHINGTON IRVING."

This letter enclosed — shall we call it the catastrophe? — a half sheet of note paper, on which the hand of the humorist of Sunnyside had traced these words: —

"WASHINGTON IRVING.

Written at the request of James K. Paulding, for 'one of the most beautiful young ladies in this or any other world' — as he says."

What a sly old stager it was, to be sure! Well, notwithstanding this horrible bit of implied distrust and lack of gallantry, Mr. Paulding forwards the document. His letter may be considered as the Epilogue to this "scene individable."

TO MISS E. P.

HYDE PARK, Duchess County. December 28th, 1855.

My dear Emily,

I have the pleasure to inclose you the autograph of Mr. Irving, written in his very best manner for the most beautiful young lady in this or any other world — meaning yourself, whom he recollects to have seen in a vision before you were born.

I wish you had been with us Christmas day — which Dr. S. has christened "Nativity" — as we had quite a party, consisting of Will and Mary, Jemmy, and Dr. C. We drank all your healths and a happy Christmas, and, as the newspapers say, "the company separated at an early hour, highly pleased with each other."

We have had for the last two days one of those gorgeous spectacles which I have sometimes seen before, but which seldom last much longer than a rainbow. The trees, and indeed the whole face of Nature, were coated with ice, and as the weather has been cold, it has remained during two days of sunshine. Diamonds, rubies, emeralds, and topazes, have decked every tree and blade of grass, and Prince Esterhazy's diamond coat was a beggar's garment compared with the gorgeous veil cast over the face of Nature. Let no one say after seeing such a sight that Winter has not its charms, as well as Spring, Summer, and Autumn, or that old men are not sometimes the most agreeable people in the world, except young ones. . . . . . . . .

I once more wish you a happy New Year, with another kiss for fear the last may not have come to hand; and am, my dear Emily,

Yours very sincerely,

J. K. PAULDING.

And, as the children say, that's all.

Here ends a correspondence between Irving and Paulding of over half a century. If any subsequent letters were written on either part, they have not been preserved. Throughout this long course of years there is no indication of any difference having occurred between the two. Mr. Paulding exhibits, always, a steady and loving regard; a readiness with a manly word of encouragement in his friend's desponding moods; a willingness to lend a helping hand, in any way, to further his interest; a concern for his reputation; and a pride, unalloyed with a particle of envy, in his fame;—which, altogether, set his character in the most amiable light.

Both were now old men, Washington Irving well on to seventy three, and James K. Paulding to seventy eight. Mr. Irving had yet nearly four years of life before him, as it proved, and when he died his friend was failing fast, surviving him about four months. It is anticipating the order of time, but it may be said here that though my father evidently felt the death of his early associate, yet, with the reticence of his character as far as the tongue is concerned, he is not remembered to have made any allusion to the subject. It dwells uncertainly in my memory, however, that, one day in the summer of 1859, when it was known that Mr. Irving's health was very precarious, and his own strength was obviously breaking, he said to me: "Well, we are running a race, and it appears to be likely that my old friend, Irving, may get the start of me, after all."

# XXV.

1856–1858. [ÆT. 78–80.]

LETTERS, TO G. KEMBLE, I. G. PEARSON, J. S. SIMS — THE DESOLATE OLD MAN — THE ANGEL OF TIME — WISDOM AND KNOWLEDGE.

MR. PAULDING began now to feel the approaches of decay. But a few days after the correspondence with Irving closed, he wrote thus of himself: —

TO GOUVERNEUR KEMBLE.

HYDE PARK, Duchess County. January 23d, 1856.

My dear Gouv,

Nothing would afford me greater pleasure than assisting at the celebration of your birthday, and if it had only come in summer instead of mid-winter I should certainly be with you. But there is no disguising or denying that I am growing old, and that, like a ricketty chest of drawers, though I may hang together if left alone in a corner, it won't do to disturb me, for fear of my falling to pieces. I mean, please God, to drink your health in a bumper or two of old wine, let what will be the consequence.

. . . . . . . . . . .

Uncle Nat and I have not been a hundred yards from the fireside for nearly two months past, and you can't imagine how I long to crawl out and sun myself like a snake in the Spring.

TO I. G. PEARSON.

HYDE PARK, Duchess County. 2nd May, 1856.

The Spring is still backward, and playing its old tricks, one step forward and two backward, like minuet dancers.

But the grass is green, and the foliage striving to put forth, and the shad are beginning to find their way among our waters. Then we have plenty of spinach and asparagus, and are beginning to cherish the glorious anticipation of green peas.

Kemble [his son] is very busy and very industrious, and in a year from this time our farm will bang all Duchess County, not excepting the famous township of Bangall at the North East corner.

It will be a great pleasure to me and Brother Nat when you once more take possession of your old quarters, and we can show the young ladies a specimen of the gallantry of the old school.

### TO J. S. SIMS.

HYDE PARK, Duchess County. June 29, 1857.

I am gradually becoming a bundle of little infirmities, and find my best remedy is to repeat to myself, "Patience, patience, patience my friend;" and I assure you it operates, if not as a cure, at least as a palliative. . . .

You talk of details "of my works in the fields, and in my garden": but for the last two or three years I have been past all that. My last exploit was burning the dry leaves in a little copse of wood, in order that the grass might have a chance of growing, the catastrophe of which was that I set fire to the tail of my coat, and burnt up some lengths of a board fence, in consequence of which my son has *tabooed* all such experiments in future. In sober truth my working days are over, though I now and then smite off the head of a bull's eye, or the turban of a dandelion, with my cane. All I can do is to sit under a tree in summer, and see the men at work, which is sufficient exercise; nay, sometimes too much: for, as you may recollect Sancho Panza got a violent pain in his bones at seeing his master tossed in a blanket, I do assure you I have sometimes got the back-ache in contemplating my men building stone walls.

### TO J. S. SIMS.

HYDE PARK, Duchess County. February 5th, 1858.

I have lately had an attack of influenza, which is a sore enemy to old men of fourscore, who have little of the power of renovation left. The ground they lose they can never regain, and I feel the effects of what was but a trifling indisposition very sensibly, both intellectually and physically. The exercise of my pen, which was rather a recreation than a labor, has become tiresome, and I have come to the conclusion that it is high time to lay aside my long cherished vocation. I am on speaking terms with the world; but, out of the circle of my family and friends, I care little about it, being no philanthropist. I leave it to the direction of Him by whom it was created. I am willing to live as long as it pleases Him; my most earnest prayer is that I may not live to weep over any more of the graves of those I love, and that I may die without pain and without fear.

It was somewhere about this time, as I suppose, that he wrote the following lines — one of the rare instances in which a sad or complaining spirit appears.

### THE DESOLATE OLD MAN.

Videlicet H. S. [? himself.]

I'm weary, yet I cannot sleep;
I can not laugh, nor can I weep;
I suffer little, less enjoy;
Ease wearies me, and cares annoy.
I stand, a withered trunk, alone,
My roots decayed, my limbs all gone.
Those whom I loved have passed away,
And those who loved me — where are they?
The past is one wide desert drear,
The future an approaching bier.
Strange that in living we outlive
All that in life can pleasure give!

And strange that still we linger here,
Not lured by hope, but checked by fear;
Not that this gloomy world we love,
But know not what the next may prove.

It is a melancholy business to follow the breaking of a vigorous man, and to see the shadow of death gradually darkening about his path. But there were flashes of the old spirit all along, and his opinions, prejudices, and whim-whams, asserted themselves on occasion as decidedly as ever.

Among other notions, he had always cherished an aversion to having any likeness of himself exhibited to the world. In a sort of preface to "Tales of the Good Woman", which is styled "Memoir of the unknown author", and in the edition of 1836, he pleasantly satirizes the Boswellian pattern of biography, and makes merry with the natural curiosity of readers as to the personal appearance and the handwriting of an author. He retained to the last this disinclination to being paraded before the public in a "counterfeit presentment"; and, during his life, none was ever given in any of his works, or otherwise. The drawing in water-colors from which the engraving prefixed to the present volume was derived was done by Joseph Wood, an American artist of great facility of hand. Mr. Paulding at the time was about thirty-five years of age. In later life, when urged to sit for a portrait, he would artfully excuse himself by saying that he never was as well-looking as at that period, and that he liked the idea of being known to his descendants as a spruce young man rather than as an old fellow.

Colonel J. Grant Wilson has furnished me an

anecdote connected with this likeness. While paying a visit to Mr. Paulding in this year, 1858, he noticed it hanging on the dining-room wall. "In reply to my enquiry as to whether that or any other portrait had been engraved, he said: 'I would never consent to have any portrait engraved for the periodicals. While I was Secretary of the Navy, the publisher of the Democratic Review wanted to put in one of his damned, scurvy, lamp-black portraits of me.'"

This is hardly above the level of gossip, and yet it helps to fill out the picture of the man. Throughout his life he was superior to the clap-trap of literature — the advertising that pretends not to be advertisement, the mutual-admiration business, the timely notice, the premonitory rumor, the awakening review, and the various arts which have elevated many into a temporary notoriety that almost looked like reputation.

But to the correspondence again.

TO J. S. SIMS.

HYDE PARK, Duchess County. Sept 16, 1858.

I returned home a few days ago, [from a visit to his son, W. I. Paulding, at Coldspring], and either brought with me, or caught since my return, a bad cold which obliged me to keep my bed a whole day, a thing which has not happened to me since I came here some fourteen years ago. This is pretty well you will say. I am now on the mending hand, but it is slow work. It takes an old horse a long while to recover his wind.

TO J. S. SIMS.

HYDE PARK, Duchess County. Oct. 16th, 1858.

My dear friend,

My only remaining brother — the last of eight brothers and sisters except myself — left us on the morning of the

12th. He died in the eighty third year of his age — being two years older than myself — easily, calmly, and like a Christian philosopher. The world will never know his worth, but those to whom he was all his life a benefactor will cherish his memory while they live, as one of the most upright, just, and generous men that ever lived. He spent his better days in saving pennies that he might give away tens of thousands. To the world he appeared anxious to make and save money; to his friends and relatives only, he was known as the most generous of men, as one who saved only to give away. He might have died a millionaire, but preferred leaving behind him hearts that will cherish his memory with affectionate gratitude as long as they beat. He has gone before, but I shall soon overtake him. I am as free from infirmities as most men of my age, but there is a monitor within which tells me that the old frame building will ere long be without a tenant. Should you never hear from me again, receive from me now the assurance of my sincere and affectionate regard. True, we have never met, but our minds have communed together, and I trust have become friends.

I introduce here a couple of little fables written by our author many years before this period, but which appear to me not out of place; the one embodying that half serious half jesting philosophy of old age in which we have had so many lessons throughout the letters heretofore quoted, and the other conveying in a few words the sum of his whole life's experience and reflection.

### THE ANGEL OF TIME.

THE angel of time, being commissioned by the Supreme Governor of the world, made proclamation that he had a hundred thousand years of additional life to bestow on the inhabitants of the earth. His trumpet echoed far and wide, penetrating the cities, the valleys, the mountains, and reaching the uttermost extremes of the universe. The people flocked eagerly from all points of the compass, to prefer their claims to a portion of the beneficent gift; but it was surprising to see that the crowd consisted of the aged alone. The children were enjoying their youthful sports, and paid no attention to the proclamation; the youths and maidens were wandering in the labyrinths of love; and the men and women of a middle age were too much engaged in the pursuits of life to think on death.

The first who preferred his petition for a few additional years was an old man of fourscore and upward, bent almost double with age.

"Thou doubtless wishest to live a little longer for the sake of thy children, and the companions of thy youth!" said the angel.

"Alas!" cried the old man, "they are all dead."

"Thou art in possession of wealth and honors?"

"Alas, no! I have lost my good name, and am miserably poor. Yet I wish to live till I am a hundred, and enjoy life yet a little longer."

The angel bestowed upon him the privilege of living a hundred years, and he went on his way rejoicing and trembling.

The next applicant for lengthened years was a feeble old man, who was carried in a litter. When he had preferred his request, the angel replied:—

"I understand. Thou art enamored of the charms of woman, of the beauties of the earth, the waters, and the skies, and wishest to behold them yet a few years more?"

"I am blind these ten years," said the old man.

"Thou art delighted with the music of the birds,

the murmuring of the waters, the echoes of the mountains, and all the harmonies of the universe, and wishest to hear them a little longer?"

"I am deaf, and scarcely hear the sound of thy trumpet."

"Thou art fond of the delicacies of food?"

"Alas! my feeble health will not permit of such indulgences. I have lived on milk and crusts of bread these seven years past, and more. I am a miserable, sickly old man."

"And still thou wishest to lengthen out thy miseries. What pleasure dost thou enjoy in this life?"

"The pleasure of living," said the old man; and the angel granted him a few years more.

The third who approached the footstool of the angel was a decrepit female, almost bent to the earth, and trembling with palsy. Her teeth were gone — her eyes buried deep in their livid sockets — her cheek hollow and fleshless — and she could hardly prefer her request, for an incessant cough, which drowned her voice, and almost choked her.

"I am come," said she, "to beg a score of years, that I may enjoy the pleasure of seeing the cypress trees I have planted over the graves of my husband, my children, my grandchildren, and the rest of my dear relatives, spring up and flourish before I die. I am bereft of all that were near and dear to me; I stand alone in the world, with no one to speak for me; I beseech thee, oh! beneficent angel, to grant my request."

"Though I grant thee lengthened days, I cannot remove thy infirmities and sufferings. They will increase upon thee," answered the angel.

" I care not, since I shall know they cannot kill me before my time."

" Take thy wish," said the angel, smiling; " go, and be happy."

" Strange ! " cried a learned man who had come to petition for a few years to complete an explanation of the Apocalypse, and had witnessed the scene. " Strange," cried he, curling his lip in scorn, " that the most helpless and miserable of human beings should still covet a life divested of all its enjoyments ! "

" Silence, fool ! " replied the angel in a voice of ineffable contempt; " it rather becomes thee, ignorant mortal, to adore the goodness of Providence, which, having ordained that men should live to be old, mercifully decreed at the same time that the love of life should supply the absence of all its sources of enjoyment. Go ! take thy wish, and finish thy commentary on the Apocalypse."

### WISDOM AND KNOWLEDGE.

One day the Calif Almansor, one of the vainest and most learned of all the descendents of the Prophet, was conversing familiarly with the great poet Fazelli, with whom he delighted to unbend from the cares of his empire. " Thou thinkest," said he to Fazelli, " that I am not wiser than my fathers. Why is it so? Doth not every succeeding generation add to the wisdom of that which preceded it ? "

" Dost thou think thyself wiser than the Prophet? ", answered the poet, bowing his head reverentially. " Assuredly not," answered the Calif. " Dost thou think thyself wiser than Solomon ? ," asked the poet, bowing still lower. " Assuredly not ", again responded the Calif. "Dost thou think thyself wiser than Moses, who communed with Allah himself?", a third time asked the poet, bowing to the ground. Almansor was for a moment very thoughtful, and held down his head. "Assuredly not", replied he, at length; "I were foolishly presumptuous to think so."

"Then how," resumed Fazelli, "canst thou prove that each succeeding generation is wiser than another that is past?"

"The aggregate of knowledge is certainly increased", replied the Calif.

"True, oh my king", rejoined Fazelli; "but knowledge is not wisdom. Wisdom points out the road to happiness and virtue; knowledge is only an acquaintance with a mass of facts, which are not necessarily connected with either wisdom, virtue, or happiness, the only objects worthy the pursuit of a wise man. The knowledge of things has certainly increased; but, oh Commander of the Faithful!, remember that wisdom is always the same; as much so as the great Power by whom it is dispensed. Thou mayest perhaps, know more of the moon, the stars, the earth, and the seas, than thy father; but of thy organization, thy soul, thy passions, appetites, the power to direct them, and the Being who bestowed them upon thee, thou knowest no more than the meanest of thy father's slaves."

"Thou sayest true", answered the Calif, bowing his head reverently — "Allah teach me humility."

"Great King," said Fazelli, "lament not thine ignorance. Every thing we cannot comprehend furnishes proof of the existence of a Being wiser than ourselves."

# XXVI.

1859–April 6, 1860. [ÆT. 81–81 yr. 7 mo. 15 days.]

FAILING HEALTH — LETTER TO W. I. PAULDING — PERSON AND CHARACTER OF JAMES K. PAULDING — LITERARY CHARACTERISTICS — THE POET'S LAST STRAIN — THE LAST LETTER — DEATH.

In the year 1859 Mr. Paulding's health began to fail decidedly. To this he alludes in a letter to W. I. Paulding, in answer to one offering to send him some fresh water, from Saratoga.

HYDE PARK. Augt. 19th.

I am pretty much as when you saw me, and am never free from pain, day or night. My disease I fancy is pretty much old age, which no waters can cure, except the Fountain of Youth in Florida. I think it best therefore to tamper with myself as little as possible, and let Nature do what little she can. . . . . . .

There is a great clearing out at Cold Spring, and poor Gouv [his son] is left alone, as it were howling in the wilderness.

At this time Mr. Paulding was sensibly becoming weaker day by day, though he still kept about the house. But it was evident that his end could not be very far off.

I know not that a more appropriate opportunity than this could be found to say a few words of his person and character.

Mr. Paulding, as I recollect him, was a man a little

above the medium height, strongly built about the bust and arms, but not so powerfully in the lower limbs; though, in the early sports of the Salmagundians, I am told he was noted as a leaper. In his youth he had soft and fine black hair, but in his later years was absolutely bald. His complexion was dark, and his eyes of an unmixed brown. His profile was more striking than his full face, and might have passed, according to fancy, for an old Indian chief, or an ancient philosopher. This was before he allowed his beard to grow, as he did for some years before his death.

His forlorn years of childhood left their impress in a certain reserve of character. Like most men of that stamp, he said the least on those subjects most near and holy to him. His affections were strong, but undemonstrative; and his friendships few, but lasting. There was not about him much of the social with the ordinary run of men, or transient acquaintance. Accordingly, if he failed sometimes to attract immediate regard in his intercourse with others, he never failed to secure their permanent respect; and the sure evidence of the sterling qualities of his character lies in the fact that those who knew him the longest and the best loved him the most.

Sometimes hasty, when his blood cooled he always became just; and there was no malice in his disposition. He was blessed with that first safeguard of a public or private man, an actual horror of debt; his integrity was scrupulous; and he held his word ever sacred.

When he came across a bubble, he could not, for the life of him, withhold his hand from pricking it; and he had an instinctive appreciation of shams—

literary, political, social, philanthropic, religious, or other.

That he had strong prejudices; many of them unfortunate, some unfounded;—cannot be denied. But they were honest. Upon no question whatever where it was incumbent on a man to express an opinion, did he fail to give it, and that not ambiguously, whether it were popular or the contrary. In this respect he was strictly what may be called a positive man.

His political views, both as to the external relations and internal concerns of the country, were extreme; but they were the established and unquestioning convictions of his mind. His jealousy of English influence, and especially of any interference on her part in the affairs of this continent, was almost morbid: and in regard to domestic policy he based his opinions on the ultra doctrine of State Rights, to which he inflexibly adhered.

Did any man's conduct or professed principles strike him as dangerous to our institutions, he detested him without measure. In whatever affected the interest, or, (and that more especially), the *honor* of the nation, he was profoundly interested. Careless of self, his anxiety was ever for what he deemed his country's good; and long after he ceased to labor for reputation or money, he labored for his idea of utility.

Every office that he held during his life was unsolicited on his part; and he was in his official character inaccessible to any corrupt influence. As the head of a Department of the Government he was impartial and efficient; at the same time, it is believed that he was as popular among his subordinates as any man could be who set out with, and enforced, the idea, that to be secretary, was to be also commander, of the Navy; while with Congress he dealt in very independent and uncommon sort: — stubbornly resisting any and every attempted encroachment on his proper executive functions.

Take him by and large, he was a man in every relation of life sound, healthful, directed by a lofty sense of honor and of honesty; with failings, doubtless, yet for the most part doing to the best of his ability the work it became his duty to do.

But it is as a literary man after all, and if at all, that James K. Paulding will hereafter engage the attention of others; and it appears to me that when the future historian of a perfected and passed-away American Literature sets about his task, he will never be able to ignore this strong piece of foundation in the temple whose glory he would illustrate.

Desultory reading he indulged in extensively, but never bound himself down to regular study. In youth he was almost dreamy; and throughout life more a man of speculation than of action. Hence the pen was his chosen instrument of industry. The influence he has exerted, and left the impress of, upon American sentiment and American literature, is very inadequately represented by the present volume and those which are to succeed it. For he was a pioneer; and it was of the very essence of a career such as his that much of his time and labor should be spent upon themes of a merely temporary interest.

The characteristics of his style Mr. Irving happily touched in a letter to Brevoort, when he wrote of "his usual stamp of originality, his vein of curious and beautiful thought, his turns of picturesque language, mingled with the faults that arise from hasty and negligent composition." In fact he looked at every thing for himself; his fancy or reflection worked itself out through peculiar channels; and he evinced a remarkable faculty of bringing before the mind's eye an entire picture, or firing a complete train of association, by a few words and sometimes by a single expression: while his carelessness or indolence in composition debarred him from attaining that eminence which a more laborious method had perhaps assured.

As for the spirit of his writings, it is thoroughly American, and therefore almost necessarily, in view of the time in which he wrote, Anti-British. He exhibits, more distinctly than any of his cotemporaries, that protest and struggle against an intellectual thraldom to the mother country which were the first steps toward future excellence at home. What Cooper tended to accomplish by competing, and that not feebly, with the Wizard of the North himself, in the delineation of types of national character; what Irving, by demonstrating that it was possible to be born on this side of the water and yet be a master of style; he essayed to bring about in right man-at-arms fashion, by direct assault. How much of the rescue from this foreign tyranny is due to him individually, and how much to natural causes operating on the grand scale, need not now be considered. Suffice to say, that, in a contest, success in which he deemed essential to the character of his country, he did what he could and as he could.

Whatever his merits, they were indigenous. In particular, all the phases of American scenery and season are illustrated with a delicacy and freshness of feeling almost without a parallel. Indeed, for one quality I do not know where he is to be matched. Not only the outward features of Nature stand forth in his picturing, but, as one may say, her very soul breathes in his language. Engaged as he was throughout the larger portion of his years, in the dull routine of official business, or the cheerless work of volunteer newspaper service in the dissemination of his political ideas, the strongest instinct of his personality was a simple and hearty delight in this beautiful material world. From the midst of rural life he sprung, and to the retirement of the country he thankfully betook himself in the evening of his life, when the heat and burden of the day had been faithfully borne. Thus it comes about that the greatest charm of his writings is this unaffected loyalty to Nature which carries us back to the Spring of English Literature. Whether it were the softness of a summer dawn, or the wild terror of a storm; the ruggedness of a mountain gorge, or the lily-dotted meadow into which it declined; his observation was wonderfully acute, and even more sympathetic. For it was not merely the visible characteristics of the earth that he caught, and fixed in words. It is not only that his sketches of scenery are graphic, but that they are imbued with a sentiment; that reflection is interwoven with description, and description interpenetrated with thought, in such harmonious blending that the one can scarcely be separated from the other. They are renderings of Nature as affected by and affecting the moods of the observer. She is translated into the language of humanity. We have the goddess and man in one accord.

Perhaps it was not for his editor to say this; but let him be pardoned though he insists upon it. Mixed up as was James K. Paulding with political or social controversies for the greater part of his life, the most essential element of his character was a deep and almost reverent love of Nature. With this his whole being was animated. His first literary effort, just sixty years before the period to which we have arrived, was, as we have seen, dedicated to her service, and the last known attempt of his muse embodied a lament that her beauties and her pleasures were no more for his sight or his enjoyment upon earth.

This was probably written in the autumn of 1859. The handwriting, for the first time, is decidedly feeble, and somewhat tremulous.

THE POET'S LAST STRAIN.

So sings the gray-haired bard his dying strain;
On earth he never will be heard again.
His fingers tremble as he sweeps the lyre,
And the chill damps of age have quenched his fire;
The starry hosts of Heaven fade away,
The sun grows dim, 'tis twilight all the day;
Nature is bed-rid, and no more displays
Fresh beauties to his weak, bewildered, gaze;
Spring, Summer, Autumn, all the same appear;
With him 'tis Winter through the livelong year.
He scarce can hear the warbler forest-free
Trilling his merry song from the old tree
Whose weather-beaten bark and leafless limb
Seem types of Death, aye whispering to him
A dreary warning, and mysterious call
To that long home, the biding place of all.
Yet may we hope that though his voice be still
For ever by the woodland and the rill,

Perchance it may be heard in Heavenly choir,
Quickened anew by an ethereal fire,
Hymning high anthems at the awful throne
Of Him who rules the Universe, alone.

And here is the last letter his hand ever traced — a kindly closing to the unreserved correspondence between him and his friend Sims. The writing is still more enfeebled, and irregular.

TO J. S. SIMS.

HYDE PARK. Jany. 8th, 1860.

My dear Sir,

I was gratified at the receipt of your letter, and learning that yourself and family were in good health. But I fear I cannot reply at length, as I have laid aside my pen entirely for almost a year past, except on indispensable occasions. Writing is both physically and intellectually irksome, and indeed difficult, to me. But I shall be happy to hear from you, and you may be assured that I shall always retain a deep interest in your happiness and that of your family, however I may fail in writing. Remember me to them all.

Yours very truly,
J. K. PAULDING.

I may observe here, now that he has for the last time spoken for himself, that there is one thing at least for which we should thank this man. Exerting for a time, and that time critical, a powerful influence on the rising literature of his country; writing much, often anonymously, and almost always in careless freedom; one merit he had, and that not a mean one. He resisted always, to the best of his ability, the encroaching spirit of licentiousness in letters. Though without the slightest affectation of Puritanism, the drift of all that he has written is pure; and though even his pen sometimes, (but not often), has strayed beyond the bounds of decorum in language, yet the scope of his works, (when viewed in the large way, as these things should be), is eminently healthy and wholesome.

And now the last scene approaches. A strong constitution broke up with difficulty, but under the pressure of no specific disease. He declined to consult any physician, simply asserting that the machinery of life was worn out, and that tinkering at it were worse than useless. His oft-recurring prayer was but half answered. He drifted onward indeed to his expected death without fear, but not without much pain. His intellect was preserved even after the power of speech, had, through weakness, left him; for, with a dear friend who found him incapable of words he attempted to communicate, by tracing letters upon the palm of one hand with the fore-finger of the other. A very few hours after this, he passed away.

At Hyde Park, on the evening of the sixth of April, 1860, having endured nigh on to twelve years beyond the allotted three score and ten, James Kirke Paulding was added to the innumerable multitudes who have gone where there is no work for men to recognize any more.

But, inasmuch as he had in his life belonged to the great guild of Literature, he shares in that recurring miracle whereby it comes to pass that a man, though dead, yet speaketh. Though the cunning of the hand be passed away forever; though the heart be stilled, never to beat again; and though even the presiding brain have lost its common hold on daily life; such a man can still appeal palpably to his fellow men, and maintain and pass on a mysterious influence into unknown depths of time.

Circumstances, during many of the latter years of his life, kept his reputation in abeyance; and he exhibited the not-uncommon spectacle of a man who has outlived his own fame. His son and editor, convinced that there is essential merit, (as certainly there is marked individuality), in much that he has written, puts forth the present and forthcoming re-publication, in the hope and persuasion that it will be interesting to a new generation of his countrymen; and that there is some matter withal, which rings so true to Nature and the human heart, that the Literature of the English tongue will not readily suffer it to pass into oblivion.

---

# INDEX.

# INDEX.

## J. K. PAULDING.



## FRAGMENTS OF AUTOBIOGRAPHY.



## PUBLICATIONS.

## LETTERS.

### From J. K. Paulding.

### To J. K. Paulding.



## SKETCHES OF NATURE.

### Prose.



### Poetic.



## SKETCHES OF PUBLIC CHARACTERS.



## MISCELLANEOUS.

### Prose.

POETRY.

## SUNDRIES.



THE END.

CAMBRIDGE: PRESS OF JOHN WILSON AND SON.

www.ingramcontent.com/pod-product-compliance
Lightning Source LLC
LaVergne TN
LVHW020108110826
845151LV00001B/103

* 9 7 8 1 4 2 5 5 4 4 1 1 9 *